Knowledge For Tomorrow

Knowledge For Tomorrow

A Summarized Commentary of World History, Nature, Health, Religion, Organized Crime, and Inspiration for the Youth.

Mr. Quinton Douglass Crawford

A.A. Ethnic Studies, A.A. Liberal Arts (Solano Community College)
B.A. Social Science (Chapman University)
Elementary: Primary Research Certificate—(Advancing the Research)
Elementary Study Certificate: (Soka-Gakkai International)

iUniverse, Inc.
New York Lincoln Shanghai

Knowledge For Tomorrow
A Summarized Commentary of World History, Nature, Health, Religion, Organized Crime, and Inspiration for the Youth.

iUniverse books may be ordered through booksellers or by contacting:

iUniverse
2021 Pine Lake Road, Suite 100
Lincoln, NE 68512
www.iuniverse.com
1-800-Authors (1-800-288-4677)

ISBN: 0-595-34030-X

Printed in the United States of America

Contents

CHAPTER 2
PHYSICAL HEALTH OF HUMANITY

<u>GRAPHICS</u>

CHAPTER 3
COLONIAL CONCEPTIONS OF EDUCATION

GRAPHICS

CHAPTER 4
WORLD HOLOCAUSTS

GRAPHICS

CHAPTER 5
RELIGION & HUMANITY,—OR—RELIGION VS. HUMANISM

CHAPTER 6
ORGANIZED CRIME

CHAPTER 7
THE CHILDREN

<u>GRAPHICS</u>

CHAPTER 8
EXTRA KNOWLEDGE

About the Author

In the writing of this book, I have used a lot of memorized information, and direct study of the selected topics. All information came from reliable resources, such as U.S. Public Records, Religion text translations, etc. I have strong feelings against holding information to myself that can be of benefit to many others. During the few months I spent writing this book, I have been a substitute teacher for the Fairfield/Suisun Unified School District, and Instructor in the local Sylvan Learning Center here in California. Through the past 13 years, I have involved myself with many local cultural, social justice, and educational programs. It is my personal passion to contribute to the positive formation of a better present and future. Enjoy!

About This Book

- This book is a proposal for revolutionary progression of the truth. It is a unique, encompassing synthesis unifying ethics, world history, ecology, humanities, common sense education, and liberty.

- It addresses the urgent problems facing humanity and the rest of our planet; such as, disrespect for nature, negative culture domination, scientific corruption, organized crime, mis-education, racial pathology, and information selectively hidden from the general public. Furthermore, it shows some solutions to these problems, and leads you towards the development of other ideas.

- The information presented in some areas is meant to expose the reader to evidence that supports some past assumptions, and corrects others. This is the author's first public comprehensive analysis of the destructive aspects, potential solutions of our problems, and verifiable information concerning claims thought of throughout the time of his research.

- This book attempts to put present predicaments into perspective, and leads to a vision of the future.

Introductory Poem: My Nature

- Study calls me to learn of my mothers & fathers in Africa, brothers & sisters of Asia, nieces & nephews of Europe, uncles & aunts among the Natives of the America's, and purity of spirit through all faiths.
  The world is my extended family.

- I honor all study that inspires the call for peace, truth, justice, and responsibility.

- Faith calls me to act in directions to correct wrongs in life. Faith inspires me to enhance the day & night. Faith inspires me to direct prayers to improving myself. Faith inspires me to direct balance to remove obstacles from my path. Faith inspires me to create positive environments in the world around me. Faith inspires me to motivate honorable actions among the youth I am honored to reach. Faith helps me balance my place in this universe, to make way for the new.

- Faith calls me to enlighten my respect of all forms of life, love, and directions to truth.

- I am a student of the universe around me. I am a teacher when I have been placed in positions to restore order with the laws of nature. Through my path of study of my heritage, I have learned that I am a disciple of correct order. Faith calls me to thrive from the energy I am bound to respect.

- Faith calls me to open eyes to sights without focus, listen to sounds of distress, touch for the creation of healing, think with foresight, speak against evil words, and pray with the balance of dream and nature.

- I awaken for the wings of the morning, and I shield the earth beneath me as a body of water at night. I flow with the energy of the day, and blend into the flow of the night.

- I am an element of the love to all life for the realization of justice. I am love for humanity to the direction of truth.

- I am an element of the love to all that embraces responsibility to mold the future of choice, with joy, prosperity, and balance.

Intellectual & Spiritual Influences of this Book

To My Family: With love to my Late Great-Grandmother Elizabeth Myers, My Late Father (Wiley Douglass Crawford), My Mom, My Brother, My Sisters, Nieces & Nephews, Aunts, Uncles, and Cousins…

My Former Schools: Anna Kyle & Scandia Elementary, Sullivan Middle School, Fairfield High, Solano Community College, "Advancing the Research," and Chapman University.

To My Friends: Author. Manu Ampim, R. Mitchell Young, Gustavo Cardenas, Brenda Abdul, Monica Zuniga, Perry Woods, Jaime Greene, Author. Michael Lyons Jr., Ivel A. Oei, Chunky Harrigan, Brandi Bennett, Caleb Watkins, Steven/Jennifer Nevels, Mike Vannoy, The Quewon Family, I. Kanika Roberson, Tumekia Watukuthaza, Gary Moland, Ahjamu Umi, Lisa Leonard, Meron Negash, Tammy Boatwright, Clara Young, Issac Carter, Bernice Garza, Glyniss Sheppard, Anthony Lane, Betty Sewell, Kelvin Lambert, Fama Thiam, Maurice Washington, Seretha Jefferson, Mustafa Ali, Jeffrey Telmo, Vonic, Skipper, Shere Khan, Jasmin, Saada Sadiq, Holli Breakfield, Tamara Johnson, Jabari Jones, Carlton Jones, the Sneed family, Jenny Cables, Guy Dagustin, Darrold Mote, Griff Bailey, Dr. Shirley Lewis, Kenya Cole, The Late—Rickshella Harrison, Lori Day, Chauncey Banks, Czar, Andrea Belser, Lisa Reed, Susan Sullivan, Warrior Woman, (love at first sight—Jennifer Whitman), SGI-USA members, (Earth Charter)—Diana Young, my former and present co-workers,…Special Honor to Departed Friend: Mr. Tyrone Wayne Thompson.

Life Storytellers: Wanda Sykes, Dave Chappelle, Chris Rock, Bill Cosby, Eddie Murphy, George Wallace, Paul Rodriguez, George Lopez, Steve Harvey, Cedric the Entertainer, Bernie Mac, David Attenbourough, Spike Lee, Marlon & Shawn

Wayans David Carradine, Bruce Lee, John Singleton, William C. Faure, Robert Powell, Matt Stone, Trey Parker, Gene Roddenberry, etc.

Activists: Prof. Manu Ampim, The Late-Dr. Chancellor Williams, The Late-Dr. John Henrik Clarke, The Late-Malcolm X, The Late Kwame Ture, The Late-Prof. Joseph Campbell, The Late-Emilio Zapata, The Late Josei Toda, Louis Farrakhan, Prof. Leonard Jeffries, Dr. Molefi Kete Asante, Dr. Ishakamusa Barashango, Dr. Maulana Karenga, Dr. Ivan Van Sertima, Mustafa Ali (Al-Islam), Dr. Daisaku Ikeda, U.N. Secretary General Kofi Annan, Former. U.S. Vice President Al Gore, Dr. Ivan Van Sertima, Winnie Mandela, Nelson Mandela, Magic Johnson, Cherokee Ville (Black Cowboy), Betty Shabazz, Author— Michael Gurian, Ricardo Pena (Mixcoatl Anahuac)

News Sources: The Final Call, World Tribune, Living Buddhism, Christian Science Journal, Watchtower.

Music Artist: KRS-One, X-Clan, Isis, Queen Mother Rage, Kid Frost, E-40, B-Legit, NAS, TLC, Capleton, DMX, Ziggy Marley, Public Enemy, The Federation, Ice-T, Salt n Pepper, Paris, Rakim, Wyclef Jean, Dark Sun Riders, Gang Starr, Guru, C-Bo, Goodie Mob, Outkast, Naughty by Nature, Bob Marley, Wu Tang Clan, Les Nubians, Killarmy, Too Short, Steele Pulse, Marvin Gaye, Erykah Badu, Prodigal Son, Scarface, Ja Rule, Poor Righteous Teachers, Brand Nubian, MC Ren, Westside Connection, Santana, YZ, Whitney Houston, Mariah Carey, Intelligent Hoodlum, 2Pac, Will Smith, Queen Latifah, Sally Nyolo, Steele Pulse, Coolio, Busta Rhymes, Dr. Dre, Snoop Dogg, Born Jamericans, Arrested Development, Def Jeff, Shaquille O'neal, Juvenile, Jungle Brothers, MC Lyte, Bone thugs—n-Harmony, Mystical, Master P., Shabba Ranks, Club Nouveau, Sade, Lionel Richie, Miriam Makeba, Stevie Wonder, Ladysmith Black Mambazo, Soul II Soul, etc.

Organizations: The Solano-Napa Library System, Soka Gakkai International, M.E.Ch.A., Vallejo Inter-Tribal Council, United Nations, Institute of Karmic Guidance, All-African Peoples Revolutionary Party, U.S. Peace Corps, Green Peace USA, Earth Charter, Temple of Hip Hop, Ausar Auset Society, 5% Nation of Islam, Black Panther Party, Black Cowboys Association, The Late-Hoopers Buck Gang, NAACP, Solano College-ASSC & ICC, Advancing the Research, Fairfield/Suisun Unified School District, and the Government of Solano County—CA, U.S. Air Force, African/Black Statewide Student Alliance(A/BSSA).

Video Art: Cartoons: The Simpsons, Captain Planet, Yogi Bear, Southpark, Beast Wars, Berenstein Bears; Yugioh…
Movies: Twin Warriors, Fist of Legend, Bulworth, Pink Panther, Blazing Saddles, Monty Python, CB4, Boys in the Hood,
Don't be a Menace to South Central while Drinking your Juice in the Hood, Star Trek IV, Spaceballs, Panther, X-Men, Kung Fu, Enemy of the State, Blade, Shaka Zulu, Born in East L.A., Malcolm X, Cradle to the Grave, Lean on Me, Posse, The Day After, Return of the Dragon, PBS-Messege of the Myth, PBS-Nature series, PBS-Nova series…

Paranormal Artists: Nancy Matz, John Edwards, Astara, Gordon-Michael Scallion

Special Appreciation for the realization for writing this book goes to all of the children and staff I have worked for:
Golden Hills School, Suisun City—Pre School (2000/2002); Suisun Elementary via the (Cal-Soap) Success Consortium—(1999/2002); the former Ulatis Elementary—(2002/2003); Fairview Elementary, Grange Middle, Crystal Middle, Armijo High, Harvest Valley School, Sylvan Learning Center of Fairfield-CA, Bransford Elementary, Tolenas Elementary, Rodriguez High, Cleo Gordon Elementary, and B. Gale Wilson Elementary—(2003/2005).

As a special note to anyone reading this book with connections towards movie production, it is time that historically correct movies documenting the true lives of King Taharka, Queen Nzinga, Nat Turner, The True "Hannibal", Marcus Garvey, Emilio Zapata, The Ancient Hawaii, Conquest of Mexico, The Nubians, etc; be made! The time is right, information is readily available, the audience is here, and the worth to humanity is enormous. The movie ticket sales of the documentation about criminals like Alexander the so-called great, fantasies like Indiana Jones, and relation to the populations are prime examples of the profitability leaning towards a factual movie of type.

Chapter 1

Disrespect for Nature

The environment may not be understood without at least beginning to understand oneself. Then observation of your relationships with nature should include considering the cultural, political and economic processes through which the environment becomes subject in human power relations. Accurate perceptions of reality lead to fair evaluation. What many may consider a crisis of the environment is really a social and cultural emergency. Critical thinking is necessary in order to recognize the relations of power involved in nature. As this is among the greatest social problems in world history, the understanding of power and wealth must change back to there true meanings. Power is simply the release of potential and potential in action. Wealth is the gathered potential of earned resources and knowledge prepared to transform into wisdom. Knowledge of self is the actuality of natural and cultural heritage awareness. Collective child, family order, teacher, and spiritual honor are gradually being weaned away as less important. Colonial ideologies have altered the conceptions of importance in virtually every group of people's, through there education, religions, and perception of economics.

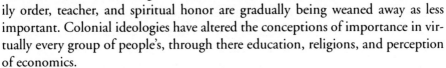

Postcolonial theory has asserted the need to carefully consider how present-day social and cultural Faiths are labeled by historical reports. Colonialism therefore, is a process of subjugation that has occurred throughout human history and in various different contexts. Modern colonialism is deeply rooted in European imperialism, although it must be understood that the world was not free of colonization beforehand. The primary difference between modern colonialism and previous forms is its intimate bond with capitalism. It is important to see colonialism as a concept with plural meanings. Among others, the western image of human relations to nature should be seen as a dualism. In social relations, a dualism shapes both the dominating and dominated identities. Colonialists see the world in a "conflict perspective" towards other people and the earth itself. Dualisms involve denial of dependency on a subordinated other; and the other is defined as servant of those that consider themselves as godly.

However, there cannot be a colonizer without a colonized. Hierarchy and polarization are required in order to maintain dominance. Central to Western culture is the identity of the master; colonization constructs identity so that the 'other' is made to internalize a sense of inferiority in order to maintain the valuation as the center. In dualism, humans are thus valued more than nature. Women, the indigenous peoples, and other colonized peoples have been seen as closer to nature and therefore of less worth.

This dehumanizing and denaturalizing view, which is fundamental for the creation of racism, sexism, colonialism, and other forms of oppression, developed with capitalist patriarchy, and Religious Supremacy Perspectives.

The religions of Islam and Christianity have had several groups within their faiths, which used the religion for justification reinforcement, to do this throughout the world. This was a tool against other peoples viewed as 'savage' animals of nature; therefore justifying slavery, domination, and genocide.

In addition, nature is often engendered, exoticized, romanticized, and sexualized as an evil. The colonization of 'other' peoples and the colonization of nature are intertwined.

PATRIARCHAL CAPITALISM

Historical development of the capitalist patriarchy essentially is a basic root of oppression and the environmental crisis. Patriarchy is the notion that the supreme beings of civilization are men & only men should control everything. Capitalist progress seeks regimental mono-cultural uniformity under profitability, solely for select humans. This conception of the way of life can be altered to accept diversity, and open balance. It is up to the people to gather, create, and accept a common sense approach to life for stability, respect, and order.

SOME WRONGS AND RIGHTS

The result of societies collectively based on common sense, deny social inequalities, while also leading to support of biodiversity. Civilizations without it lead to the opposite. Several great research-authors like a man named "Bruce Willems-Braun (1997)," explored how current discourses about nature are infused with colonialism. [I highly suggest the purchase of his writings for specific details beyond this text.] His analysis focused a postcolonial lens on "the politics of nature" in British Columbia, Canada; in order to contest the assumptions and stability of concepts, and representations brought to bear in current environmental debates.

- He contests common sense and the so-called 'norm,' because what constitutes either may hide and perpetuate developed colonial power relations. A general quote stating that "Power begins at the level of Conception," from Dr. Kwame Ture, 1995," fully applies here

The definition of nature has implications for people and the environment lived on. The separation of nature and culture in the dominating western culture, near east, and most European religious conceptions permit the construction of the landscape as a resource, instead of a cultural one. Concurrently and complicity, dual oppositions are portrayed by the media and parties involved in conflicts over the environment, resulting in the marginalizing and silencing of certain affected groups, such as the First Nations (Indigenous Peoples of the America's). This of course is the same for all indigenous peoples of lands now dominated by descendants of colonization and enslavement worldwide. Colonization is the subordination and marginalization of others, both humans and life in the environment. This is an example of racial pathology effecting the environment.

The same can be seen from invading species of plants and animals in a new environment. The two are not distinct entities but are inextricably linked. Therefore, environmental issues are necessarily social issues, just as social issues are environmental issues. Ignorance of this connection will only cause further subjugation of our world. In fact, colonialism is perpetuated the same ways environmentalists speak about many of today's humans taking over natural ecosystems.

"Yes," Ideals for nature are linked to conceptions of freedom. Liberating humanity and nature is a complex revolutionary goal with multiple possibilities. Nevertheless; if this is a goal, we must strive for in thinking of environmental and social justice. Perhaps a first step is for most of us to realize we live on a colonized land. Postcolonial views of life can analyze knowledge and experiences represented by nature.

The great author Mr. Nöel Sturgeon (1997) observed that, "indigenous knowledge and cultures are often idealized or silenced in euro centric literature." This perspective is common among those that have openly observed the old world history textbooks and American history books that imply indigenous peoples of the world as less significant, savages, or non-existent.

Prejudice is not a true high mental function, but may be considered an instinct designed to function for self-preservation. In relation to human civilizations, prejudice and racist conceptions have historically became weeded out of the societies. This is a natural order of ways for advanced societies, but those that state themselves as advanced societies without order with the natural world and humanity within it, exist out of balance, unless there nature is to destroy and conquer. Life is a struggle to create and maintain happiness, prosperity, and awareness.

ON THE PRINCIPLES

The principles for humans to consider living by are both present in various ancient societies, and in a multitude of environmental organizations. Organizations like; The Earth Charter, Greenpeace, Earth First, The Defenders of Wildlife, among others, have excellent principles for the ways of life that can be modernized from the human/nature based ways vs. the mechanical/calculated ways most people mistake as advanced today. The following collections of principles are probably what humans should embrace for a more joyful future:

A. Recognize that all beings are interdependent and every form of life has value regardless of its worth to human beings.

B. Affirm faith in the inherent dignity of all human beings and in the intellectual, artistic, ethical, and spiritual potential of humanity.

The South American Amazon basin, called the "lungs of the world," consists of grassy savanna, as well as tropical rainforest. The ecology here is under rapid destruction by the agricultural fields of soybeans and expanding cattle ranches. The soy being raised here is mainly for cattle. Due to the fear of Mad Cow disease, soy producers have benefited from increased demand as cattle feed from wealthy countries for meat cows, rather than animal-based feed. This is only the latest in a series of factors that have allowed a company named the André Maggi Group to spearhead, along with the Brazilian government, the expansion of soy in Mato Grosso and adjacent states since the 1980's, with disturbing consequences. Soy may now be the most dangerous driver for deforestation in South America.

C. Promote social and economic justice, enabling all to achieve a secure and meaningful livelihood that is ecologically responsible.

D. Transmit to future generations values, traditions, and institutions that support the long-term flourishing of Earth's human and ecological communities.

E. Protect and restore the integrity of Earth's ecological systems, with special concern for biological diversity and the natural processes that sustain life.

F. Promote the recovery of endangered species, ecosystems, and technologies that restore the health of the biosphere.

G. Control and eradicate non-native or genetically modified organisms harmful to native species and the environment, and prevent introduction of such harmful organisms.

H. Manage the use of renewable resources such as water, soil, forest products, and marine life in ways that do not exceed rates of regeneration and that protect the health of ecosystems.

I. Manage the extraction and use of non-renewable resources such as minerals and fossil fuels in ways that minimize depletion and cause no environmental damage.

J. Take action to avoid the possibility of serious or irreversible environmental harm even when scientific knowledge is incomplete or inconclusive.

K. Place the burden of proof on those who argue that a proposed activity will not cause significant harm, and make the responsible parties liable for environmental harm.

L. Ensure that decision-making addresses the cumulative, long-term, indirect, long distance, and global consequences of human activities.

M. Prevent pollution of any part of the environment and allow no build-up of radioactive, toxic, or other hazardous substances.

N. Avoid military activities damaging to the environment.

O. Reduce, reuse, recycle the materials used in production and consumption systems, and ensure that residual waste can be assimilated by ecological systems.

P. Ensure universal access to health care that fosters reproductive health and responsible reproduction.

Q. Adopt lifestyles that emphasize the quality of life, instead of quantity of materials.

R. Recognize and preserve the traditional knowledge and spiritual wisdom in all cultures that contribute to environmental protection and human well-being.

S. Empower every human being with the education and resources to secure a sustainable livelihood, and provide social security and safety nets for those who are unable to support themselves.

T. Promote the equitable distribution of wealth within nations and among nations.

U. Require multinational corporations and international financial organizations to act transparently in the public good, and hold them accountable for the consequences of their activities.

V. Promote the active participation of women in all aspects of economic, political, civil, social, and cultural life as full and equal partners, decision makers, leaders, and beneficiaries.

W. Honor and support the young people of our communities, enabling them to fulfill their essential role in creating sustainable societies.

X. Implement comprehensive strategies to prevent violent conflict and use collaborative problem solving to manage and resolve environmental conflicts and other disputes.

Y. Eliminate nuclear, biological, orbital, and toxic weapons and other weapons of mass destruction.

Z. Recognize that peace is the wholeness created by right relationships with oneself, other persons, other cultures, other life, Earth, and the larger whole of which all are a part.

"SUSTAINABLE DEVELOPMENT IS A DYNAMIC PROCESS WHICH ENABLES ALL PEOPLE TO REALIZE THEIR POTENTIAL, AND IMPROVE THEIR QUALITY OF LIFE IN WAYS WHICH SIMULTANE-OUSLY PROTECT AND ENHANCE THE EARTH'S LIFE SUPPORT SYS-TEMS."

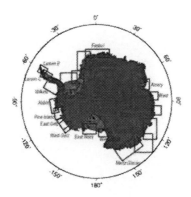

Melting areas of: Antarctica, 2004. Image credit: NASA

PRINCIPLES OF ENVIRONMENTAL JUSTICE

Delegates to the First National People of Color Environmental Leadership Summit held on October 24–27, 1991, in Washington DC, drafted and adopted 17 principles of Environmental Justice. Since then, *The Principles* have served as a defining document for the growing grassroots movement for environmental justice.

WE, THE PEOPLE OF COLOR, gather together as the Multinational People of Color Environmental Leadership Summit, to begin to build a national and international movement of all peoples of color to fight the destruction and taking of our lands and communities, do hereby re-establish our spiritual interdependence to the sacredness of our Mother Earth; to respect and celebrate each of our cultures, languages and beliefs about the natural world and our roles in healing ourselves; to insure environmental justice; to promote economic alternatives which would contribute to the development of environmentally safe livelihoods; and, to secure our political, economic and cultural liberation that has been denied for over 500 years of colonization and oppression, resulting in the poisoning of our communities and land and the genocide of our peoples, do affirm and adopt these Principles of Environmental Justice:

1) **Environmental Justice** affirms the sacredness of Mother Earth, ecological unity and the interdependence of all species, and the right to be free from ecological destruction.

2) **Environmental Justice** demands that public policy be based on mutual respect and justice for all peoples, free from any form of discrimination or bias.

3) **Environmental Justice** mandates the right to ethical, balanced and responsible uses of land and renewable resources in the interest of a sustainable planet for humans and other living things.

4) **Environmental Justice** calls for universal protection from nuclear testing, extraction, production and disposal of hazardous wastes and poisons and nuclear testing that threaten the fundamental right to clean air, land, water, and food.

5) **Environmental Justice** affirms the fundamental right to political, economic, cultural and environmental self-determination of all peoples.

6) **Environmental Justice** demands the cessation of the production of all toxins, hazardous wastes, and radioactive materials, and that all past and current producers be held strictly accountable to the people for detoxification and the containment at the point of production.

7) **Environmental Justice** demands the right to participate as equal partners at every level of decision-making, including needs assessment, planning, implementation, enforcement and evaluation.

8) **Environmental Justice** affirms the right of all workers to a safe and healthy work environment without being forced to choose between an unsafe livelihood and unemployment. It also affirms the right of those who work at home to be free from environmental hazards.

9) **Environmental Justice** protects the right of victims of environmental injustice to receive full compensation and reparations for damages as well as quality health care.

10) **Environmental Justice** considers governmental acts of environmental injustice a violation of international law, the Universal Declaration On Human Rights, and the United Nations Convention on Genocide.

11) **Environmental Justice** must recognize a special legal and natural relationship of Native Peoples to the U.S. government through treaties, agreements, compacts, and covenants affirming sovereignty and self-determination.

12) **Environmental Justice** affirms the need for urban and rural ecological policies to clean up and rebuild our cities and rural areas in balance with nature, honoring the cultural integrity of all our communities, and provided fair access for all to the full range of resources.

13) **Environmental Justice** calls for the strict enforcement of principles of informed consent, and a halt to the testing of experimental reproductive and medical procedures and vaccinations on people of color.

14) **Environmental Justice** opposes the destructive operations of multi-national corporations.

15) **Environmental Justice** opposes military occupation, repression and exploitation of lands, peoples and cultures, and other life forms.

16) **Environmental Justice** calls for the education of present and future generations, which emphasizes social and environmental issues, based on our experience and an appreciation of our diverse cultural perspectives.

17) **Environmental Justice** requires that we, as individuals, make personal and consumer choices to consume as little of Mother Earth's resources and to produce as little waste as possible; and make the conscious decision to challenge and reprioritize our lifestyles to insure the health of the natural world for present and future generations.

INCOMPLETE LIST OF ENDANGERED ANIMALS

1. African Elephant: Poaching & environmental loss.
2. Alabama Sturgeon: Over fishing, human pollution, and environment loss.
3. All Ducks: Poaching, human pollution, and environment loss.
4. All Kingfishers: Poaching, human pollution, and environment loss.
5. All Otters: Poaching, environment loss, and human pollution.
6. All Tigers: Poaching and environment loss are main reasons.
7. Amur Leopard: Poaching and environment loss are main reasons.
8. Asian Elephant: Poaching and environment loss are main reasons.
9. Asiatic Cheetah: Poaching and environment loss are main reasons.
10. Aye-Aye: Poaching and environment loss are main reasons.
11. Bactrian Camel: Environment loss.
12. Black Bear: Poaching, human population, environment loss.
13. Black Rhinoceros: Poaching and environment loss are main reasons.
14. Blue Whale: Poaching, pollution, and UV damage of food supply.
15. Blue-bellied Parrot: Poaching, human pollution, and environment loss.
16. Broom's Pygmy-possum Poaching and environment loss are main reasons.
17. California Condor: Poaching, human pollution, and environment loss.
18. Chinese Paddlefish: Human pollution, over fishing, and environment loss.
19. Clan William Redfin: Poaching, human pollution, and environment loss.
20. Cochabamba Mountain-finch: Poaching, environment loss.
21. Common Carp: Poaching, Over-fishing, and environment loss.
22. Cuvier's Gazelle: Poaching and environment loss are main reasons.
23. Fin Whale: Poaching, human pollution, and UV death of food supply.
24. Florida Cougar: (Poaching and environment loss are main reasons.
25. Galeda Baboon: Poaching and environment loss are main reasons.

26. Giant Armadillo: Poaching and environment loss are main reasons.

27. Giant Panda Poaching and environment loss are main reasons.

28. Golden Lion Tamarin: Poaching and environment loss are main reasons.

29. Gouldian Finch: Poaching, human pollution, and environment loss

30. Hairy-nosed Wombat: Poaching and environment loss are main reasons.

31. Hawaiian Crow: Poaching, human pollution, and environment loss

32. Hyena: Poaching, human population.

33. Iberian Lynx: Poaching and environment loss are main reasons.

34. Manipur Brow-Antlered Deer: Poaching and environment loss are main reasons.

35. Mauritius Kestrel: Poaching, human pollution, and environment loss

36. Monarch Butterfly: Poaching and environment loss are main reasons.

37. Mountain Gorilla: Poaching and environment loss.

38. Mountain Pika

39. Prairie Dog: Poaching, human pollution, and environment loss

40. Red Wolf: Environment loss, poisoning, and poaching.

41. Short-tailed Chinchilla: Poaching and environment loss are main reasons.

42. Siberian Sturgeon: Poaching, over fishing, habitat loss.

43. Silver Shark: Poaching, human pollution, and environment loss.

44. Snow Leopard: Poaching and environment loss are main reasons.

45. Texas Ocelot: Poaching and environment loss are main reasons.

46. Western Giant Eland: Poaching and environment loss are main reasons.

47. Whooping Crane: Poaching, human pollution, and environment loss.

48. Caribou: Poaching, human pollution, and environment loss.

49. Porcupine: Poaching, human pollution, and environment loss.

50. Albatross: Poaching, human pollution, and environment loss.

51. Badgers: Poaching, human pollution, and environment loss.

And millions of others!

Environmental loss also includes factors from global warming. The most natural method to stop the problem, and allow nature to repair the damage done is actually for a drastic reduction in the population and needs of the humans that are responsible, directly and indirectly. The greater good of all surpasses the comforts of the few. Sustainable civilization must replace the temporary technology, NOW!

POACHERS & PIRATES

"One of the few methods to harm, or stop poaching entirely, is to allow equal assault on poachers." An estimate of millions of victimized animals currently indicates that poachers take as many or more fish and other living parts of various ecosystems as legitimate sportsmen do during the legal seasons of designated locations, possibly more. Poachers do not confine kills to legalized species. Endangered and Threatened Wildlife are also included. Poachers are criminals that should have the death penalty for the level of crimes they commit. Poachers take animals for a variety of reasons.

The hides, skins and other parts may be used for clothing, food, folk medicine, jewelry, and trophies. A number of animals are captured live and used in the pet, falconry, or live trophy animal trade. Some people poach because of deeply rooted beliefs that these activities are acceptable. Some poach just for the thrill of killing. They may also poach to market themselves as a great guide, or to promote a product.

They operate year round with any method that produces results. Many poachers are also involved in other illegal activities. A majority of the criminals are supplying unnecessary demands from people in the South East Asia, the Southern Pacific, Montana-USA, and a few in other places. Here in the early 21st century, within the open ocean, there are people that still operate as pirates. These criminals purposely kill dolphins, whales, and other innocent life in the seas, for profits. The demanders, suppliers, and methods of  transporting the innocent animals must be immediately destroyed, to prevent further damage to earth's ecosystems. Self-Preservation of our own species is no longer, and has never been more important than the entirety of the systems of life. An individual can be reborn, but a species is more significant.

THE ATMOSPHERE

By burning fossil fuels such as oil, coal, and gas; we are pumping billions of tons of carbon dioxide, and other greenhouse gases, into our atmosphere. The enormous quantities of these polluting gases are creating an un-natural "greenhouse effect," thickening the natural canopy of gases in our atmosphere and causing our climate to heat up now with less and less cooling, or what is called "global warming." This is among the greatest social problems of today and the near future.

Global warming is a serious and immediate problem. Global warming is not simply about warming temperatures. It means that we are profoundly changing the world's ecological systems and the structure of civilizations around the world. The very system that made life possible on Earth is breaking down. The constant temperatures in the western Arctic are increasing at three to five times the global rate, causing glaciers to melt and sea levels to rise, and dramatically altering environments. In the Antarctic, enormous ice shelves as large as U.S. states are breaking off because of warming temperatures. Recently, movies like "The Day After Tomorrow" from mid 2004, demonstrated potential effects of this. Some psychics, and prophecies mention this often.

As the world temperatures rise, various polar and glacial ice sheets melt, ocean currents will change, and sea levels will rise, as they are doing now. Many places, at or near sea level, can be flooded over the next 50 years. Changing ocean temperatures and currents will cause even more extreme weather; including severe El Niño events, more floods, stronger hurricanes, longer droughts, off-seasonal weather, further damage to virtually all ecosystems, longer heat waves, etc. These weather disasters in turn will lead to more forest fires, faster spread of diseases, water shortages, dramatic declines in all animal life, etc.

The year 1998 marked the 20th consecutive year of above-normal global surface temperatures, according to NASA.

More than 5,000 scientists worldwide have determined that human activities are changing our climate and upsetting the natural balance of our atmosphere. The fossil fuel industry is, funneling billions of dollars into advertising and lobbying to oppose actions that may hinder abnormal global warming. The fact that the United States has 4% of the world human population, and is emitting over

25% of the worlds polluting greenhouse gases makes it a prime target for those in high passion for the future, to alter this unjust situation.

In light of this international problem, the U.S. government; among others, should be taking the lead in developing alternative forms of energy, and curbing greenhouse producing gas emissions. Instead, many U.S. government officials, like in other countries, bow to corporate influences, and using taxpayer's money to give enormous subsidies to the fossil fuel industry, for privileges. A great number of the world's leaders have attempted to address the problem of global warming by creating an international treaty called the Kyoto Protocol in the early 1990's, which sets up targets to reduce greenhouse gas emissions. The Earths natural ozone layer in the upper atmosphere is also in danger!

BLEACHING LIGHT

The Earths stratospheric ozone levels have declined steadily over the last 5-decades according to NASA, and many environmental scientists worldwide. The ozone layer acts like a giant sunshade, protecting the biosphere from much of the sun's harmful ultraviolet radiation. Evidence is present and available that a significant thinning of the ozone layer is under way. Gradual bleaching of the coral reefs, radical declines in amphibian populations, rising counts of skin cancer, and eye problems, are occurring worldwide. During the last 5–10 years, the ozone layer above the northern hemisphere has been reduced by about 10–14 percent, over normal natural loss and gain. It is estimated to take another 100 years for the full atmospheric recovery, if complete inoculation of bad industry is done, and natural environments are repaired, or replaced with comparable natural environments.

If not, the time for recovery will extend beyond that, and endanger life on earth permanently. Some people think people should leave the earth to escape the damage humans have done. Or to avoid the future major earthquakes like those expected in California, Tsunami's like the ones in late 2004, and other super storms of the early-mid 21st century.

It is completely unrealistic for human societies to build arrogance to the level of reapplying humans off the planet. Humanity as a whole, would not survive such a project, as interconnectedness is a requirement of living. This is a part of the basis of what "Al Gore" constantly mentioned in lectures from 2000–2003. The increases in UV radiation in 2003, due to Ozone Deterioration has contributed to the disruption of many ecosystems. Worldwide, mushroom growth is showing signs of reduction, due to the effects of UV-B on the nitrogen assimilating activities of microorganisms.

The diminishing ozone layer is beginning to reduce the supply of natural nitrogen and oxygen to ecosystems; such as, marshlands, forest wetlands, ocean environments, grasslands, and tropical areas. Most plants grow slower, smaller, and mutate as they develop into adult plants when exposed to large amounts of UV-B. Increased UV-B also inhibits pollen germination, and stops the process of seed germination.

The New York Times had a great article in 2004. It mentioned about a fact that scientists continue to have concerns over the weakening of Earth's magnetic field. The deterioration of the Earth's magnetic field began around 150 years ago and has recently begun to fade faster. The strength of the field has decreased by 17 percent and has reduced the magnetosphere's ability to protect the planet from solar storms and radiation bursts.

Dr. Charles Jackman of NASA reported that solar storms might soon be able to destroy large amounts of the ozone, which protects us from ultraviolet light. Next to the combo-damage done by European technological needs, and consumer greed, this is the second greatest threat to life on earth.

People in certain societies should stay in touch with statistics and advertising. You should notice that advertisers are probably more in touch with scientific evidence for the sales of UV protective skin and eye care products. Unlike pharmaceutical companies, which produce artificial products to require you to take more artificial products due to side effects; Many but not all, of the companies look at the dangers for you and promote there products accordingly.

DUE TO THIS PROBLEM, THE FOLLOWING LIFE FORMS ARE NOTICEABLY AFFECTED:

Atlantic Cod, Atlantic/Pacific Salmon, Phytoplankton, Porpoises, Dolphins, Whales, Krill, Eels, Reef Slugs/Snails, Anemones, Arctic Char, Zoo-Plankton, Phyto-Plankton (Major link in the Food-Chain), Fur Seal, Sea Lions, Otters, Polar Bears, Penguins, The Worlds Coral Reefs, Squid, Mollusks, Harbor Seals, Halibut, Tanner Crabs, among other forms of life!

WAKE UP!

Military Weapons, Waste Chemicals, Pesticides, and other European/Euro-American-style wastes are sent into the world's oceans as a secret dumping ground. Green Peace is one great organization that has helped to stop, or slow the process of this happening. It is one dimensional to think of land, sea and air as isolated compartments when they are not. What effects one part of the environment will eventually affect all land life! A Malaysian freighter lost power to its main engine on December 7, 2004 and ran aground near a wildlife refuge in the Aleutian Island chain. The ship was carrying 483,000 gallons of heavy bulk fuel and another 21,000 of diesel fuel. Although this was an accident, like the Exxon Valdez, this happened much closer to a sensitive wildlife refuge.

An ancient method of producing fertilizer is gaining popularity in various populations around the world. Under the assumption of it being a modern invention, a human-waste compost latrine system called EcoSan, is helping many people in the villages of Mozambique. The use of decayed animal waste is a natural method to produce sustainable food production and development. Traditionally, the recycling of waste by-products into the farming system has been through the rotation of crops, integration of certain plants, and/or combination of season scheduled use of the waste by-products of the community as fertilizer. As the waste is composted, harmful pathogens die, leaving a rich fertile soil-base material. Colonization and enslavement have broken several known ways that sustained the people for centuries.

Even the most annoying natural insect is important. Recently, weather changes have begun to happen, but it is never too late to make corrections. The return to normal is a gradual transition. In the interests of progressing civilizations, we must all also engage in true renewable energy, etc. In the USA, "The Wisconsin Energy Bureau recently found that the use of renewable energy generates about three times more jobs, earnings and sales output in Wisconsin than the same level of imported fossil fuel use and investment." (*Solar Today*, S/O '96, www.ases.org/solar, ases@ases.org, 303-443-3130.)

MANIPULATION

Disrespect of Nature is a Social Problem that also extends to manipulation of bacteria, viruses, and food production beyond simple domestication of livestock. Unlike traditional crops or animal breeding, "genetic engineering" enables scientists to cross genes from bacteria, viruses, and even humans into plants and animals. Strawberries and flounder could never breed, but with genetic engineering, genes from fish have been inserted into strawberries and other common foods.

There are already over 80 million acres of (GMO)—"Genetically Modified Organisms," crops growing in the U.S. alone, with no long-term study of the impact these crops. They tend to ignore potential effects on the local environment, since money and/or short-term feeding are priorities, not true health. There are a multitude of ancient methods that are much more productive, and healthier than those many village scientists, etc., agriculturalists that have been trained by foreign people with side interests.

<u>**Some Noted Problems**</u>:

- Biological Pollution: While chemical pollution has been the scourge of the 20th century, biological pollution from GMO crops poses even more hazards. Unlike chemicals that are released into the environment, GMOs are living beings that can reproduce and spread uncontrollably, with no possibility of containment or clean up.

- Increased Chemical Use: An analysis of over 8000 University field tests has shown that farmers who grow GMO soybeans use 2–5 times more herbicides than farmers who grow natural soy varieties.

- An increase in food allergies, SIDS, etc., are now being traced to genetically modified foods (GMO's)

- Super weeds: Studies have shown that GMO crops can cross-pollinate with related weeds, possibly resulting in "super weeds" that become difficult to control. One recent study found that a genetically modified plant was 20 times more likely to breed with a related weed than with natural plants.

The biotech industry claims that eating GMO food has harmed no one. But doctors and scientists warn that there is not enough evidence to ensure that these foods are safe in the human diet. In fact, there is ample evidence of the risks of GMOs:

- Allergies: Transfer of allergens through the genetic engineering is documented. GMO's now on the general market contain protein complexes that have never been assessed for their allergenic potential.

- Nearly 75% of the foods in the Supermarkets today are GMO's.... (2004)

- Antibiotic Resistance: The rise of diseases that are resistant to treatment with common antibiotics is already a serious medical concern. Doctors warn that the use of antibiotic resistance genes in GMO crops may add to this risk. (Over-Use also is a serious concern)

- Herbicide Residues and Cancer: Over 75% percent of the GMO crops growing in the U.S. are engineered to withstand high doses of toxic weed killers. Those "herbicide tolerant" crops (HTCs) will lead to more herbicides, pesticides, and other chemicals in human food, pet food, drinking water, and the environment. Products are sold domestically and internationally.

- Several medications are being manufactured with GMOs, with many known side effects.

The environment and the views of what social problems are, tend to have extreme links. Humans like all life, rely on the health of the local and worldwide environment. We as arrogant humans, often disregard the importance of the world we live in. It is like living in a house with your family, spraying toxins around your food, never uses birth control, commits incest, has everyone urinating on walls, smokes, and never takes out the trash. Families which disregards the health threats of this situation represent the manner of care that the Euro-centric view over nature has strongly instigated around the world, since the 1500's.

BIO-WEAPONS

Militaries and corporations in various nations; such as the United States, Syria, North Korea, The states of the Former Soviet Union, Taiwan, South Africa, England, Israel, Iran, China, Germany among others, have played key roles in developing biological weapons over the centuries. Biological warfare is the use of pathogens—bacteria and viruses that damage the body—to harm an enemy's population. They can be released to one person, put in social congregations, etc., and spread to infect thousands, or millions. Some are highly infectious, and can spread across a population with terrifying speed.

The mechanical processes of developing these weapons have been becoming simpler to attain and operate for paramilitary, terrorist labeled organizations, and crazy leaders in established nations. Populations of humans in Africa, South America, Pacific Islands, Asia, North America, and Central America have been victims of bio-weapons testing, and other direct actions of war; according to the U.N., Hammas, European governments, CIA, testimony from residents, and former agents.

Pathogens like manipulated Ebola, Anthrax, Bubonic, HIV, have been selected as either weapons of mass destruction or weapons of mass disruption to hold levels of control, whether for long-term economic or political reasons. Q-Fever and the V.E.E.-virus were considered for use through order from the U.S. Pentagon against the nation of Cuba during the Soviet-Cuba Missile Crisis time of U.S. history. The emergence of particular viral and bacterial infections among several human populations during social change conditions, are common factors that can be observed as suppression agents. The intentional spread of chicken/small pox, influenza, and other illnesses, to indigenous Americans by colonial Europeans, and recent genocidal attempts in Iraq, central Africa, and Mexico are other examples.

Abuse of nature in any way, against the balance, always turns against the abuser. Genetic manipulation; like those used to make genetically modified foods, are also used to alter genes in viruses and bacteria's to make them lethal, or more lethal (super-viruses/bugs). This process can make; for example, viruses that produce pneumonia symptoms through toxin production and alteration of human immunological functions, making the body attack itself. They can also become super-virulent enough to avoid destruction by multimillion dollar medications, which usually are pre-selected for production and release by one or more governments that have played parts in it's dispense.

Of all these, again, many could have a motive to launch a biological weapon attack in the near future. Some countries presently creating biological weapons include: Iran, Iraq, Libya, Syria, North Korea, Taiwan, Israel, Egypt, Vietnam, Laos, Cuba, Bulgaria, India, South Korea, South Africa, China and Russia. The real question is what are the real issues that have caused the creation of so many angry people? Answers can only be given with all and neutral perspectives.

In the scope of geo-politics, institutional racism, and racial pathology, through a review of recent history, one is likely to see the initial presence of the super-viruses called HIV, Ebola, and the more moderate Hanta Virus more than suspicious for there location origins. The Hanta Virus was first identified on Navajo Indian land, the Ebola Virus is either an intentional or accidental super-virus release, and the HIV virus was first reported in Southern Africa from persons injected through what was called an international vaccination project, which was funded through the European, Soviet, Colonial South Africa, and the U.S., World Health Organization of the U.N., in it's early identified years of the 1950's–1960's. While it may be obvious that the storage of biologically dangerous containers in or near what are titled minority populations may be to blame for the spread of the Hanta Virus; the HIV and Ebola virus, among others are warfare agents gone out of control.

When a fact like this is brought to the public the government often alters it immediately, or corporation involved. Nature would produce these viruses many centuries ago, and natural defenses would of developed by now, if many of them were meant to be. There are only a few exceptions nature is forming in defense today.

TRUE HUMAN NATURE

Cultural differences can clearly be understood by virtually anyone by sheer observation. Culture is expressed through the arts, language, dress, and collective wisdom passed on to the young by its elders. Like all life forms, humans are also in constant struggle as groups and individuals to attain & maintain happiness. On a basic level, it is health, prosperity, and knowledge of self that in it's various interpretations includes love. Love is realized as a universal energy, because the energy of love flows as the basic harmony of existence. Men in virtually all cultures view love as an element of prosperity, the ego is based on the endeavors and what they can show others. Women in virtually all cultures view love as an element of health, the ego is based on the love in their life and what they have around them. This is an expected natural development due to the roles induced both by natural and adopted paternal social structures.

Each variation of human is a part of the family of life on Earth. Life sciences of ancient and modern cultures have proven that we are one of many creatures that developed from past life forms, and developed into other forms in constant evolution. Spiritual Sciences prove that we are all more than the basic physical perception, and connections with all elements of existence are a part of us as well. It must be understood that current stated of violent behavior against nature are not endemic to all peoples. The major generalization that man is responsible for the injustices done to life around us needs to be corrected, so the ethnic cultural base behavior can be understood as being learned from the colonial expansionists, and missionaries from foreign spiritualities.

The struggle to attain the things one wants, and the things one needs, tends to be confused in many societies. The conceptions of financial wealth are taught to be an issue of competition among institutions of government, and some religions. There are no logical explanations that justify disparities of the value of money from country to country; such as, Haiti, Brazil, Ghana, and Armenia, against the values of money of Canada, The United States of America, The European Union, Japan, or South Africa.

Capitalism should not be confused with Democracy, and Socialism should not be confused with Communism. It is a basic nature among communal based peoples such as the indigenous Africans, indigenous Americans, their descendants, and many other peoples to think in preference for living in a socialist-democracy.

Capitalism and Socialism are economic systems that harvest either "me/mine" perceptions, or "our/us" perceptions of what is right. Democracy and Communism are political systems. One inspires collective agreement among the people, and the other is dictatorial.

Some religious cultures have developed a dualist perspective against nature. Nature from the Islamic and Judeo-Christian (Post-Council of Nicea), victimizes nature as a corrupt, sinful, evil force that must be controlled. This conception brings about anti-nature prejudice. The conception that land and life exists for man, and reproduction is a power that must be regulated for profitable interests spring from these bases for dominance. Housing creations are a part of this, as the placement and designs for most human housings are based in the theory that human dwellings are more important than anything else. The placement of humans in and over natural environments is out of balance in most places. If virtually every advanced civilization can create a city in balance with the world around them, why don't the so-called architects do it now?

ARTIFICIAL JOY (DRUG ABUSE)

The desire for satisfaction of needs for pleasure is the main basis for addiction. The most known example of this is the use of drugs to stimulate a sense of pleasure, or separation that is hoped to become permanent. Drugs are mainly used by individuals to produce a sense of distraction from a current state of mind, euphoric joy, or a temporary sense of high empowerment. Each of these sensations are temporary fixes that have no true support system, unlike those created by persons acting on their knowledge and faith to do the same things. Some people involved in the consumption of artificial agents, or even natural ones without respect to themselves, are simply followers of a group that believe in artificial joy, while some also believe in a need to punish themselves for various reasons.

Most ancient civilizations had principles, and/or limitations of supply of alcoholic drinks. In Egypt, beer was used during certain ceremonies, and limited in its use to ceremonies. This is done to some extent today, but devoid of any spiritual significance, which has been the regulating intent towards the use of such agents in non-technocratic social structures. Sadly, the use of such agents, have become agents of destruction today, with extremely little account towards its roles in addiction, behavioral manipulation, and resulting physical actions.

GOVERNANCE

Nations with Socialist-Democracies, firm economic relations, and participation of the cultures, tend to have the happiest people. The concept of nation has started to return to a basic concept of citizenship of the Earth, as many peoples were developing before imperial colonization. Communal social organization, not elite subjugation of social order is a natural tendency of most people's. This way can be trained out of people with bad education valuing the individual over the group, money and land grabbing over sharing & giving, and supreme leaders, or corruption, over collective leadership.

This degradation seems to be a natural progression in places were foreign concepts of governance are pushed into people. Positive changes are up to the people with knowledge of self, heritage, and aspiration in action. All governments are of the people, not for oppressors. It is un-natural for any living social structure to maintain damaging elements and/or poor leadership.

World history and archeological evidence states that communications before colonial developments stemmed from ancient African ties starting about 6,000 years ago. It is only within the last 4000 years or so, that disruption from corrupted Islamic, Catholic, Judeo-Christians, and Early Capitalists spread their beliefs through force, manipulation, and false perceptions of power.

Only those in each of these religions, whether they were a majority under rule by a few that led the people wrong, or the few within the faith that acted in recognition as true followers for humanity can be justified as honorable persons of those faiths. Some of the transformations were happening in the America's and eastern Asia.

The adoption of the parliamentary structure by many of the peoples of Europe has been an important advancement for there societies. However, what is advanced or just works for one group of humanity may not be correct for another. As seen in many news clips, actual fighting within Indonesian governmental bodies, which are adoptions of foreign ways, is one of the perfect examples.

Stable governmental structures of a society depend on the cultural orientation of the people. The traditions developed over the 100's of centuries are a part of the make-up of any people, and cannot be erased from any people in a few generations.

DOMESTIC ANIMAL ABUSE

In country, suburban, and many low-income urban areas, the use of dogs, chickens, and some other animals for violent and/or sexual gratification has become an epidemic.

The ignorant underground illegal business of Pit-Bull fights among mainly European (white), African Americans and Asian boys; as well as, specially designed weapon-wear for rooster fights set-up by low-income Latino Boys are some of the most evil abuses of life in the United States. Poorly educated males, & some females mostly commit the actions. This is an example of species-ism, lack of respect, poor education, and extreme capitalistic thinking.

This social problem can currently be seen well; for example, in Conway-South Carolina, Mexico City, Los Angeles-California, Detroit-Michigan, and many other cities worldwide. This information should not surprise anyone; rather it should only be reminding you that this problem of disrespect is probably where you live too. Law enforcement at least in the U.S., penalize against animal abuse. It is up to you to report to them whenever you suspect activities like this happening. Just like street racing, prostitution, and drug dealing by bored, un-guided life-risking youth are popular activities, this is another underground type of gambling. This is the type of behavior that poachers, murderers, drunk drivers, and other ignorant people exhibit.

End of Chapter #1
To be continued...

Chapter 2

Physical Health of Humanity

Eating out is an ancient practice. In Kemet (Egypt), a restaurant offered a single dish of wild fowl, cereal, and onions. Today most foods are not nearly as healthy. Some fast food restaurants try to get you to buy the deceptively unhealthy foods by using cute animals. Not only does this type of advertisement offend people, cute animals don't necessarily mean that the food is healthy. Many of the basic ailments that humans have, tend to be based on the toxicity of there digestive systems. While this is not the only factor, the human digestive system is highly susceptible to harboring specialized parasites, digested food by products, pesticides, and other elements throughout the body, and especially the intestines. The nutrients you digest are fed to your cells through your blood stream. If your intestines are dirty with non-beneficial bacteria, and do not function properly, you may not be absorbing all the elements you need.

Self-Toxification can result from diet choices, but mainly by ingestion of substances that are, or should be illegal. Self-Toxification by diet is done from un-eliminated waste material accumulating on the intestinal walls. This action becomes a breeding ground for bad bacteria, fungi, viruses, and parasites, which tend to release toxins and you can also Re-absorb your own waste into your bloodstream, which can act as slow poisoning of your body, leading to susceptibility to diseases, and other disabling factors. We as humans have six basic cleansing organs, but several new ingredients created or allowed by medically euro-centric educated persons, have abilities to damage the body beyond the natural capacities to handle them.

MONEY OR MEDICINE

Although some diseases are genetically initiated, most problems are controllable, correctable, and even curable with natural care. The root cause of minor and major diseases is flawed nutrition, along with a susceptibility based on a poorly nourished pregnancy, and sometimes a genetic tendency. Capitalistic interests against the interests of humanity have been allowed to maintain continual control, over medication disbursal and prices, by the very people that complain the most. People around the world are currently facing one of the largest challenges in current human history. The financial interests of the multi-billion dollar pharmaceutical industry/cartel threaten the right to health.

There is no such thing as a "Ritalin Deficiency." One of the things many doctors are trained to ignore are mineral and vitamin deficiencies. It is not fair to blame the problem on the daily workers, or many of the doctors directly effected within this industry cycle. Those to blame are the people accepting these problems without true challenge; the persons in-charge of releasing the medications, the government agencies that allow pay-offs, corporations based on profit instead of people, and the principles founding and/or justifying there actions. I suggest examining **www.nomorefakenews.com** as one additional source of information.

Over medication is a tendency that many HMO & PPO doctors are trained to accept when it comes to decisions about assigning medications? Acknowledgement of nutrient deficiencies, toxic build-up in the intestinal tract and elsewhere, artificial food ingredients, poor nutrient quality due to bad farming tactics, and/or parasites tend to be severely ignored in the analysis a multitude of health problems. Similar problems are involved in the dentistry field of chemicals and elements they are trained to use. Again, it is not the fault of the persons working in these fields as care assistants, nurses, doctors, etc., whether it is the fault of those in control of the supply of materials, education, and funding of these professionals; as well as blind acceptance of the average symptom suppressing medications, instead of feeding any deficiency.

The marketplace of the pharmaceutical industry is from disease; and its future growth is dependent on the further expansion of the disease market, or continued ill health of the potential customers. The pharmaceutical cartel, FDA, Tri-Lateral Commission, small arms trade, some health insurance corporations, and many life insurance corporations have been working together for a balance of death, illness, and price fixing. Are they working for you, or for your money?

A 2002 report from the JAMA (Journal of the American Medical Assoc.) stated in general that throughout the 1990's, nearly 90% of the doctors that wrote guidelines about common diseases like; diabetes, chronic fatigue syndrome, high blood pressure, etc., revealed relationships with drug companies. Almost 60% had financial relations with companies whose medications were considered in their guidelines. The problems are much greater than this. It is a real and obvious form of organized crime.

The FDA gets funding directly from the drug industry. In 1992, an anti-humanistic law was passed that is intended to have the FDA controlled by the pharmaceutical industry. It was not debated in congress, and there have never been votes against it. More and more simple ailments are being classified as diseases. Once it is classified as a disease, legally there can be no natural, inexpensive remedy that can cure or prevent it, according to their written for profit rules. The FDA says only a drug can legally help, and the final word on what is a "disease." Remember, the American Medical Association is not mandated of solve the medical problems of American citizen's. It is designed to protect medical doctors and the industry.

MEDICINE CHANGE

The rudimentary and institutional functioned medical training is commonly known and used in what is known as Toxi-Molecular Medicine. It is the administration of drugs at Sub-lethal quantities; to cover-up the disease process, disguise the difficulties of an ailment, and avoids the real cause. The examples of the medicines fully accessible by the public are commonly seen on many television promotions for depression, heartburn, herpes, etc, etc. The medicines available for many doctors, pharmacists, and the general public are almost always a symptomatic relief with potentials for dangerous side effects, never cures.

The pharmaceutical cartel in response, creates reliance on the part of the patient, and often complicates the doctor's job. Several medical professionals are trained to ignore, or subsequently erase valuable clues of the source of ailments. Some drugs save lives of ill patients, just like surgery etc. Millions of people have been realizing that Nutrition deficiencies are the real cause, and much cheaper to satisfy than the drugs from the average hospital. If the doctors of today don't become nutritionists, the nutritionists will become the doctors of tomorrow.

Orthomolecular Nutritionists believe that the treatment of infectious and degenerative diseases should be a matter of varying the concentration of vitamins, minerals, trace elements, amino acids, enzymes, hormones, etc., which are in the body. The optimum nutritional micro-environment of every cell in the body is vital to achieve or restore optimal health. The list of necessary nutrients is the same for every human being, but the relative amounts needed by each general race or individual is as different as the shape of a body. It is impossible to create a daily nutrition plan for every human. It can be generally assumed that milk from cows treated with genetically engineered bovine growth hormones, are affecting children's growth.

Everyone is different physically because of the food eaten, physical stature, mental aptitude, emotional stress, lifestyle environments, inherited biochemical and physiological composition, drinking water ingredients, and many other factors, determine your uniqueness. Nutrition is not just about preventing or reversing disease, it is about living favorably, where you have room to stretch your physical, mental, and spiritual muscles, without overstepping the threshold at which cellular health in any of the systems of the body become endangered.

NOURISHMENT FOR REAL HEALTH

Problems like diabetes II, attention deficit disorder, asthma, and others have natural cures, many unnatural causes, and very few natural ones. If internal damage is too extreme from excessive chemical damage, continual parasitic damage, and/or rare genetic problems, the slow long-term transformation from unhealthy to healthy bodies through whole food type supplements may require extra help. It is a wonder that the word origin of the word "diabetes" is so hard to find? Please remember that "research and common sense state that, you are what you eat, drink, breath, absorb, and think; even the toxins."

About 80% of the foods in the U.S. contain agents responsible for either long-term negative health problems, chemical build-up causing continuous organic damage, or create biological challenges which lead to susceptibility to other chemicals you may currently be able to naturally cleanse out of your body. The ancestors of each population of the human family starting around twenty million years ago lived on lean meat, fruits, seeds, grubs, roots, herbs, honey, cleaner water, cleaner air, and increasingly better traditions. Our bodies and digestive processes evolved on those diets. To be healthy, we must imitate that diet and eat raw foods, lean meats, and a minimum of dairy and grains.

Because of soil depletion of the essential minerals, the food that comes from the soil, and ultimately our bodies are deficient in these important trace minerals and likewise degenerative diseases are epidemic. The minerals Praseodymium and Yttrium have potentials of doubling the average lifespan. Rubidium and Cesium have been successful against cancer. Zinc is important in wound healing and also for the production of Super oxide dismutase (SOD), an element highly deficient in the average African American male. Iron and copper are basics for hemoglobin production. Germanium is an adaptogenic mineral that helps to fight all diseases. Even small levels of strontium and asbestos are used in some ways.

New Delhi's Center for Science and the Environment tested 12 Pepsi and Coca Cola products and released a report stating "each sample had enough poison to cause in the long term cancer, damage to the nervous and reproductive systems, birth defects and severe disruption of the immune system." (Www.organicconsumers.org/). Most people know that short-term deficiencies of food, water or rest can result in memory difficulties, and other short-term problems, but again, most people have no clue of long term effects made by combinations of seemingly safe ingredients, or lack of adequate nutrition. The IQ of the average student can be raised by simply changing to healthy foods, proper eating scheduling, correct sleeping hours, and mainly through ridding consumption of refined sugars. Human diseases like cancer, diabetes, etc., are considered to thrive in acidic, oxygen poor blood. Each point on the pH scale is said to be 10x more acidic than the previous number; for example 9 to 7 may be 10x, more deadly than 8 to 7. Diet sodas may have the highest acid content.

High blood acidity is called "ACIDOSIS." This is known as a lethal condition of the blood and root of many diseases as stated before. Food contains both acid and alkaline forming elements. In some, acid forming elements dominate, in others alkaline forming elements dominate. According to modern biochemistry, inorganic elements like sulphur, copper, phosphorus, potassium, sodium, magnesium, and calcium determine the acidity or alkalinity of the body.

Acidic condition inhibits nerve action, alkalinity stimulates nerve action. One who has a balanced condition can think and decide well. An extended amount of time such as 3–6 weeks consistently, prove beneficial in virtually everyone. Cold showers make the blood alkaline, while hot showers make the blood acidic. If your blood develops acidic conditions, your body deposits the more acidic substances in specific areas/organs of the body. When this condition continue's some cells die. As so, the dead cells themselves decay and turn into acids. However, some other cells may adapt by becoming abnormal cells called malignant cancer. Malignant cells may grow indefinitely and without order. This is what we call cancer.

Omega-3 fatty acids are among the few natural elements lacking in a majority of behavior problem student diets. Over the last One Hundred years, low Vitamin C intake, by males, has led to sperm damage across the general population.

What this means is that birth defects are, and will become more common. Did you ever wonder what populations of people these types of toxins marketed towards?

At the Earth Summit at Rio De Janeiro (June 1992), a report was released documenting the decline of nutritional minerals in farm and range soils, by continent, over the last hundred years. Here is a summary of the report: **Continent**	**Minerals % Depleted over 100 Years**
North America	85%
South America	76%
Asia	76%
Africa	74%
Europe	72%
Australia	55%

Water-Soluble Minerals are constantly being washed out of the soil and into the ocean. Until these minerals are regularly replaced in farm soils through the widespread use of seaweed, volcanic ash, and rock powders as fertilizers, you must find another way to get these minerals in your diet.

Many diseases in industrialized nations are linked to a deficiency in both trace and major minerals. Until the planet is subject to another rage of volcanic ash eruptions, asteroid collisions, or an ice age with the glaciers scouring out more minerals from the earth to renew the topsoil, we will have to make use of supplements. While our bodies can continue to function-however poorly-without vitamins, we must have minerals to survive. Critical minerals like selenium, zinc, magnesium, calcium, copper, and iron are now only marginally present in the soil. Organically grown foods are healthier because they are free from pesticides, but that is no guarantee that all the minerals we need are in that soil. Currently, well over half of the foods consumed by Americans are processed convenience foods. Organic foods are better than chemically treated ones, but if the minerals are not in the soil that the food grew in, the food will not contain them. In other words, the foods may be almost as bad as those with pesticides.

> "On June 14, 2003 Doctor. Mathias Rath made a complaint of genocide and other crimes against humanity against the pharmaceutical industry." (Reading Suggestion) Full story at:
> http://www.4.dr-rath-foundation.org

About 90% of the population of humans in North America, are infected by a parasite; such as a type of worm, or protozoa, according to the U.S. Center for Disease Control (2004). Nearly the same statistics can be stated of people worldwide. Most common symptoms like anemia, fatigue, digestive problems, etc., can be symptoms of an infection. There can be 10 different kinds of problems, parasites included; that can cause the same physical problem. Humans contract pesticides and parasites through several means; like infested portions of soil, non-organic fruits & vegetables, meats, mosquitoes, as well as infested people and pets.

MILK, OR NOT MILK

A synthetic hormone called rBGH (recombinant bovine growth hormone) that was approved by federal officials is within many dairy products in the U.S. Many of the milk cows in the U.S. are injected several times a month. The U.S. Food and Drug Administration (FDA), and the U.S. Department of Agriculture (USDA) support the anti common-sense agri-chemical companies. The so-called "FDA," declared rBGH as a safe product for use in milk cows. The FDA official responsible for the labeling policy not allowing consumer notice of rBGH containing dairy products is a Michael R. Taylor, a former partner of King &

Spaulding, the Washington, D.C. law firm that fought on behalf of Monsanto. Taylor, a lawyer, is a classic product of the generally republican sense of capitalistic order. From the year 1980, he worked for the FDA for 4 years as an executive assistant to the commissioner. In 1984 he joined the King & Spaulding Agency and remained there until 1991; during that time the law firm represented Monsanto while the company was seeking FDA approval of rBGH.

In 1991, President Bush (senior's) FDA Commissioner, David A. Kessler, Jr., revolved Taylor back into FDA as assistant commissioner for policy. Kessler himself was retained by President Clinton, as was Taylor. He signed the federal register notice warning grocery stores not to label milk as free of rBGH, therefore giving Monsanto a powerful boost in its fight to prevent consumers from knowing whether or not another toxin was in there food.

Researchers has discovered that rBGH-treated cows are very likely to have milk with more antibiotics, shortened shelf life, lower protein content, more tumor-promoting chemicals like IGF-I, which has been implicated in cancers of the colon, ovary, liver, smooth muscle, and breast. As many people have noticed, girls and boys are reaching puberty a few years younger than when many people that are adults have. The percentage that is above the natural potential 20% is highly prevalent. Over 50% of the children in the U.S. are physically developing faster than age expectations. Increased milk production with rBGH is estimated to cost taxpayers an additional $200 million from the general public into some chemical company's account. Up to 130 other genetically engineered food products are scheduled for approval by FDA in the next few years.

MICROWAVE EFFECTS

The effects on organic materials inside of the closed microwave over are usually not limited there. Headaches, extreme fatigue, cataracts, macular degeneration, possible eye cancer, certain rashes, and some types of nerve damage occur from microwave radiation poisoning. Most cooked foods are not properly digested because the nutrients molecules tend to be hard to digest. What then happens is that the immune system is weakened, memory retention is challenged, fatigue, and other problems occur. Most individuals still have no clue of the harm from PCS, and other cellular phones. We expose ourselves to un-researched radiation by putting the microwave transmitter in contact with their heads for extended, or constant amounts of time.

THE SKIN

The skin is the largest organ of virtually every animal on earth. Like many others, human skin absorbs an amount of most chemicals it touches. What we absorb can affect us either negatively or positively. The skin is the biggest membrane type organ. Human skin is our most important defense barrier against infections, as well as your largest organ for eliminating waste liquid. Petroleum products can clog your pores, blocking toxins from leaving your body. You know the results of clogged pores.

CHEMICALS & THE SKIN
(Propylene Glycol)

Damages your skins protective barrier, depletes moisture preservation abilities, dissolves proteins; encourages bacterial & parasitic growths.

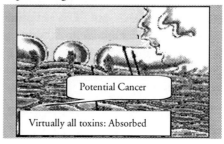

As discussed later in this chapter, on the shelf products are normally unsafe products. In 1938, the FDA granted self-regulation to the cosmetics industry. This meant that harmful products did not need to be listed, or marketed with government approval. Most of the 27,000 chemicals used in the U.S., have not been tested for long-term toxic effects. In a typical day, you might be exposed to over 200 different chemicals, many of which are suspected of causing cancer or juggling hormones. The so-called EPA, and other inadequate businesses, are beginning to accept the facts that the average industrial produced chemicals, may be messing with functions that control growth, reproduction, digestion, mental conditions, healing and immunity factors.

THE AIDS VIRUS

To be simply plain, I believe in the evidence stating AIDS (Auto-Immune Deficiency Syndrome) is caused by "HIV," which is a synthetic virus. This virus has no commonality in society except in the sporadic planting of the virus throughout the world over the past few decades, and mass media attention in the U.S. during the early 80's. It is determined that the agency called "Global 2000" represents the suspected shadow government where a few elitist white men in such organizations as the Trilateral Commission, Council of Foreign Relations, Illuminati, Skull & Bones, and other racist based organizations, seem to have designed plans by which well over two billion of the world's people are to expire because of synthetic agents, and designed wars.

The National Security Study Memorandum 200 that was created in 1974 by a Henry Kissinger, was adopted and approved by many of the nations of the world. On March 16, 1970 by President Richard Nixon approved the U.S. Public Law 91-213, authorizing HIV/AIDS and the development of HIV/AIDS as a matter of Public Law of the United States of America.

(MSG) MONOSODIUM GLUTAMATE

Some scientists tell us that MSG places humans at risk to poor health. MSG turns into glutamic acid within the body. The toxic effects of glutamic acid on damaging brain cells are available to research online. Glutamic acid can be considered a neurotoxin, because it has damaging and deadly effects on neuron cells. Studies in the 1970s demonstrated that at least 25% of the U.S. population reacted to MSG in negative ways. Since then, MSG has still been allowed to remain a growing part of the processed foods made in the U.S. Glutamic acid ingested as MSG enters the placenta during pregnancy, and crosses the blood-brain barrier during fetal development. It is generally accepted that the young are particularly at risk from ingestion of MSG. Currently; this ingredient is sold in bulk throughout Asia and being pumped into Africa. Ingredients stated as natural flavoring, are common ploys to hide this slow poison.

Animals that have absorbed glutamic acid during the fetal stage, or in the first 12 days of life tend to suffer learning deficits either immediately or in later life. The first published report of adverse reactions to MSG appeared in 1968, within a letter published by "*The New England Journal of Medicine.*" Some symptoms complained of are: numbness at the back of the neck, gradually radiating to both arms and the back, general weakness, and heart palpitations." Persons with an epileptic, ADHD, or other mental related problem should reasonable be advised to avoid foods rich in "MSG." Remember, MSG and Aspartame are Neurotoxins. From time to time, case reports have been published describing instances of adverse reactions associated with ingestion of MSG, but the FDA does not do anything because of pay-offs and coercion against the legislature to prevent profit loss change.

Hyperactive activity in children, severe "burning" headache, upper abdominal pain and pressure, hypertension, migraine headaches, myocardial infarction, brain tumors, neurosis, asthma, functional colitis, Fibromyalgia, vertigo, adrenal fatigue, and manic depression, are some symptoms associated with

MSG poisoning. Again, poisoning can occur over a long period of time, build-up negative reactions, or more commonly known as virtually instant. If you take blood pressure meds, be aware that some have effects on the lungs.

There are reports of adverse reactions associated with MSG in published literature, and most of those are reports of badly flawed research, pretending to have found no relationship between MSG and any sort of adverse reaction to it. They have funded, at least in part, by Ajinomoto's International Glutamate Technical Committee and/or others in the glutamate industry. Those industry-sponsored reports that claim to have demonstrated that MSG is "safe" far outnumber studies reported by independent researchers. The reasons for what might at first seem to be a discrepancy are ugly but straightforward. Those who generate studies that pretend to find that MSG is "safe" are invariably paid to do so, directly or indirectly, by the glutamate industry.

No food or drug company, and certainly not the U.S. Food and Drug Administration (FDA), adequately researches the potential toxicity of a food additive. Moreover, people who do studies that displease the industrial giants have been known to be smeared, harassed, loose jobs, have suspicious accidents, or people die. This type of behavior suggests that we are dealing with a cartel, not a group of businesses.

The FDA, both in its Adverse Reactions Monitoring System (ARMS) and elsewhere, has in its files numbers of letters from people reporting problems with MSG. In a Memorandum to the Health Hazards Evaluation Board of the FDA dated October 6, 1989 and June 8, 1990, entitled, "Adverse reactions associated with monosodium glutamate (MSG) ingestion,"

A "Linda Tollefson" had detailed the symptoms that had been reported to ARMS per dates received. The lists included headache, nausea, diarrhea, faster heart rate, change in mood, abdominal cramps, dizziness, localized pain and tenderness, sleep problems, change in vision, fatigue, weakness, abnormal changes in body temperature, difficulty breathing, facial swelling, non physically caused joint pain, numbness, blood pressure changes, difficulty swallowing, and more. (Tollefson insultingly concluded that after considering all of the material available to her, "...Nothing was submitted that suggested MSG is a human health hazard.") What does common sense tell you?

Endocrine disorders; conditions such as gross obesity, stunted growth, learning disabilities, and behavior disorders can be caused by MSG-induced damage to the endocrine system; glaucoma and retinal degeneration. As mentioned earlier, obesity, reproductive disorders, learning problems, ADHD, can many times be linked to neuroendocrine dysfunction caused by exposure of infants and small children to MSG. This product is mainly manufactured in California and shipped for sale into Thailand, Mexico, and other places, etc.

FLUORIDE

Fluoride compounds in water is called fluoridation. Many toothpaste and non-organic supplement tablets (including some vitamins) are not tested for safety before approval. Recent independent research by scientists not associated with dental trade organizations has shown the following:

1. **Neurotoxins Lower IQ**
    In 1995, neurotoxicologist and former Director of toxicology at Forsyth Dental Center in Boston, Mass, Dr. Phyllis Mullenix published research showed that fluoride build-up occurred in the brains of animals exposed to moderate levels over a short time. Damage to the brain occurred and the behavior patterns of the animals was adversely effected. Offspring of pregnant animals receiving relatively low doses of fluoride showed permanent effects to the brain, which were seen as hyperactivity (ADD-like symptoms). Young animals and adult animals given fluoride experienced the sluggishness. The toxic effects of fluoride on the central nervous system have been confirmed by previously classified government research.

2. **Causes of Cancer**
    The Department of Health in New Jersey found that bone cancer in male children was between two and seven times greater in areas where water was fluoridated. U.S. Environmental Protection Agency (EPA) researchers confirmed the bone cancer-causing effects of fluoride at low levels in an animal model. A recent has shown that fluoridation of water is linked to uterine cancer deaths.

3. **Changes Bone Structure and Strength**
    Fluoride gradually builds up in the bones and causes adverse changes to the bone structure. Some studies have shown that fluoridation leads to increases in hip fractures. Tensile strength of the hip is destroyed over time by fluoride ingestion.

4. **Causes Birth Defects and Prenatal Deaths**
    A toxicologist in the United Kingdom recently found that prenatal deaths in a fluoridated area was 15% higher than in neighboring non-fluoridated areas. The fluoridated area had a higher socio-economic status and would have been expected to have less prenatal deaths. The fluoridated area also had a

30% higher rate of Down's Syndrome. Chile banned fluoridation because of research by the world-renowned researcher, Dr Albert Schatz, which showed a link to infant deaths due to fluoridation.

5. **Impairs Immune System**
Fluoride impairs the functioning of the immune system over time. Chronic problems tend to occur over several years of use.

6. **Causes Acute Adverse Reactions**
Chronic Poisoning Effects: gastrointestinal symptoms, stomatitis, joint pains, polydipsia, headaches, visual disturbances, muscular weakness, and extreme fatigue.

7. **Fluoride Causes Osteoarthritis**
Published studies from Rhuematology International report in 2001, found links between fluoride exposure and the development of osteoarthritis. The level of fluoride exposure that causes osteoarthritis is common in the United States.

8. **Causes Permanent Disfigurement of the Teeth in Many Children**
A very large and increasing number of children are experiencing dental fluorosis that is a permanent adverse structural change to the teeth.

9. **Inhibits Key Enzymes**
As fluoride builds up in different parts of the body over decades, disrupts the actions of many key enzymes, and organs, such as the Pancreas.

10. **Banned in Many Countries**
Fluoridation is not legal in many countries. Please look-up Fluoride Status of Countries.

COMMONLY KNOWN HOUSEHOLD CHEMICALS

DMDM Hydantoin & Urea (Imidazolidinyl): Two of the many preservatives that release formaldehyde which causes joint pain, skin reactions, allergic reactions, depression, headaches, chest pains, ear infections, chronic fatigue, dizziness, and loss of sleep. Exposure may also irritate the respiratory system, trigger heart palpitations or asthma, and aggravate coughs and colds. Other effects include weakening the immune system and cancer. Alternative: Lonicera Japonica

Triclosan: A synthetic "antibacterial" ingredient—with a chemical structure similar to Agent Orange! The EPA registers it as a pesticide, giving it high scores as a risk to both human health and the environment. It is classified as a chlorophenol, a class of chemicals suspected of causing cancer in humans. Its manufacturing process may produce dioxin, a powerful hormone-disrupting chemical with toxic effects measured in the parts per trillion; that is only one drop in 300 Olympic-size swimming pools! Hormone disruptors pose enormous long-term chronic health risks by interfering with the way hormones perform, such as changing genetic material, decreasing fertility and sexual function, and fostering birth defects. It can temporarily deactivate sensory nerve endings, so contact with it often causes little or no pain. Internally, it can lead to cold sweats, circulatory collapse, and convulsions. Stored in body fat, it can accumulate to toxic levels, damaging the liver, kidneys and lungs, and can cause paralysis, suppression of immune function, brain hemorrhages, and heart problems. Tufts University School of Medicine says that triclosan is capable of forcing the emergence of "super bugs" that it cannot kill. Its widespread use in popular antibacterial cleansers, toothpastes and household products may have nightmare implications for our future. Alternative: Search for organic anti-bacterial agents, and/or hot steam.

FD&C Color Pigments: Synthetic colors made from coal tar, containing heavy metal salts that deposit toxins onto the skin, causing skin sensitivity and irritation. Absorption of certain colors can cause depletion of oxygen in the body and death of some cells. Animal studies have shown almost all of them to be carcinogenic.

Fragrances: Mostly synthetic ingredients can indicate the presence of up to four thousand separate ingredients, many toxic or carcinogenic. Symptoms reported to the FDA include headaches, dizziness, allergic rashes, skin discoloration, violent coughing and vomiting, and skin irritation. Clinical observation proves fragrances can affect the central nervous system, causing depression, hyperactivity, irritability, inability to cope, and other behavioral changes. Alternatives: Aroma therapeutic, Organic Essential Oils.

Try contacting some manufacturers yourself: The typical responses might be:

(1) Denial: "It's completely safe," or, "We never heard of that."

(2) Avoidance: "You'll have to talk to someone else" or "We can't talk about that."—or,

(3) Ignorance: "I've never heard about that."

All information provided in this chapter is publicly available through government and public access online resources.

ASPARTAME

Something approved by the U.S. Food and Drug Administration (FDA) composed of natural ingredients, would be assumed to be safe to eat, drink, swallow, or put on your skin, right? What about aspartame? Millions of people use aspartame, an artificial sweetener worldwide.

ASPARTAME CAN BE IN THESE LISTED PRODUCTS:

Instant breakfasts	Pharmaceuticals and supplements,
Breath mints	including over-the-counter medi-
Cereals	cines
Sugar-free chewing gum	Shake mixes
Cocoa mixes	Diet Soft drinks
Coffee beverages	Sugar-free Pudding
Frozen desserts	Tabletop sweeteners
Gelatin desserts	Tea beverages
Juice beverages	Instant teas and coffees
Laxatives	Topping mixes
Multivitamins (normally not in	Wine coolers
whole food supplements)	Yogurt
Milk drinks	

Aspartame; like many other dangerous products, have a bad history of premature approval and have toxic ingredients as a so-called sugar substitute. Aspartame can also increase your appetite due to the sweetness and normal craving generated to rid oneself of the aftertaste.

The FDA approval may signal a green light for safe consumption for some people, but a high percent of complaints registered with the FDA are for adverse reactions related to aspartame, including several deaths directly linked to the effects. Unscientific studies, suspicious approval methods, and ingredients, reveal the dangers of this artificial sweetener. Aspartame and MSG are Neurotoxins, but are in many of the foods and drinks sold in the U.S. and to millions of other people. The only safe sweetener products seem to be Honey, Stevia, Brown Cane Sugar, and a few others.

PUBLIC RECORDS ON ASPARTAME

The components of aspartame are reported to lead to a wide variety of ailments. Some of these problems occur gradually while others are immediate, acute reactions. Chemically, this substance is actually a neurotoxin that has the ability to do considerable damage, and suppress natural functions. If you feel a bit of a cringe when you consider using this stuff, your body is telling you "I don't want it." A few of the many more known disorders associated with aspartame include the following:

BIRTH DEFECTS

A study funded by Monsanto to study possible birth defects caused by consuming aspartame was cut off after preliminary data showed damaging information about aspartame. I suggest purchasing the book: **While Waiting: A Prenatal Guidebook.** "It is stated in this book that aspartame is suspected of causing brain damage in sensitive individuals." A fetus may be at risk for the effects, and SIDS may be one result. Some researchers have suggested that high doses of aspartame may be associated with problems ranging from dizziness and subtle brain changes to mental retardation. Look for the reports that are not funded through Aspartame using associations.

CANCER & ASPARTAME

The approval of aspartame is a violation of the U.S. Delaney Amendment, which is supposed to prevent cancer-causing substances such as methanol (formaldehyde) and DKP from entering our food supply. An early 80's FDA toxicologist testified before the U.S. Congress that aspartame was capable of producing brain tumors. This made it illegal for the FDA to set an allowable daily intake at any level. If the FDA itself elects to violate the law, who is left to protect the health of the public?"

DIABETES & ASPARTAME

The American Diabetes Association (ADA) actually recommended this chemical poison to persons with diabetes, but according to research conducted by a diabetes specialist, aspartame:

1) Leads to the precipitation of clinical diabetes.

2) Causes poorer diabetic control in diabetics on insulin or oral drugs.

3) Leads to the irritation of diabetic difficulties such as retinopathy, cataracts, neuropathy and gastro paresis.

4) Causes convulsions.

5) May cause liver, pancreas, and kidney damage, or facilitate any damage occurring.

6) Hinders the action of certain nutrients, and may add to such magnesium deficiency conditions.

Another researcher stated that excitotoxins such as those found in aspartame could precipitate diabetes in persons who are genetically susceptible to the disease. Aspartame and other toxins seem to be low-level population control agents.

EMOTIONAL DISORDERS & ASPARTAME

Several studies of low brain serotonin levels, depression, and other emotional disorders have been linked to aspartame and often are relieved by stopping the intake of aspartame.

Of course, extra help may be needed after this toxification.

EPILEPSY/SEIZURES & ASPARTAME

With the large and growing number of seizures caused by aspartame, it is sad to see that the Epilepsy Foundation is promoting the "safety" of aspartame. At Massachusetts Institute of Technology, 80 people who had suffered seizures after ingesting aspartame were surveyed. The Community Nutrition Institute concluded the following about the survey: "These 80 cases meet the FDA's own definition of an imminent hazard to the public health, which requires the FDA to expeditiously remove a dangerous product from the market."

Both the U.S. Air Force's magazine, Flying Safety, and the Navy's magazine, Navy Physiology, published articles warning about the many dangers of aspartame including the cumulative delirious effects of methanol and the greater likelihood of birth defects. The articles note that the ingestion of aspartame can make pilots more susceptible to seizures and vertigo. Twenty articles sounding warnings about ingesting aspartame while flying have also appeared in the National Business Aircraft Association Digest (NBAA Digest 1993), a paper warning about aspartame was presented at the 57th Annual Meeting of the Aerospace Medical Association (Gaffney 1986), Aviation Medical Bulletin (1988), The

Aviation Consumer (1988), Canadian General Aviation News (1990), Pacific Flyer (1988), General Aviation News (1989), Aviation Safety Digest (1989), and Plane & Pilot (1990).

A hotline was even set up for pilots suffering from acute reactions to aspartame ingestion. Over 600 pilots have reported symptoms including some who have reported suffering grandma seizures in the cockpit due to aspartame. Why don't we hear about these things?

WHY WE DO NOT HEAR ABOUT ASPARTAME, FOR REAL:

1) The industry financially suppresses countering information from spreading to the public.

2) Lack of awareness by the general population. Aspartame-caused diseases are not reported in the newspapers like plane crashes. This is because these incidents occur one at a time in thousands of different locations across the United States.

3) Most people do not associate their symptoms with the long-term use of aspartame. For the people who have killed a significant percentage of their brain cells, and poisoned other parts of their bodies they would normally not associate an illness with aspartame damage.

How aspartame was approved is a lesson in how chemical and pharmaceutical companies can manipulate government agencies such as the FDA, "bribe" organizations such as the American Dietetic Association, and flood the scientific community with flawed and fraudulent industry-sponsored studies funded by the makers.

During the late 1970's. A Dr Jacqueline Verrett, Senior Scientist in an FDA Bureau of Foods Review Team created in August 1977, reviewed the Bressler Report (a report that detailed G.D. Sealer's abuses during the pre-approval testing) and later said: "It was pretty obvious that somewhere along the line, the bureau officials were working up to a whitewash."

In 1987, Verrett testified before the US Senate stating that the experiments conducted by Searle were a "disaster." She stated that her team was instructed not to comment on or be concerned with the overall validity of the studies. She stated that questions about birth defects have not been answered.

She continued her testimony by discussing the fact that it has been shown to increase uterine polyps and change blood cholesterol. People that work in positions for the public should not work in motivation for money; they should work in motivation of principle. The November, 1992 Townsend Letter for Doctors reported on a study revealing that 37 of 49 top FDA officials who left the FDA took positions with companies they had regulated. They also reported that over 150 FDA officials owned stock in drug companies they were assigned to manage.

Many organizations and universities receive large funds from companies connected to the NutraSweet Association, one of a group of companies that promote the use of aspartame.

In January 1993, the American Dietetic Association received a $75,000 grant from the NutraSweet Company. The American Dietetic Association has stated that the NutraSweet Company writes there own "Facts Sheets." What is the FDA doing to protect the consumer from the dangers of aspartame?

—In 1992, the FDA approved aspartame for use in malt beverages, breakfast cereals, and refrigerated puddings and fillings. In 1993 the FDA approved aspartame for use in hard and soft candies, non-alcoholic favored beverages, tea beverages, fruit juices and concentrates, baked goods and baking mixes, and frostings, toppings and fillings for baked goods.

- In 1991, the FDA banned the importation of Stevia.

- The powder of this leaf has been used for hundreds of years as an alternative sweetener. It is used widely in Japan with no adverse effects. Scientists involved in reviewing stevia have declared it to be safe for human consumption—something that has been well known in many parts of the world where it is not banned. Some people believed that Stevia was banned at that time to keep the product from taking hold in the United States and cutting into sales of aspartame. Recently, the U.S. allowed Stevia to be sold to the public. What is the U.S. Congress and Administration doing to protect the consumer from the dangers of aspartame? Aspartame consumption is not only a problem in the United States—it is being sold in over 70 countries throughout the world.

(Anonymous E-Mail Messege, 5-21-04)

RECOMMENDED READING: *"THE DEADLY DECEPTION"*

"The Deadly Deception" cites chapter and verse of the cover-up by Searle and the FDA. Here are some highlights from the book "The Deadly Deception":

1969—Dr. Harry Waisman fed ASPARTAME mixed with milk to monkeys. One died after 300 days of ASPARTAME and five others had grand mal seizures. Searle deleted this negative study when the company submitted safety evidence to the FDA.

1971—Dr. John Olney, a research psychiatrist, told Searle that aspartame caused "holes in the brains of mice."

1975—Many of the test animals fed ASPARTAME developed TUMORS. These were not reported to the FDA.

1977—Despite the many complaints about ASPARTAME, William Conlon and Thomas Sullivan, the US attorneys, took no action due to pay offs, in the five years the statute of limitations for a grand jury investigation expired.

1981—Dr. Arthur Hull Hayes, Jr. was appointed the new FDA Commissioner and overruled the Public Board of Inquiry's recommended ban of ASPARTAME. It was approved as a "food additive," and exempt from continued research. {What other health problems are there in our world since?}

1984—100,000 people swallowed 7-million pounds of Aspartame products, with multiple health effects since. Several so-called chronic diseases have become more common worldwide.

PROBLEMS LINKED TO MSG IN CONJUNCTION WITH ASPARTAME

Cardiac	Neurological	Respiratory
Arrhythmia	Depression	Asthma
Atrial fibrillation	Mood swings	Shortness of breath
Tachycardia	Rage reactions	Chest pain
Rapid heartbeat	Migraine headache	Tightness in the
Palpitations	Dizziness	chest
Slow heartbeat	Light-headedness	Runny nose
Angina	Loss of balance	Sneezing
Extreme rise or drop	Disorientation	**Urological/Genital**
. in blood pressure	Mental confusion	Swelling of the
Circulatory	Anxiety	prostate
Swelling	Panic attacks	Swelling of the
Gastrointestinal	Hyperactivity	vagina
Diarrhea	Behavioral problems	Vaginal spotting
Nausea/vomiting	..in children	Frequent urination

Stomach cramps	Attention deficit	Nocturia
Irritable bowel	disorders	**Skin**
Swelling of	Lethargy	Hives (may be both
hemorrhoids	Sleepiness	..internal and
..and/or anus area	Insomnia	external)
Rectal bleeding	Numbness or paralysis	Rash
Bloating	Seizures	Mouth lesions
Muscular	Sciatica	Temporary tightness
Flu-like achiness	Slurred speech	or
Joint pain	Chills and shakes	..partial paralysis
Stiffness	Shuddering	..(Numbness or
Endocrine	**Visual**	tingling)
Pancreas Poisoning	Blurred vision	. of the skin
Etc.	Difficulty focusing	Flushing
	Pressure around eyes	Extreme dryness of
		..the mouth
		Face swelling
		Tongue swelling
		Bags under eyes

ANCESTRY & HEALTH

African-American, Native American, etc., ancestry is also an important indicator of the ability of anyone having tendencies towards, early damages; rare genetically initiated diseases, etc. It must be recognized that none of the races of humans had such a large amount of ailments like Hypertension, Diabetes, STD's, etc, until colonization; hyper-capitalistic industrial growth, and extreme political mismanagement have taken control of this time. Pesticide chemical damage, average chemical Toxification, etc, causing noted as chronic illnesses and cancers are not based on genetic weaknesses.

One should be very careful towards the blanket identification of a majority of chronic problems listed as coming from a family member. Nearly 90% of the chemicals produced today for general personal use, cooking, additives on foods, etc., also create the same so-called chronic genetically initiated problems. Don't blame your family, but know if you eat organic, you're still a target.

The African-American population is formed mainly, from a genetic mixture across African and Indigenous Peoples of the Americas. Like all types of humans, each race has specific physical strengths and weaknesses. Our bodies are designed for the conditions they originated from. Foreign and artificial elements of consumption are un-natural to many, and therefore should logically be expected to cause harm or challenge, if un-adapted. The same is generally true of a person from one culture to another, but of the same race.

FOOD GUIDE AND DEFICIENCY PROBLEMS

The populations of people around the world that suffer from fast food addiction and processed food dependence are the main persons in rising counts of diabetes type II. They tend to be low in the following nutritional elements: magnesium, chromium, zinc, vitamin C, potassium, calcium, water, vanadium, B6, manganese, folic acid, and alpha lipoic acid. It is normally the case that the person is extremely low in the elements magnesium and chromium, if they become diabetic. Besides the average American having an average of only 40% of the digestive bacteria needed to maintain good health, the average person in the USA is 80 % deficient in the mineral magnesium alone, as of 2004, according to several nutritional researchers.

Among the best sources of assurance to replenishment these and other elements are from whole-food multivitamin/multiminerals, with pro-biotics. Several herbs are also beneficial and cleansing your body of toxins as ancient peoples have in conjunction with faith shouldn't be too bad of a goal either.

	Doctors under the Control of the Pharmecuetical Cartel are the Third Leading Cause of Death Some studies show that doctors account for over 250,000 deaths per year. Most don't do it intentionally, but due to a lack of knowledge, human error, and over-influence from drug companies or government, that is the result.	

WHAT ARE THE DANGERS OF PROCESSED WHITE SUGAR (SUCROSE)?

-Use of Honey, Stevia, or unprocessed sugar is suggested-

Sugar contributes to weakened defense against bacterial infection.
Sugar can cause kidney damage.

Sugar can reduce helpful high-density lipoproteins (HDLs).
Sugar interferes with absorption of calcium and magnesium.
Sugar suppresses the immune system, and is a leading motivator for food allergies.
Sugar upsets the body's mineral balance, and can decrease growth hormones.
Sugar can cause hyperactivity, anxiety, concentration difficulties, and crankiness.
Sugar can cause drowsiness and decreased activity in children.
Sugar negatively effects school performance.
Sugar can produce a significant rise in bad cholesterol.
Sugar can weaken eyesight, and can contribute to eczema.
Sugar can speed the aging process, causing wrinkles and gray hair.
Sugar can promote tooth decay.
Sugar raises the level of a neurotransmitter called serotonin, which can narrow blood vessels.
Sugar can cause hypoglycemia.
Sugar may lead to chromium deficiency.
Sugar can cause copper deficiency.
Sugar can lead to periodontal disease.
Sugar can overstress the pancreas, causing damage.
Sugar can cause tendons to become brittle.
Sugar can motivate headaches, including migraines.
Sugar can cause an increase in alpha, delta, and theta brain waves, which can alter the ability to think.
Sugar can cause candidiasis (yeast infection).
Sugar can motivate the formation of gallstones.
Sugar can motivate the formation of kidney stones.
Sucralose shrinks thymus glands.
Sucralose enlarges liver and kidneys.
Sucralose causes atrophy of lymph follicles in the spleen and thymus.
Sucralose reduces growth rate.
Sucralose decreases red blood cell count.
Sucralose causes hyperplasia of the pelvis.
Sucralose may cause extension of the pregnancy period or premature abortion.
Sucralose causes memory and other brain problems.
Sucralose concentrates in the liver, gastrointestinal tract, and kidneys over time.
Sucralose is generally 98% pure, the remaining 2% containing Lead, Arsenic, Triphenilphosphine Oxide, Methanol, Chlorinated Disaccharides, and Chlorinated Monosaccharide.

AVERAGE AMERICAN HOUSEHOLD TOXIC CHEMICALS— INGREDIENT DIRECTORY

1,4-dioxane Look-Up Ethoxylated surfactants	A carcinogenic contaminant of cosmetic products. Almost 50% of cosmetics containing ethoxylated surfactants were found to contain dioxins. **From Material Safety Data Sheet (MSDS):** 1,4-DIOXANE MAY EXERT ITS EFFECTS THROUGH INHALATION, SKIN ABSORPTION, AND INGESTION. 1,4-DIOXANE IS LISTED AS A CARCINOGEN. EFFECTS OF OVEREXPOSURE: 1,4-DIOXANE IS AN EYE AND MUCOUS MEMBRANE IRRITANT, PRIMARY SKIN IRRITANT, CENTRAL NERVOUS SYSTEM DEPRESSANT, NEPHROTOXIN, AND HEPATOTOXIN. ACUTE EXPOSURE CAUSES IRRITATION, HEADACHE, DIZZINESS, AND NARCOSIS. CHRONIC INHALATION EXPOSURE CAN PRODUCE DAMAGE TO THE LIVER, LYMPHATIC SYSTEM, AND KIDNEYS, AND BLOOD DISORDERS. MEDICAL CONDITION AGGRAVATED BY EXPOSURE PRECLUDES FROM EXPOSURE THOSE INDIVIDUALS WITH DISEASE OF THE BLOOD, LIVER KIDNEYS, CENTRAL NERVOUS SYSTEM, AND THOSE SUSCEPTIBLE TO DERMATITIS.

2-bromo-2-nitropropane-1, 3-diol (Bronopol)	Toxic: Causes Allergic Dermatitis. Look-Up Nitro sating agents
Alcohol, Isopropyl (SD-40)	A very drying and irritating solvent and dehydrator that strips your skin's natural acid mantle, making us more vulnerable to bacteria, moulds and viruses. It is made from propylene, a petroleum derivative. It may promote brown spots and premature aging of skin.
Anionic Surfactants	Anionic refers to the negative charge these surfactants have. They may be contaminated with nitrosamines, which are carcinogenic. Surfactants can pose serious health threats. They are used in car washes, as garage floor cleaners and engine degreasers—and in 90% of personal-care products that foam. Sodium Lauryl Sulfate (SLS) Sodium Laureth Sulfate (SLES) Ammonium Lauryl Sulfate (ALS) Ammonium Laureth Sulfate (ALES) Sodium Methyl Cocoyl Taurate Sodium Lauryl Sarcosinate Sodium Cocoyl Sarcosinate Potassium Coco Hydrolyzed Collagen TEA (Triethanolamine) Lauryl Sulfate TEA (Triethanolamine) Laureth Sulfate Lauryl or Cocoyl Sarcosine Disodium Oleamide Sulfosuccinate Disodium Laureth Sulfosuccinate Disodium Dioctyl Sulfosuccinate etc
Benzalkonium Chloride	Highly toxic, primary skin irritant. Look-Up Cationic surfactants **From Material Safety Data Sheet (MSDS):** MATERIAL IS HIGHLY TOXIC VIA ORAL ROUTE.

Benzalkonium Chloride	EFFECTS OF OVEREXPOSURE: MISTS CAN CAUSE IRRITATION TO THE SKIN, EYES, NOSE, THROAT AND MUCOUS MEMBRANES. AVOID DIRECT CONTACT. SYMPTOMS: MUSCULAR PARALYSIS, LOW BLOOD PRESSURE, CNS DEPRESSION AND WEAKNESS. INGESTION: IF CONSCIOUS, IMMEDIATELY DRINK LARGE QUANTITIES OF FLUID TO DILUTE AND INDUCE VOMITING. CALL PHYSICIAN.
Butylated Hydroxyanisole (BHA)	Known to cause allergic contact dermatitis.
Cationic surfactants	These chemicals have a positive electrical charge. They contain a quaternary ammonium group and are often called "quats". These are used in hair conditioners, but originated from the paper and fabric industries as softeners and anti-static agents. In the long run they cause the hair to become dry and brittle. They are synthetic, irritating, allergenic and toxic, and oral intake of them can be lethal. Stearalkonium chloride Benzalkonium chloride Cetrimonium chloride Cetalkonium chloride Lauryl dimonium hydrolyzed collagen
Chloromethylisothiazolinone and	Causes contact dermatitis
Cocoamidopropyl Betaine	**From Material Safety Data Sheet (MSDS):** CAN CAUSE EYE AND SKIN IRRITATION.

Cyclomethicone	Look-Up Silicone derived emollients
DEA (diethanolamine), MEA (Monoethanolamine), & TEA (triethanolamine)	Often used in cosmetics to adjust the pH, and used with many fatty acids to convert acid to salt (stearate), this then becomes the base for a cleanser. TEA causes allergic reactions including eye problems, dryness of hair and skin, and could be toxic if absorbed into the body over a long period of time. These chemicals are already restricted in Europe due to known carcinogenic effects. Dr. Samuel Epstein (Professor of Environmental Health at the University of Illinois) says that repeated skin applications…of DEA-based detergents resulted in a major increase in the incidence of liver and kidney cancer. **From Material Safety Data Sheet (MSDS):** Health Hazard Acute And Chronic: Product is severely irritating to body tissues and possibly corrosive to the eyes. Explanation Carcinogenicity: Amines react with nitro sating agents to form nitro amines, which are carcinogenic.
DMDM Hydantoin	Contains formaldehyde.
Ethoxylated surfactants	Ethoxylated surfactants are widely used in cosmetics as foaming agents, emulsifiers and humectants. As part of the manufacturing process the toxic chemical 1,4-dioxane, a potent carcinogen, is generated. On the label, they are identified by the prefix "PEG", "polyethylene", "polyethylene glycol", "polyoxyethylene", "-eth-", or "-oxynol-". Look-Up 1,4-Dioxane

FD&C Color Pigments	Synthetic colors made from coal tar. Contain heavy metal salts that deposit toxins onto the skin, causing skin sensitivity and irritation. Animal studies have shown almost all of them to be carcinogenic.
Fluoride	Excessive Use: Neurotoxin effects may cause ADD, SIDS, Chronic Immune System Disorders, Organ Activity Problems (i.e. stomach, pancreas, intestines), and Enzyme Suppression in the bodies of all mammals.
Formaldehyde	Formaldehyde is a known carcinogen (causes cancer). Causes allergic, irritant and contact dermatitis, headaches and chronic fatigue. The vapor is extremely irritating to the eyes, nose and throat (mucous membranes).
Fragrance	Fragrance on a label can indicate the presence of up to four thousand separate ingredients, many toxic or carcinogenic. Symptoms reported to the USA FDA include headaches, dizziness, allergic rashes, skin discoloration, violent coughing and vomiting, and skin irritation. Clinical observation proves fragrances can affect the central nervous system, causing depression, hyperactivity, and irritability.
Imidazolidinyl Urea	The trade name for this chemical is Germall 115. Releases formaldehyde, a carcinogenic chemical, into cosmetics at over 10°C. Toxic. Look-Up Formaldehyde
Isopropyl Palmitate	A fatty acid from palm oil combined with synthetic alcohol. Industry tests on rabbits indicate the chemical can cause skin irritation and dermatitis. Also shown to be comedogenic (acne promoting)

Lanolin	Any chemicals used on sheep will contaminate the lanolin obtained from the wool. The majority of lanolin used in cosmetics is highly contaminated with organo-phosphate pesticides and insecticides.
Liquidum Paraffinum	Liquidum Paraffinum is an exotic sounding way to say mineral oil.
Mineral Oil	Petroleum by-product that coats the skin like plastic, clogging the pores. Interferes with skin's ability to eliminate toxins, promoting acne and other disorders. Slows down skin function and cell development, **resulting in premature aging**. Used in many products (baby oil is 100% mineral oil!) Any mineral oil derivative can be contaminated with cancer causing PAH's (Polycyclic Aromatic Hydrocarbons). Manufacturers use petrolatum because it is unbelievably cheap. Mineral oil Liquidum paraffinum (also known as posh mineral oil!) Paraffin oil Paraffin wax Petrolatum
Nitro sating Agents	The following chemicals can cause nitro amine contamination, which have been determined to form cancer in laboratory animals. There are wide and repeated concerns in the USA and Europe about the contamination of cosmetics products with nitro amines. 2-bromo-2-nitropropane-1, 3-diol Cocoyl Sarcosine DEA compounds Imidazolidinyl Urea Formaldehyde

Nitro sating Agents	Hydrolyzed Animal Protein Lauryl Sarcosine MEA compounds Quaternium-7, 15, 31, 60, etc Sodium Lauryl Sulfate Ammonium Lauryl Sulfate Sodium Laureth Sulfate Ammonium Laureth Sulfate Sodium Methyl Cocoyl Taurate TEA compounds
Paraben preservatives (methyl, propyl, butyl, and ethyl)	Used as inhibitors of microbial growth and to extend shelf life of products. Widely used even though they are known to be toxic. Have caused many allergic reactions and skin rashes. Highly toxic. **From Material Safety Data Sheet (MSDS):** EMERGENCY OVERVIEW: WARNING! HARMFUL IF SWALLOWED OR INHALED. CAUSES IRRITATION TO SKIN, EYES AND RESPIRATORY TRACT. MAY CAUSE ALLERGIC SKIN REACTION. SKIN CONTACT: CAUSES IRRITATION TO SKIN. SYMPTOMS INCLUDE REDNESS, ITCHING, AND PAIN. MAY CAUSE ALLERGIC SKIN REACTIONS. EYE CONTACT: CAUSES IRRITATION, REDNESS, AND PAIN.
Paraffin wax/oil	Paraffin Wax is mineral oil wax. Look-Up Mineral Oil
Phthalates	Toxic gender bending chemical used as a plasticizer in food wraps and many pliable plastics and containers. Also used in hairsprays and some cosmetics including nail varnishes from where it is readily absorbed into the system. All 289 people

Phthalates	in a recent test for body load of chemicals tested positive for phthalates. Phthalates are implicated with low sperm counts and also causing sexual abnormalities and deformities.
Polyethylene Glycol (PEG) compounds	Potentially carcinogenic petroleum ingredient that can alter and reduce the skin's natural moisture factor. This could increase the appearance of aging and leave you more vulnerable to bacteria. Used in cleansers to dissolve oil and grease. It adjusts the melting point and thickens products. Also used in caustic spray-on oven cleaners. Look-Up Ethoxylated surfactants
Propylene/Butylene Glycol	Propylene glycol (PG) is a petroleum derivative. It penetrates the skin and can weaken protein and cellular structure. Commonly used to make extracts from herbs. PG is strong enough to remove barnacles from boats! The EPA considers PG so toxic that it requires workers to wear protective gloves, clothing and goggles and to dispose of any PG solutions by burying them in the ground. Because PG penetrates the skin so quickly, the EPA warns against skin contact to prevent consequences such as brain, liver, lymphatic system, and kidney abnormalities. But there isn't even a warning label on products such as stick deodorants, where the concentration is greater than in most industrial applications.

Propylene/Butylene Glycol	**From Material Safety Data Sheet (MSDS):** Health Hazard Acute And Chronic INHALATION: May cause respiratory and throat Irritation, central nervous system depression, blood and kidney disorders. May cause Nystagmus, Lymphocytosis. SKIN: Irritation and dermatitis, absorption may directly harm the Lymphatic System. (Possible leading cause of diabetes type II) EYES: Irritation and conjunctivitis. INGESTION: Pulmonary oedema, brain damage, hypoglycemia, intravascular hemolysis. Death may occur.
PVP/VA Copolymer	A petroleum-derived chemical used in hairsprays, wave sets and other cosmetics. It can be considered toxic, since particles may contribute to foreign bodies in the lungs of sensitive persons.
Quaternium-7, 15, 31, 60, etc	Toxic, causes skin rashes and allergic reactions. Formaldehyde releasers. Dr Epstein reports in his book Unreasonable Risk "Substantive evidence of casual relation to leukemia, multiple myeloma, non-Hodgkin's lymphoma and other cancers" **From Material Safety Data Sheet (MSDS):** SKIN: PROLONGED OR REPEATED EXPOSURE MAY CAUSE SKIN IRRITATION. MAY CAUSE MORE SEVERE RESPONSE IF SKIN IS DAMP. MAY BE A WEAK SKIN SENSITIZER IN SUSCEPTIBLE INDIVIDUALS AT GREATER THAN 1% IN AQUEOUS SOLUTION.

Rancid Natural Emollients	Natural oils used in cosmetics should be cold pressed. The refined vegetable oils found on supermarket shelves and many health food stores which lack color, odor and taste are devoid of nutrients, essential fatty acids, vitamins and oils—all valuable skin conditioning agents! They also contain poisonous "trans" fatty acids as a result of the refining process. Another important factor to consider with creams made from plant oil is the use-by date. The most beneficial plant oils (like rosehip, borage and evening primrose oils) are polyunsaturated, which means they oxidise and go rancid fairly quickly (about 6 months). Most off-the-shelf cosmetics have a shelf life of three years. Rancid oils are harmful, they form free radicals, which damage and age your skin.

Silicone derived emollients	Silicone emollients are occlusive—that is they coat the skin, trapping anything beneath it, and do not allow the skin to breathe. Studies have indicated that prolonged exposure on the skin to sweat, by occlusion, causes skin irritation. Some synthetic emollients are known tumor promoters and accumulate in the liver and lymph nodes. They are also non-biodegradable, causing negative environmental impact.
	  Dimethicone
	  Dimethicone Copolyol
	  Cyclomethicone
	Silicone was and still is used as breast implants. Tens of thousands of women with breast implants have complained of debilitating symptoms. Anecdotal evidence indicates silicone to be toxic to the human body. For more detailed information on the dangers of silicone simply key "silicone toxicity" into the Google search engine

Sodium Laureth Sulfate (SLES) Ammonium Laureth Sulfate (ALES)	When combined with other chemicals, SLES and ALES can create nitro amines, a potent class of carcinogens. It is frequently disguised in semi-natural cosmetics with the explanation "comes from coconut". **From Material Safety Data Sheet (MSDS):** WARNING! CAUSES SKIN AND EYE IRRITATION! AVOID CONTACT WITH EYES, SKIN AND CLOTHING. THE MATERIAL WAS CLASSIFIED AS A MODERATE TO SEVERE EYE IRRITANT.
Sodium Lauryl Sulfate (SLS) & Ammonium Lauryl Sulfate (ALS)	Used in car washes, hand soap, dish soap, garage floor cleaners and engine degreasers—and in 90% of products that foam. Animals exposed to SLS and ALS experience eye damage, central nervous system depression, labored breathing, diarrhea, severe skin irritation, and even death. Young eyes may not develop properly if exposed to SLS and ALS because proteins are dissolved. SLS and ALS may also damage the skin's immune system by causing layers to separate and inflame. It is frequently disguised in semi-natural cosmetics with the explanation "comes from coconut". Look-Up Nitro sating agents & Look-Up Anionic Surfactants **From Material Safety Data Sheet (MSDS):** EYE CONTACT: INSTILLATION OF A 29% SODIUM LAURYL SULFATE SOLUTION INTO THE EYES OF SIX ALBINO RABBITS PRODUCED SEVERE IRRITATION. THE MATERIAL WAS CLASSIFIED AS A SEVERE SKIN IRRITANT.

Stearalkonium Chloride	A chemical used in hair conditioners and creams. Causes allergic reactions. Stearalkonium chloride was developed by the fabric industry as a fabric softener, and is a lot cheaper and easier to use in hair conditioning formulas than proteins or herbals, which do help hair health. Toxic.—Look-Up Cationic surfactants
Talc	Scientific studies have shown that routine application of talcum powder in the genital area is associated with a three-to-fourfold increase in the development of ovarian cancer.
TEA (Triethanolamine) Laureth Sulfate	Synthetic emulsifier. Highly acidic. Over 40% of cosmetics containing Triethanolamine (TEA), are contaminated with carcinogens, called nitro amines. **From Material Safety Data Sheet: Special Hazard Precautions:** PRODUCT IS SEVERELY IRRITATING TO BODY TISSUES AND POSSIBLY CORROSIVE TO THE EYES. HANDLE WITH CARE. AVOID EYE & SKIN CONTACT. AVOID BREATHING VAPORS IF GENERATED. IF THERE IS DANGER OF EYE CONTACT, WEAR A FACE SHIELD. Explanation Carcinogenicity: AMINES REACT WITH NITROSATING AGENTS TO FORM NITROSOAMINES, WHICH ARE CARCINOGENIC.
Toluene	**From Material Safety Data Sheet (MSDS):** POISON! DANGER! HARMFUL OR FATAL IF SWALLOWED. HARMFUL IF INHALED OR ABSORBED THROUGH SKIN.

Toluene	VAPOR HARMFUL. FLAMMABLE LIQUID AND VAPOR. MAY AFFECT LIVER, KIDNEYS, PANCREAS, CIRCULATION SYSTEM, OR CENTRAL NERVOUS SYSTEM. CAUSES IRRITATION TO SKIN, EYES AND RESPIRATORY TRACT. INHALATION: INHALATION MAY CAUSE IRRITATION OF THE UPPER RESPIRATORY TRACT. SYMPTOMS OF OVEREXPOSURE MAY INCLUDE FATIGUE, CONFUSION, HEADACHE, DIZZINESS AND DROWSINESS. PECULIAR SKIN SENSATIONS (E. G. PINS AND NEEDLES) OR NUMBNESS MAY BE PRODUCED. VERY HIGH CONCENTRATIONS MAY CAUSE UNCONSCIOUSNESS AND DEATH. INGESTION: SWALLOWING MAY CAUSE ABDOMINAL SPASMS AND OTHER SYMPTOMS THAT PARALLEL OVER-EXPOSURE FROM INHALATION. ASPARTAMEIRATION OF MATERIAL INTO THE LUNGS CAN CAUSE CHEMICAL PNEUMONITIS, WHICH MAY BE FATAL. SKIN CONTACT: CAUSES IRRITATION. MAY BE ABSORBED THROUGH SKIN. EYE CONTACT: CAUSES SEVERE EYE IRRITATION WITH REDNESS AND PAIN. CHRONIC EXPOSURE: REPORTS OF CHRONIC POISONING DESCRIBES ANEMIA, DECREASED BLOOD CELL COUNT AND BONE MARROW HYPOPLASIA. PANCREAS, LIVER AND KIDNEY DAMAGE MAY OCCUR. REPEATED

Toluene	OR PROLONGED CONTACT HAS A DEFATTING ACTION, CAUSING DRYING, REDNESS, AND DERMATITIS. EXPOSURE TO TOLUENE MAY EFFECT A DEVELOPING FETUS.

PESTICIDES IN/ON YOUR FOOD:

- Macozeb
- Daminozide
- Carbaryl
- Captan
- Dicloran
- Folpet, Chlorothalonil
- ETU, Methamidophos

- UDMH
- Chloropyrifos
- Azinphos-Methyl
- Diazonon
- Dimethoate
- Acephate
- Permethrine
- Methyl-parathion
- Omethoate
- DDT
- Phosmet
- Methamidophos, among others...

With all of these chemicals involved in the daily life of most U.S. citizens and those of many other countries, it should be of no surprise that problems such as diabetes, high blood pressure, ADHD, ovarian cancer, breast cancer, and many birth defects are becoming much more common. The human body is able to adapt to the consumption of a multitude of foods, but chemical damage may not allow the body to function normally. Industrial companies and pharmaceutical corporations that produce these chemicals, as well as various insurance companies, have invested interests in the damage certain household toxins, pesticides, and the drug reliance patterns that may be planned as a result.

Recently it has been confirmed that most Americans have dietary deficiencies. According to the studies, Americans tend to be deficient in virtually all vitamins, minerals, essential amino acids and essential fatty acids. Unfortunately, deficiencies in these areas are seriously suppressed to the benefit of pharmaceutical companies, which endeavor to control the awareness and facilitation of information to health care facilities, etc. A full majority of over the counter vitamins and minerals are not compatible with human physiology. It is best to find supplements made from whole food natural companies.

SOME NUTRIENT INFORMATION

VITAMIN A (Retinol)
VALUE: foundation for most retinal regeneration of the four light-absorbing pigments in the eye.
Broccoli, Carrots and some other vegetables provide **beta-carotene**, which the liver converts into other forms.
DEFICIENCY SYMPTOMS: Skin Blemishes, Night-Blindness, other problems may be related. Excess Vitamin A is stored in the liver, but can be toxic in large doses, especially in children. Best taken from food sources, and whole-food based vitamins....(See health text).

VITAMIN B-1 (Thiamine)
VALUE: Plays a key role in the body's metabolic cycle for generating energy; aids in the digestion of carbohydrates; essential for the normal functioning of the nervous system, muscles & heart; stabilizes the appetite; promotes growth & good muscle tone./
DEFICIENCY SYMPTOMS: May lead to mental depression & constipation; weakness & feeling tired; nervous irritability; insomnia; the loss of appetite; paralysis & loss of weight; vague aches & pains; heart & gastrointestinal problems....(See health text).

VITAMIN B-2 (Riboflavin)
VALUE: Necessary for carbohydrate, fat & protein metabolism; aids in the formation of antibodies and red blood cells; maintains cell respiration; necessary for the maintenance of good vision, skin, nails & hair; alleviates eye fatigue; promotes general health./
DEFICIENCY SYMPTOMS: May result in sluggishness; itching and burning eyes; cracks and sores in the mouth & lips; bloodshot eyes; purplish tongue; dermatitis; retarded growth; digestive disturbances; trembling; oily skin....(See health text).

VITAMIN B-6 (Pyridoxine)
VALUE: Necessary for synthesis & breakdown of amino acids, the building blocks of protein; aids in fat and carbohydrate metabolism; aids in the formation

of antibodies; maintains the central nervous system; aids in the removal of excess fluid of premenstrual women; promotes health skin; reduces muscle spasms, leg cramps, hand numbness, nausea & stiffness of hands; helps maintain a proper balance of sodium & phosphorous in the body.
DEFICIENCY SYMPTOMS: May result in nervousness, insomnia, skin eruptions, loss of muscular control, anemia, mouth disorders, muscular weakness, dermatitis, arm & leg cramps, loss of hair, slow learning, and water retention….(See health text).

VITAMIN B-12 (Cobalamin)
VALUE: Helps in the formation & regeneration of red blood cells, thus helping prevent anemia; necessary for carbohydrate, fat & protein metabolism; maintains a healthy nervous system; promotes growth in children; increase energy; needed for Calcium absorption.
DEFICIENCY SYMPTOMS: May lead to depression, tiredness, nervousness, pernicious anemia, poor appetite, growth failure in children, brain damage, neuritis, and degeneration of spinal cord, lack of balance….(See health text).

NIACINAMIDE (VITAMIN B-3)
VALUE: Improves circulation and reduces the cholesterol level in the blood; maintains the nervous system; helps metabolize protein, sugar, & fat; reduces high blood pressure; increases energy through proper utilization of food; prevents pellagra; helps maintain a healthy skin, tongue & digestive system.
DEFICIENCY SYMPTOMS: May result in mental depression, nervousness, irritability, fatigue, insomnia, pellagra, gastrointestinal disturbance, headaches, vague aches & pains, loss of appetite, skin disorders, muscular weakness, indigestion, bad breath, canker sores….(See health text).

PANTOTHENIC ACID (VITAMIN B-5)
VALUE: Participates in the release of energy from carbohydrates, fats & protein, aids in the utilization of vitamins; improves the body's resistance to stress; helps in cell building & the development of the central nervous system; helps the adrenal glands, fights infections by building antibodies.
DEFICIENCY SYMPTOMS: May lead to restlessness, painful & burning feet, skin abnormalities, retarded growth, dizzy spells, digestive disturbances, vomiting, stomach stress, muscle cramps….(See health text).

PABA (PARA AMINO BENZOIC ACID)
VALUE: Aids healthy bacteria in producing folic acid; aids in the formation of red blood cells; contains sun screening properties; aids in the assimilation of Pantothenic acids; returns hair to its natural color.

DEFICIENCY SYMPTOMS: May cause depression, nervousness, extreme fatigue, irritability, eczema, constipation, headaches, digestive disorders, and hair turning prematurely gray....(See health text).

FOLIC ACID (VITAMIN B-9)
VALUE: Necessary for DNA & RNA synthesis, which is essential for the growth and reproduction of all body cells; essential to the formation of red blood cells by its action on the bone marrow; aids in amino acid metabolism.
DEFICIENCY SYMPTOMS: May result in gastrointestinal disorders, anemia, Vitamin B-12 deficiency, pre-mature gray hair....(See health text).

BIOTIN
VALUE: Aids in the utilization of protein, folic acid, Pantothenic acid, and Vitamin B-12, Glucose-energy facilitation, promotes healthy hair.
DEFICIENCY SYMPTOMS: May lead to depression, extreme exhaustion, drowsiness, loss of appetite, muscle pain, elevated blood sugar levels, and grayish skin color....(See health text).

CHROMIUM
GENERAL: U.S. government studies show that 9 out of 10 Americans do not get enough chromium in their diet and that chromium deficiency is a widespread problem, with various symptoms; including elevated blood sugar levels. Chromium levels decrease gradually with age, while strenuous exercise, pregnancy, diabetes and stress can all cause the body to use up its chromium stores even faster **VALUE**: *Works with insulin in the metabolism by stabilizing blood sugar levels; cleans the arteries by reducing Cholesterol & Triglyceride levels; helps transport amino acids to where the body needs them; helps control the appetite; medical research has shown that persons with low levels of Chromium in their bodies are more susceptible to having cancer and heart problems and becoming diabetic.*
DEFICIENCY SYMPTOMS: May result in excessive fatigue, low energy level, obesity, depressed growth, glucose intolerance in diabetics; arteriosclerosis, and heart disease....(See health text).

VITAMIN D
VALUE: Absorption of calcium from the intestine, bone formation, and melanin balance. The body creates it when ultraviolet light (mostly UV-B) strikes the skins melanocites. Also present in fish livers, and some rare fruits.
Deficiency: Rickets inadequate conversion of cartilage to bone in children, softening of the bones in adults....(health text).

VITAMIN E (Tocopherol)
VALUE: An important antioxidant, key factor in sex and other hormones.
DEFICIENCY: anemia, damage to the retinas, slow healing, and other effects...(see health text).

VITAMIN K
VALUE: needed for the protein synthesis of blood clotting, and other healing functions....(See health text).

MAGNESIUM
GENERAL: U.S. government studies show that our soils have been depleted of magnesium for decades so the plants we eat do not contain the levels they used to. Consuming fatty foods or alcohol inhibits magnesium absorption and nearly 40% of the magnesium in our foods leaches out during cooking.
VALUE*: Plays an important role in regulating the neuromuscular activity of the heart; maintains normal heart rhythm; necessary for proper calcium & Vitamin C metabolism; converts blood sugar into energy.*
DEFICIENCY SYMPTOMS*: May result in nervousness, confusion, excessive fatigue, calcium depletion, heart spasms, muscular excitability, kidney stones, unbalanced insulin, etc....*(See health text).

ZINC
GENERAL: It had been thought that a zinc deficiency did not exist in the United States. But recent studies indicate that most Americans are deficient in zinc, either due to poor choice of diet, food processing, and food grown in nutrient poor soil./**VALUE***:* Is an antioxidant nutrient; necessary for protein synthesis; wound healing; vital for the development of the reproductive organs, prostate functions and male hormone activity; it governs the contractility of muscles; important for blood stability; maintains the body's alkaline balance; helps in normal tissue function; aids in the digestion and metabolism of phosphorus.
DEFICIENCY SYMPTOMS*: May result in excessive fatigue, low energy level, decreased alertness, impaired cognition, delayed sexual maturity, prolonged healing wounds, white spots on finger nails, retarded growth, stretch marks, and susceptibility to infections....*(See health text).

OMEGA-3 FATTY ACIDS

Omega-3 essential fatty acids tend to be systematically removed from our food supply in order to improve its shelf life, and must be re-supplemented. An insufficiency of omega-3 oils (especially an essential fatty acid known as DHA [decosahexanoic acid]) in the diet has been linked to depression.

This may be related to the impact of dietary fatty acids on the composition of nerve cell membranes. While it is thought that the cell is programmed to selectively incorporate the different fatty acids it needs to maintain optimal function, a lack of essential fatty acids (particularly the omega-3 oils) and an excess of saturated fats and animal fatty acids leads to the formation of cell membranes that are much less fluid than normal. A relative deficiency of essential fatty acids in cellular membranes substantially impairs cell membrane function. Since the basic function of the cell membrane is to serve as a selective barrier that regulates the passage of molecules into and out of the cell, a disturbance of structure or function disrupts the cell's ability to control its internal environment.

Because the brain is the richest source of fatty acids in the human body, and because proper nerve cell function is critically dependent on proper membrane fluidity, alterations in membrane fluidity impact behavior, mood, and mental function. The current recommended daily intake by the FDA of DHA is 200mg .... (See your health text).

SOME ESSENTIAL AMINO ACIDS

<u>TRYPTOPHAN</u>
Natural relaxant helps alleviate insomnia by inducing normal sleep; reduces anxiety and depression; increases the level of serotonin; helps in the treatment of migraine headaches; helps the immune system; helps reduce the risk of artery & heart spasms; works with Lysine in reducing cholesterol levels.
DEFICIENCY SYMPTOMS*: May result in depression, insomnia, anxiety, disturbed sleep, migraine headaches, impaired immune system, heart disease and high cholesterol levels.*...(See health text).

<u>LYSINE</u>
VALUE: Insures the adequate absorption of calcium; helps form collagen (which makes up bone cartilage & connective tissues); aids in the production of antibodies, hormones & enzymes. Recent studies have shown that Lysine may be effective against herpes by improving the balance of nutrients that reduce viral growth.
DEFICIENCY SYMPTOMS*: May result in excessive fatigue, irritability, inability to concentrate, bloodshot eyes, retarded growth, hair loss, anemia & reproductive problems....*(See health text).

<u>ALPHA-LIPOIC ACID</u>
VALUE: Alpha-Lipoic Acid is a vitamin-like anti-oxidant that helps neutralize cell-damaging free radicals. It also helps to metabolize blood sugars in the body,

especially in muscles where it promotes energy. The human body produces this naturally; but just like biotin, chromium, magnesium, and vanadium, Diabetics tend to be extremely deficient in these nutrients....(See health text).

Sorry, not all nutrients are listed! Magnesium has a great deal to do with hypertension, mental balance, and energy production. Everyone should look into what foods and nutrients they may be deficient in, before resorting to drugs.

It is interesting that so many people forget that for thousands of centuries, people developed traditions that translated into exercises, eating correctly, medical care that was more advanced in certain civilizations, and balance with the environment. Current farming methods and pollution are depleting soil minerals, adding to consistently rising deficiency ailments like diabetes, anemia, etc. Remember water is needed, not just suggested.

HANDLING THE DEAD

While continually going through periods of learning, at no time in history has any human group created medicines that require more medicines that create toxic effect. Environmental responsibility extends from the ecosystems of our planet, to responsibility for the inside of you. In the United States, even the "Ceremony of Death;" since the U.S. Civil War, has become a commodity to gain extraordinary profits, while true family control is discouraged and institutionalized. The same has digressively become a fact in several countries around the world, mainly under capitalistic philosophies.

HOSPITALS

As of 2004, the medical profession in the U.S. is undergoing an interesting experience that is harmful.

The businesses that profit from increased ailments of the people are also organized to take healthy profits from the economic ailments of the medical institutions. Many hospitals are on the verge of bankruptcy throughout the U.S.A., and other places because of inadequate adaptation from acute infections to an increase in encouraged chronic illnesses, and the formation of the pharmaceutical cartel, which are highly controlling of the finances, medical consultation information, and base education of doctors.

Nutritional education is one element of education that is fiercely resisted for medical professionals. Pharmecuetical drugs are around the 3rd leading causes of death in the U.S.A. Similar problems with more and more extreme situations are exemplified in hospitals around the world. Very few hospitals around the world are designed without the influence of death and illness profiteering agents. The changes have to come from the demands of the people to those in power, because power is really not in the hands of the medical professionals, but they are worth everyone's praise.

FAITH

Your beliefs set the stage for your healing. Positive attitudes stimulate growth, just as intent prayer can stimulate changes. Negative attitudes impede it. It's important to rid yourself of counterproductive attitudes that you may not even realize you have. If you examine your beliefs, choose life enhancing ones, you'll create optimal wellness. No organ stands apart from your thoughts. Your beliefs program your neuro-chemicals. We are composed of flesh and blood, but also of subtle energy. Feeling energy can be very sensual, an extension of love, a knowing of connectedness to others.

Learning to tap into your body's energy is healing. It's essential that we learn to access the stillness within through prayer, personal meditation, contemplation, and/or connecting with nature in order to gain answers about our health. As with virtually all faiths, a part of the spiritual prayers are to spend a few minutes each day devoted to listening to this voice. It may appear as a gut feeling, a hunch, an image, a sound, a memory, or a knowing. Every ninety minutes during the REM stage of sleep, humans dream. Dreams provide answers about health, relationships, career choices, and any new direction in existence. The secret is to remember.

MUSIC

As an art, music is an expression of balanced creativity in action. As a science, music is an instrument of healing and communication. Through the use of music throughout the eons of human history, music has mainly been expressed in use as a science. Humanity has created various forms of music with and without lyrics. The form of music called Hip Hop is the transformation of subjects and objects in an attempt to explain your consciousness. Traditional music changes over time as an expression of the health, direction, communications, and consciousness of good & bad of the society.

Enlightenment, awakening, and remembering what was lost are states of being that require one to become open to what they desire. Music is a tool that opens persons to the art and the science of itself, with or without complimentary song, or poetic balancing lyrics. As a science, music is not only a form of communication; it is an ancient tool of the healing arts.

RELATIONSHIPS

You are what you eat, drink absorb, think, and sometimes bond with. The law of attraction is the property of who and what we have in our lives. It is the must of always being a perfect match for the pattern of our thinking. If you are short on friends, it is sometimes because you have chosen to be someone who needs a friend, there is a fear of you, or you haven't searched correctly. To solve the need, you must give up your desire for them and be open to being a friend of the type of person you want in your current life. Sometimes the person(s) needed in your life are not the ones you expect. It is a form of karma. This does not mean any type of religious prayer for someone; it means a balanced silent desired outreach for becoming the mirror of your interest.

All relationships are like the image in a mirror, reflecting back at some aspect of your own being. If you don't like what you see in that mirror, you need to change the aspects of you that you have built to want the connection with the undesired relationship. As humans, we have the ability to create our own reality, once we understand and learn to intelligently apply the spiritual laws that govern our lives. To gain a friend, first, you must choose to be a friend.

In various societies, the traditional interpersonal aptitudes learned to be correct for relationships have been being altered by the influx of foreign ideals. In some places around the world, the ideals have been a positive, but as others they are self-destructive. Many societies that have been altered in the recent past to be male-dominated with physical harm as an expected element are slowly giving way to equality and positive communication ones. The sensationalization of relationships in recent years by placing the acts of courtship, marriage, and divorce are a new low in the capitalization of the base of living life. The honor and respect that sustains the importance of love has gradually, and radically been being stripped away to less important factors of life such as lust, greed, and fame on commercializing television shows, online ratings, and radio.

These acts are similar to, and endemic to the pattern of illegitimate social advancement known of the ancient Europeans Roman society, with the replacement of rampant forced homosexual sex, baby killing, and deadly tournaments; with highly encouraged frivolity, manipulation of reality, racial pathology, self-created wars, etc, etc. Most societies of the world accepted the natural fact of the existence of homosexuals, but under current social rule, those with that natural physical state are to be considered another race of people.

In the same societies, the action of child molestation can be measured as a norm of the population, both by males and females as a misguided attempt to empower themselves, attain gratification, and supposedly to teach the same, while also degrading the youth as a servant/tool for the pleasure of the offender(s).

With the advent of increased female rule over the elements of humanity, the care-taking principles that are naturally endemic to most of the female gender should help to repair the damage that has been done to the world's peoples. For the past few centuries, humanity has been born into an increasingly damaged social and ecological structure, centered on the servitude of the Anglican and Arabic male, and gradually turning towards becoming a technocracy, not a civilization. The changes are occurring, but it will likely take another world war before the radical changes leading to a fair, just, and balanced humanity of all families will be the norm.

Supplements Recommended to Research

Goji Fruit, Noni Fruit, Aloe Vera Juice, Rooibos, Mangosteen, Yellow Dock, Turmeric, Rhadiola, Blueberry, Q-10, Magnesium Glycinate, Fenugreek, Royal Jelly, Dahlia, Oats, Griffonia S., Spirulina, Flax, Nopal, Gymnema Sylvestra, Olive Leaf, Holy Basil, Banaba, Rosemary, Tamanu, Oregano, Yucca, Essiac, Capsaicin, etc.

Here's the way free radicals damage you

1. Damages and kills cells directly,
2. Depletes the oxygen content of the body's fluids, and
3. Hinders the circulation and subsequently the immune and hormone system.

Look up the "United Senate Document #264" to see how the mineral deficiency in plants results in the mineral deficiencies and disease in those who eat those plants.

Example: Junk e-mail that promotes pharmaceutical drugs. What about those untold side effects?

Subject: re:[7] [LETU]
Date: 12/21/2004 4:47:36 AM Pacific Standard Time
From: eicqlo@ip145.82.cnz.com

Dear valued customer.!
90% discounts on all 2000 pharmacy titles!
Viagra—64$
Cialis—96$
Vicodin—310$
Valium—70$
Xanax—75$
Ambien—68$
Paxil—70$
Prozac—70$
Zoloft—70$
Lipitor—70$
Glucophage—60$
Levitra—85$
Propecia—72$
Celebrex—72$
Soma—65$
Vioxx—70$
Zyban—80$
Meridia—75$
Xenical—70$
See it yourself: http://arabicumerals.com/?a=712

And of course I have to mention that none of the information here is meant to diagnose, treat, or cure any disease….as a required mention from FDA rules… blah, blah, blah. Or they may try to punish me for going against the cartel linked activities.

Chapter 3

Colonial Conceptions of Education

One of the primary goals of colonial education has been to delete the ancestral language; which is a culture base. A foundation of culture is language, and the education instilled in most colonies was also to force other cultural Faiths of Europe. The center of the world & financial importance of Europe for its material things have helped to set other cultures in the belief that they should believe and make themselves poor. Many of the basic mythological functions have been denigrated to this purpose. The notions called 'colonization' and 'De-globalization' (as in the transformation from original to European domination of relations) is in the prominent historical & political literature mostly known today.

The word "colonization" makes one think of political and economic domination of one population by another. This form of control is usually associated with military power, which is based on most histories, and is typically used to effect such domination. This has been made more obvious by the European colonization of the world over the past four centuries, at least until the independence of African and Asian countries in the middle of the twentieth century. The terms

71

"colonization" and "neo-colonialism," have often been used to describe the economic relation of what they call "Third World Countries" with their former colonial centers.

LANGUAGE SHIFT

When languages of what are called the Third World, are an issue of thought, power has usually been invoked as an important factor that has favored the language of the powerful, over those of the dominated. If you focus on the fates of world languages among the colonized, oppressed, or powerless rural populations of Africa, the fact that the vitality of a language depends very much on factors other than power. The European view of making changes in other cultures for their favor or likeness was for the long-term benefit of cultural and economic control of others.

Many African languages have been subverted; due to competition of languages of power, by peers that have guaranteed a surer economic survival. This is also true in the America's and the Pacific Islands, but to a smaller extent on the peoples of the continent called Asia.

LANGUAGE TRANSFORMATION

In order to understand the above view, it helps to also think of colonization in terms of population genetics. When a population relocates in a new territory, regardless of whether the latter is or is not inhabited by an indigenous population, For example; the 18th-century French colonists on Reunion, and Mauritius islands, recorded those places as uninhabited. This was as much a form of colonization as the settlement of several Caribbean islands by Europeans during the 16th–18th centuries.

The establishments of trade forts, torture camps; in Africa, Asia, and the America's during the 16th through 20th centuries was initial environmental control. The political, historical, spiritual, and economic domination of several African, South Pacific, Asian, and peoples of the America's from the 17th to today are present, and trained to be accepted. Bear in mind that even the spread of Indo-European populations in Europe involved as much of settlement colonization as the domination of the Americas and Australia.

From a point of view of language contact, the consequences of colonization have not been uniform. One of the major damages done in most of these acts of war is the invalidation of the native languages. Although several languages have disbursed in the processes of suppression for example; Celtic languages in Western Europe, Navajo, Amharic, Aboriginal, etc., new ones have also emerged—e.g., Creole, Patois, Geechee, etc., have developed out of cultural resistance to contact with negative oppression. It is not always the colonized populations that have lost their languages. Sometimes, it is the colonists and colonizers who have, as in the case of the Norman French in England, or the Tutsi (former Nilotic) in Rwanda and Burundi, or the Peranakan Chinese in the Straights of Malacca. There are other interesting places where the old and new languages coexist, but normally the conquering culture dominates the expressions.

It is not difficult to produce a general theory of what happens when a population colonizes another. Language vitality and variations can help determine the development of new language varieties. Despite similarities among them, what happens in one history is not necessarily replicated in another. To be sure, we cannot overlook similarities, such as the fact that language loss has been the most catastrophic during the creation of settlement colonies, and new language varieties have emerged in trade colonies.

On the other hand, one must still note differences from one colony to another, regardless of whether the members of the relevant group can all be identified as plantation or non-plantation settlement colonies, or as trade or exploitation colonies. Settlement colonies of North America still differ from those of Latin America, plantation colonies of the Atlantic and Indian Ocean were not quite the same as those of the Pacific, and exploitation colonies of Africa were not quite the same as those of Asia.

It can be said; for instance, that current global economics and the spread of English have not been as dangerous to indigenous languages in Asia as in the Americas. There is certainly a sense linguistic globalization, meaning a directed centralizing language. However, it does not take long to notice that globalism in global war does not necessarily mean 'worldwide'. Global war is not synonymous with world war. This may help raise the facts that organizations founded of colonial institutions like the United Nations, are not truly positive organizations, due to their base of power, principles, and history. Reports on wars, theories of wealth, and the educated, are predicated as though the European or Arab descended people are the only and best at all things.

This concept is perpetuated a little less each year in most countries of the world, and being replaced by the images of local peoples.

THE SO-CALLED "THIRD WORLD"

Current processes of cultural restoration are starting to transform local education to represent the aspects of the people, just as religion is slowly changing. The above state of affairs should have been evident, as the kind of global economy in place in North America, for instance, is far from being universal. Although one can claim that it is being spread all over the world, it is far from being in place in Third World countries. In fact, if multinational economic trends continue to grow on their present patterns, Third World countries are very likely to miss the boat entirely, and not participate in it. Global economics in North America have a lot to do with different aspects of its industrial structure being interconnected. Much of its industries would shut down if there were a generalized power outage.

Its economic networks would break down if there were no adequate transportation and communication infrastructure in place. The replacement of spiritual societies, have slowly been happening around the world, into technocracies, and simple material aspirations are highly rewarded. The spiritual ways of thinking are being re-valued by many people, and social persecution has slowly decreased, worldwide.

An aspect of education must also include changes needed in world religions. Possible positive changes that can help transform our world conceptions are in the later chapter on religion. Conception is a foundation of reality. Conceptions of real economics are false, in that it allows inequalities among those that function with it. Ancient and current economic theories among the peoples of the world have subtly been deemed as primitive, and/or less important than the methods trained to be accepted.

Many countries participate in the current global economic system, only to the extent that they have become parts of networks of industrial interdependencies that blur their national boundaries, for brief survival, not independent support. Many so-called "Third World Countries," participate only as marginal players in these networks because money value is controlled by specialized post-colonial organizations (World Bank, etc.,).

When a particular common language, such as English or French, is required for communication among the different branches of such multinational companies, not all employees of these companies are expected to be fluent in the native language, especially where most of the labor is involved in the production of raw materials to be processed outside the country, or a large proportion of the adult population is unemployed and thus seriously disfranchised from the economic system. In such places, the vast majority of the populations continue to function in their ancestral or other local vernaculars, which they in fact adopt as their identity marker to distinguish themselves from the minority of effluents.

To my knowledge, Caribbean territories reflect some of the earliest experiences of loss of ancestral languages by the enslaved Africans in the North America region, and the Native Arawak and Carib Indians. The European settlement colonies were made in the sixteenth century. In most of them, the Creole vernaculars that later on replaced these languages have become identity markers for the present masses of the disenfranchised. Things are not necessarily so different in economically prosperous former colonies where English or other Western European languages appear to play an important function and can be claimed to endanger their indigenous languages.

For instance, much of the participation of Hong Kong, India, Singapore, and the Philippines in multinational networks depends on the usage of English as a worldwide language. While in many parts of the United States and Canada, it would be difficult to travel and communicate with the local population without speaking English, knowledge of only English can be frustrating while traveling in Taiwan, Malaysia, and Brazil. This shows that some forms of resistance are effective against the suppressive tactics of imperialists.

The above statement does not demonstrate that those places have not suffered any language loss, nor that Neo-colonial globalization has played no role in this process. As implied above; in becoming the major business language of Taiwan, Chinese has seriously endangered the Formosan languages, which are more indigenous to the Island, in about the same way that Japanese has caused the attrition of Ainu, just like English and the termed "Romance languages" have driven the extinction most of the Celtic languages that preceded them in Europe. The great prevalence of Malay as the vernacular of Malaysia has certainly been at the expense of several other indigenous languages. Usage of these indigenous languages in wide and diverse sectors of the national economies has nurtured their vitality by providing them some value.

In terms of costs and benefits relative to English as a global language, the association with lucrative functions in local, national, and/or regional economies is limited for most Asian populations. The need for English has thus been confined to the role of the elite. English interfaces the local, national, and global economies.

COLONIZATION TYPES

The vitality of many languages are relative to the economic ecology. It may help to restate that English and other central controlling cultures have endangered other languages, or driven them to extreme secrecy. In settlement, exploitation, and trade colonies, it is also important to know that current globalization is a by-product of earlier Islamic expansionism, and European colonization since the 11th century. However; it is helpful to remember that current globalization is not equally extensive or integrated everywhere, or for the benefit of all. It is simply the restructuring of power to maintain long-term control of the powers the so-called minority/third world nations hold. Everyone should be aware that it has normally been less than ¼ of European descendants directing evil deeds, 2/3 following along with minimal information, and the rest against or complacent, just like today's expressions of descendants worldwide.

The power roles can easily be changed! The state of globalization in a particular country currently reflects the extent of its economic success, under the perspective conceptions of wealth by European cultures, foreign religions, and technocracy influences impeding on the society. To some extent, the colonized countries with enduring ties are given a superior value. Remember, the great United Nations was founded for the purposes of supporting the originating colonial powers. Why not make a better organization?

Distinguishing trade, settlement, and exploitation colonies must be considered. Trade colonies (such as those on the west coast of Africa from the 15th to the 19th centuries and mostly remembered for the association with the slave trade/Sankofa) were among the first to develop. This happened typically soon after Europeans explored new territories and established trade relations with the Natives on more or less unrestricted terms, which usually changed later on, at the expense of indigenous populations. The common relationships were patchy and generally led to the gradual development of new language forms like pidgins; typically based on a European language on the western coast of Africa but by a Native American language in the Americas.

In the latter part of these centuries, the trade colonization was concurrent with settlement colonization. Many European colonists, Arabized colonial victims, among others that followed these tracks of existence around the world, settled to build new homes, or better lives than what they had left behind. The nature of regular interactions among different populations in these new colonies often led to protracted competition and selection among the languages and dialects they brought with them, leading to shifts from some to others, the loss of several of them, and to the emergence of new language varieties typically dominated in structure by the dominating culture language(s). Some of these have been identified as Creoles (typically in plantation settlement colonies).

Trade colonies have not been reported to cause any significant language endangerment, let alone language death, to be associated directly with this colonization style, even when trade was abused to enslave and deport some of the indigenous populations. Many Native Americans lost their languages either because they were decimated by ills and wars, or because they were forced to relocate to places where they couldn't continue to speak their languages. Another measure was because they eventually got to function in the new, European-style economic world order which imposed a new language of business and industry. Unlike the trade colonies, settlement colonies everywhere gradually evolved to some form of social and economic integration that has endangered languages other than those of the colonizing European nation, or one adopted by it.

The balance sheet has of course involved more losses than gains, but we must always remember that the outcome of population and language contact in settlement colonies anywhere, including Australia and New Zealand, has not consisted of losses only. After the Abolition of slavery in the U.S., plantation settlement colonies evolved ever more efficiently on a hybrid model between the non-plantation settlement colonies and the exploitation colonies. Worldwide, most of the former plantation settlement colony victimized peoples have not conformed/industrialized, so they are called Third World Nations.

Jamaica is a good example since "Patois"(National language of Jamaica) has gained in vitality and a new divergent variety called Dread Talk. The above considerations are simply a reminder that, just as colonization has not been uniform worldwide, the vitality of languages has not been uniformly affected everywhere. In future research, it will help the examination of indigenous social structures by understanding which populations have correlation with true economic interdependence, and to what extent the patterns of interaction across languages, or dialect boundaries have to do with the process of language endangerment.

It is also worth determining the extent to which settlement is advanced in a particular territory and what can be learned about the factors that bring about language endangerment. Differences in method of colonization, resistance, and region, are why proportionally more Native American languages have survived in Canada than in the USA, and why are there more indigenous languages still spoken in Latin America than in North America?

Are these differences a consequence of variation in colonization patterns within the settlement style (including patterns of interaction with the indigenous populations), are they a consequence of variation in the physical ecologies of the settlement colonies, or do they reflect a combination of both factors? Can the size and nature of the Amazon Forest be overlooked as a factor in the survival of indigenous languages in a large part of South America?

Many indigenous languages have survived the against exploitation colonies. Although both settlement and exploitation colonies developed from trade colonies; in part as the consequence of the damage, forced foreign language integration or use has altered the base culture.

European commercial greed in wanting to control the sources of raw materials and other products needed in Europe, very few colonizers planned or decided to build new homes in the exploitation colonies. As the term exploitation colony suggests, colonies were to be exploited for the enrichment of the foreign desire to control. The colonizers were generally civil servants, or company employees who served limited terms and had to retire back in Europe.

With the help of missionaries and their schools, they generally developed an intermediary class of indigenous bureaucrats or low-level administrators through which they communicated with the local populations or they themselves learned the most important of the local languages, but they encouraged no more than this local colonial elite to learn scholastic varieties of their languages.

Instituting economic systems that generally reaped raw materials to be processed in metropolitan industry, the colonizers fostered a two-tiered economic system (rich & poor) in which the overwhelming masses of the populations continue to communicate in their own ethnic languages or in (the new) locally-based language forms, such as Lingala and Kinshasa in the Congo, Sango along the Ubangi River, Kis-Swahili in East Africa, Nahuatl in Mexico, Wolof in Senegal, Songhay in parts of West Africa east of Senegal (along Arab north-south trade routes), Hausa in Nigeria, Fanagalo in the Copper Belt extending from South Africa to Zambia, Mandingo, Bazaar Malay in Southeast Asia, etc., etc.

In a few places, such as Nigeria, Cameroon, and Papua New Guinea, pidgins based on European languages were being learned naturalistically (by trial-and-error attempts to communicate in these languages, without a teacher) by the masses of the populations who participated in the low ranks of the colonial economy. They did not eliminate the development of other indigenous-based languages, such as Pidgin Ewondo in Cameroon or Police Motu in Papua, New Guinea.

Overall, colonial languages have been just an addition to local repertoires of languages and constituted little threats to the more indigenous ones, which were protected by the clear division of labor in their functions, with the more indigenous ones functioning as vernaculars and the colonial ones. Socioeconomic changes of the late colonial and post-colonial periods, with many of the new language becoming urban vernaculars and with relatively more and more lucrative jobs based in urban centers and operating in them gave a competitive edge to the new indigenous language.

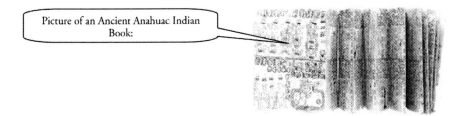

Picture of an Ancient Anahuac Indian Book:

STRUGGLE FOR RECLAMATION

Standard Languages that wane in the cities have tended to do the same in so-called developing rural areas. Several versions of sustainable development in the ancient ways tend to be overlooked. The economic control of the so-called "Third World Economies," and increasing relative economic importance of urban centers and their lure which led to a rural exodus, compounded to further erode the beneficial significance of rural indigenous languages. The multi-billionaires, Tri-Lateral, and the esteemed so-called World Bank friends maintain the concept. These have been eroded not by the foreign language integration, but by the indigenous peoples alteration of values.

One must really remember that in the evolution of languages, the balance sheets from the contact of Europe with other countries looks different in settlement colonies than in their exploitation counterparts. An important reason is that the Europeans were less invested socially and psychologically in the exploitation colonies than were the colonists in settlement colonies. The settlement colonies thought of the locations as their homes, and the patterns of their interactions with the indigenous populations gradually changed from reactionary to comfortable, with the involvement of the Natives in the local economy growing from marginal to engaged in the foreign structures. This is very evident in indigenous Hawaiian, the Philippine, Tahitian, and many other peoples, which are now divided by imposed nationalities.

Also, unlike in exploitation colonies, where the European colonizers remained a small, though powerful, minority, the colonists in non-plantation settlement colonies became the overwhelming majorities and instituted socio-economic systems that function totally in their own dominant language.

Once dismissed, and now titled minorities, the Natives in former settlement colonies have felt more and more pressure on themselves to shift to the majorities' languages for their economic survival, especially after their physical ecologies have been transformed in ways that deprived them of the alternative of practicing their traditional economic systems.

In terms of costs and benefits, as a function of the changing socio-economic ecologies, it was only natural for the Natives to shift to the colonial languages. Unlike in exploitation colonies, language shift was critical to the survival of the Natives in settlement colonies, at the cost of losing many of their traditions.

In most former exploitation colonies, the Natives did not even feel the pressure to shift, because they remained the overwhelming majorities who in the rural areas have been barely affected by the economic and political transformations undergone by their territories, including the formation of nation states. The options most of them had were either to continue operating in their traditional world or to work in the low cost colonial and post-colonial labor system that does not require a European language.

As a matter of fact, the new world order in former exploitation colonies is such that even the elite participating in the interfacing sector of the economy have had no pressure, except from their own personal attitudes, to give up their indigenous languages.

If anything, unless they decided to sever links with their ancestral customs, the pressure has been just the opposite: one must preserve one's competence in the ancestral languages in order to continue interacting with one's relatives in the rural areas.

Two factors have especially protected the indigenous languages from being driven out by foreign languages:

1.) The indigenous populations have remained numerically quite superior to the colonizers;

2.) The overwhelming majority of them have formed a proletariat that has barely assimilated the external values brought by the colonizers.

The closest approximation of these European values is evident in the development of urban societies, in which traditional and European-colonial ways have mixed and the new indigenous linguistics, favored by the colonial systems, have gained economic power, and prestige, and have gradually displaced the ancestral ethnic languages. They are the ones that can be said to have endangered indigenous languages, to the extent that some rural populations have shifted to the urban expressions, and abandoning some of their traditional cultural values for those of the city. On the other hand, the absence of economic correlates of this appeal of urban values has slowed down the effect that the current linguistic stratification could have had on rural vernaculars. The city has also frustrated some of its residents.

Some disenchanted individuals have returned to their rural roots and speak their ancestral languages with zeal.

In the same vein, unemployment in cities and the ever-growing size of the proletariat in African and other Third World countries have also disfavored usage of European languages. There are fewer and fewer incentives for speaking these languages that have sometimes been interpreted as means of exploitation. Even in more prosperous former exploitation colonies such as Singapore and Malaysia, European languages have continued to function primarily as bridges with the world outside one's home, or outside one's ethnic group or neighborhood, or outside one's country. Otherwise, it remains natural to communicate with members of one's inner group in an indigenous, or non-European language.

We should thus not overrate the importance of European languages regarding language endangering. The experience in former exploitation colonies has certainly not been the same as in former settlement colonies, as much as European colonization in general has spread European languages to territories where they were not spoken 400 years ago. Former plantation settlement colonies reveal features of both exploitation and settlement colonies. They are like the latter in that the indigenous languages have generally disappeared, due to the rapid and dramatic deaths of their speakers or regarding the relocations of indigenous peoples to places where they stopped speaking their languages.

The colonies are also similar in that several immigrants lost the languages of their motherlands. As explained in, they were originally integrated as small minorities in the homesteads, which were isolated from each other. They had nobody with whom to speak their languages within the homestead, and in the rare events that they happened to know somebody on another homestead who spoke the same language, there was not enough regular interaction that would have permitted the retention of that common language.

Attrition and loss were simply caused by lack of opportunities to interact in the native languages. The situation is somewhat reminiscent of how rural populations absorbed city populations over a few decades. The process of language shift can be gradual or sudden, just as cultural and economic shifts do.

ELEMENTS OF CULTURAL SURVIVAL

Like in many colony cities worldwide, the African slaves formed the overwhelming majorities of the plantation societies. People of European descent have been a small minorities, with small subsets of them emerging as affluent. Yet, the countries that evolved from such plantation societies still contain large proletarian majorities that speak Creole and identify socio-economically with it. Because of lack of incentives in an economic system depending on foreign markets and industry, participating only marginally in the world's global economy, and becoming poorer and poorer, Creole has gained more vitality in relation to the language varieties spoken by the upper class. In places like Jamaica and Haiti, one learns quickly that the prestige of a language does not necessarily entail its vitality.

The underprivileged do not necessarily aspire to the varieties spoken by the more affluent members of their societies, especially if the varieties won't improve their conditions. As a matter of fact being economically disfranchised is often a good reason for despising those prestigious varieties.

Prestige alone won't favor a particular language (variety) over others. Shifting to a particular language is typically associated with particular benefits to be derived from its usage, especially economic ones. Otherwise, speakers stick to the languages they have traditionally spoken, although they may learn another one for interaction with outsiders. However, even this behavior is benefit-driven. Most so-called Third World populations will not shift to European languages, because the alternatives are not likely to improve their conditions. In the first place, the division of labor that relies on indigenous linguistics in the lower sectors of the economy (in which most of the workforce is engaged) makes it unnecessary to target a European language, because of the jobs associated with them.

Immigrants to the so-called New World and Australia shifted to the dominant languages because they had emerged as the only languages of the colonies' economic systems and they had something to gain from the shift, or at least they avoided the danger of not being able to compete at all on the new job markets. Most slaves wavered on their languages because they often had nobody else to speak them with, an important reason why their children never bothered learning their parents languages (just like children in African cities) since they had the false image that everything was to be gained in speaking the colonial languages, only.

Now the question arises of whether linguists can help some languages thrive by encouraging their speakers to have pride in their ancestral heritage, even if they lack control over situations that have led them to give up their languages. Over the past decade language endangerment has become a major preoccupation among linguists.

UNEVEN DISTRIBUTION

The issues have sometimes become confusing, especially when language preservation and language maintenance are confused as one and the same thing, and the very linguists whose party line is that language is primarily oral and spoken have privileged the school system and the written medium as ways of saving the endangered languages.

Very little research has been invested in understanding the ecology of language and what it takes to sustain the vitality of a language, especially in territories where several languages have coexisted seemingly happily with one another under an efficient division of labor in the repertoires that contain them. As stated in the Introduction, this essay is a general theoretical response to the above characteristics of that literature, to show that languages do not kill languages, but their own speakers do, in giving them up, although they themselves are victims of changes in the socioeconomic ecologies in which they evolve.

Solutions that focus on the victims rather than on the causes of their plights are just as bad as environmental solutions that focus only on affected species, instead of the whole ecologies of support.

European colonization of the past four centuries has definitely contributed to the predicament of languages around the world, as it has introduced new socioeconomic world orders that have pre-empted the usefulness of some languages. However, it is helpful to put things in a historical perspective too. Language shift and language losses are neither new nor recent phenomena. Evidenced by the fact that only 3% of the world's languages are spoken in Europe, this is one of the most densely populated parts of the world.

The prevalence of English (a Germanic language) in the United Kingdom and of Roman languages in a large proportion of Western Europe has been at the expense of Celtic languages, only a handful of which are still spoken today. The Germanic languages are now spoken in territories that used to be Celtic. The Indo-European languages have spread and prevailed in territories formerly inhabited by other populations, as evidenced by rare survivals such as Basque and Finnish.

We should try to understand why and how Basque and Finnish survived the dispersal of Indo-European languages, while the majority of others vanished, and we should investigate similarities and differences between what happened then and what is happening now, and why some populations just cannot preserve their languages against the invaders while some invaders have actually given up their own languages. Linguists have typically mourned the loss of linguistic diversity. Rarely have they focused on the speakers themselves in terms of motivation (other than the obvious pressure on them) and costs-and-benefits to their survival.

The usual concern with loss of ancestral traditions is nothing more but a politically correct way of bemoaning loss of interesting resources for linguistics. Seldom have linguists addressed the question of whether the survival of a language would entail more adequate adaptations of its speakers to the changing socioeconomic ecologies. Short of claiming that cultures are static, and failing to notice that the populations who have shifted to new languages have concurrently developed new and hybrid cultures. Linguists have also considered the fact that such populations have lost their ancestral cultures.

The question arises of whether the ancestral cultures are necessarily more adaptive to the current world order than the new ones, just like the question of whether the peculiarities of the lost or endangered languages are more informative about "Universal Grammar," than are the new patterns of variation and language diversification that follow from their appropriation of languages spoken by the more powerful group. There has really been no true assessment of costs and benefits to speakers and mostly the costs and benefits to linguistics have been at the center of the relevant debates.

It should help to recall that much of the concern for language endangerment has been modeled on environmentalists concerns about the degradation of our physical ecology due to modern industry. Like linguists, environmentalists are ecologists, generally biologists, more precisely population geneticists who have specialized on the co-evolution of species and their environments.

We would really be their counterparts if there were a research area in linguistics that specializes on the co-evolution of speakers, their socioeconomic ecologies, and their languages. The concern for language endangerment seems to have caught linguists off guard and we have been prescribing remedies without the requisite understanding of the socioeconomic dynamics that have affected the vitality of languages negatively or positively in different parts of the world throughout the history of mankind.

ECOLOGY OF LANGUAGE FUNCTION

There is also another important point of difference. Environmentalists are concerned with the environment relative to humans, the way we humans should coexist with other species, and how we are affected by what affects them, thus the need for biodiversity relative to our survival. Humans have generally, been distinguished by environmentalists from that ecology.

However, things are not so similar regarding languages. These means of communication do not have independent lives from their speakers. Humans and their socioeconomic activities are the ecologies of languages, as speakers are both creators and their hosts. What affects speakers socio-economically often affects their languages.

The physical ecologies of speakers are by transitivity also those of languages, and speaker's adaptations to these ecologies when they change affect languages too. Changes in the vitality of languages can be interpreted as part of a speaker's adaptation to changing ecologies. As much as we would like to sustain some form of linguistic diversity parallel to biodiversity, it is difficult to pursue this goal without assessing clearly the ways in which the relevant socioeconomic ecologies have changed and consequently the actual nature of costs and benefits to speakers in the ways they have adapted to these changes.

The bottom line is that languages are tools that must remain useful to speakers and arguments for the maintenance of particular languages should not overlook the role that such languages will play in the efforts of speakers to cope with ecological changes affecting them. The observation that speakers make their languages to serve their needs should not be taken lightly.

Although languages wind up emerging as windows into the cultures and histories of particular populations, they exercise the important function of helping speakers communicate with each other and thereby manage conditions or ecologies that affect their survival. Unless giving up a particular language in favor of another is likely to affect negatively the survival of a particular population in a changing socioeconomic ecology, linguists must really justify what particular benefits or selective advantage its maintenance is likely to bring its speakers under those particular conditions.

NATURAL CHANGE

Most linguistic anthropologist arguments have revolved around the maintenance or preservation of particular cultures. Arguments for preservation should not be confused with arguments for maintenance. As long as preserving a language means freezing it in some form, especially writing, so that interested individuals who remain familiar with their systems can have glimpse into a frozen part of its speaker's cultural history, there is no particular social problem with that. The endeavor is just as good as the preservation of particular artifacts as evidence of the material culture of a particular people at some stage of their history.

Most arguments for maintenance have also suggested that cultures and languages are static. Such discourse could also have been developed against language change. It has ignored the fact that speakers make their languages as they speak and cultures are being shaped as members of particular communities behave in specific ways. These are dynamic systems that keep evolving as people behave linguistically and otherwise and as they keep adapting them to new situations. That is, languages co-evolve with their speakers.

Passive Language shift is the main cause of language endangerment and death. It is part of adaptive co-evolution, as speakers endeavor to meet their day-to-day communicative needs. It is not so much that linguistic changes are bringing about cultural changes but that linguistic changes echo cultural changes. That is language shift is no more but an adaptive response to changes in a particular culture, most of which is what I have identified as a socioeconomic ecology. Arguments for language maintenance without arguments for concurrent changes in the present socioeconomic ecologies of speakers seem to ignore the centrality of native speakers in the whole situation.

Suggesting that speakers will preserve their culture, if they continue speaking them, is ignoring the fact that they may not stop speaking their language if they value its association with their ancestral culture over their necessary adaptation to an environment. The position in the average literature on the subject matter is also tantamount to assuming that language and culture go hand in hand, that only one language can best mirror or convey a particular culture, and that another language cannot be adapted to convey it.

It can convincingly argue that language and culture are separate, but it really is not possible to win. Language is a key element of culture, whether you consider non-verbal and/or verbal. The literature of African English and French, for instance, have made it quite obvious that a language can be adapted to a different culture which gives more meaning to the consideration of language appropriations.

Population shifts to another language has always had the option of adapting the new language to their ancestral culture. After all it is generally influenced by their substrate systems and typically develops into a new variety. We can perhaps argue that a language mirrors a culture because it is itself part of a culture. Changes affecting it reflect changes in a particular culture. A problem then arises when nothing is being done or advocated to change the ecology, to which speakers adapt. Linguists are different from environmentalists whom have realized that survival of a particular species depends largely on restoring the ecology in which it thrives.

Linguist proposal's for rescuing endangered languages suggests that speakers must continue their traditional communication, regardless of the changing socioeconomic ecologies. Somebody should explain how adaptive such resistance to changing ecologies is or how a language can continued to be spoken as a vernacular when the ecological structures that used to support it barely survive. Since there are countries such as Taiwan, which have succeeded in appropriating the Western capitalist economic system without losing much of the Chinese culture and language, it is obviously clear that other countries could have taken that path.

It should help to know why they did not choose it. The question also remains whether things can be reversed in nations whose cultural and linguistic experiences have been different and under what realistic conditions, bearing in mind that under certain ecological conditions speakers shift to the language that promises to benefit them the most.

If the current ecology cannot be changed, linguists should focus realistically on language preservation, rather than maintenance. Investing more time into understanding language shifting, the loss of some languages, the emergence of new ones, and the losses vs. gains at different states in history, would be beneficial. We will then be able to deal with language endangerment with justifications other than benefits and costs to linguistic study. Speakers as individuals, adapting to socioeconomic changes that affect them, should play central roles in the literature important to our planet and in the environmentalist discourse, than their languages.

Elements of world history suggest that linguistic behavior is profit-driven. Many people tend to invest only in forms and structures that maximize their social linguistic capital, and whatever is beneficial to them for economics. It is perhaps not by accident that in highly diverse societies multi-linguists are the most profitable persons in the society, because communicating is a central role in all interactions.

In societies that are typically monolingual, multi-linguists can travel outside their communities, and interact with outsiders. Not everybody has a vested interest in speaking more than one language. A profile of individuals or communities that give up their languages in favor of others will be informative in future research.

COLONIZATION AND GLOBALIZATION OF OPPRESSION

The current literature on language endangerment has presented the phenomenon primarily as one of the negative side effects of European expansion and colonization of most of the non-European world over the past half millennium. It is true that the geographical and political extents of European expansion have been unprecedented, for instance when one compares the size of the British Commonwealth, as discontinuous as it has been, with that of the Roman Empire a millennium earlier.

However, putting things in perspective, one can also realize that the difference in size is also a function of differences in modes of communication. About 1,500 years ago, the size of the Roman Empire was certainly also unprecedented, in fact too large to have central control over, at least under the communicative conditions of the time.

Easier and faster transportation systems since the 15th century have enabled the European conquest of territories much farther away from home. Easier and faster means of communication (especially with the invention of the telegraph and telephone, of the radio and television, and now of the internet) have facilitated the political, military, and economic controls of bigger and bigger colonies, making the world look even smaller. Improvements in control techniques have also facilitated the control of more and more aspects of the colonies.

Today's colonization differs from colonization of the earlier times more in size and complexity than in kind. It is not so common to refer to the dispersal of the Bantu populations from the southern Nigeria, the Western Cameroon areas, into central and southern Africa. Nor is it common to refer to the peoples throughout Asia that are repressed by Arab language supremacists. Arabic and many languages have a beauty of there own, but some people think the language they speak is the most, or only important one to have. This type of belief is counter-productive towards the aspiration of a peaceful, just, and common sense world.

In reality, the main colonial peoples throughout history have been consisting their military, political, economic, relationship, and religious domination nature from their hunter-gatherer heritage & nature.

Basque has survived both the Indo-European and Roman Colonization's. The present linguistic map of Europe represents consequences of many language shifts, under wars and colonization, for Roman, Germanic, etc., language superiority. Celtic languages became dilapidated in a wide area, from the lands recently called Germany onto Ireland. We stand to learn a lot by trying to understand similarities and disparity among early forms of colonization, renaissance periods, and the European Expansion of the past 400 years outside Europe.

The Romans have colonized for instance both British Isles, and the southern part of Western Europe. In both parts, Latin was the colonial language. Early times of colonization of the British Isles was by the Germanics and Romans. Iberia (now Spain & Portugal) have been conquered, by the Arabs and Visigoths, only centuries ago. The land now called "France," was dominated by the Frankish, and later by the Germans for a very short time. Out of the two only the Frankish have had an effect on the peoples linguistic expression.

It is also important to stress the fact that like in Africa and Central America; for instance, it was after the colonizers had left that the important proportions of the indigenous populations shifted to the colonizers language(s). Why didn't the Arab, Visigoth, Frankish, and Norman colonization of Iberia, France, and England have the same effects regarding the vitality of indigenous and colonial languages as the Roman and Germanic colonization's of the same territories? Did all these cases involve colonization of the same style, such as settlement or exploitation? If so, how did they vary?

COLONIZATION STYLES

There are similarities between the conquests of England and North America in the styles of their colonization of natives. When the Germanics settled in England, they drove the Celts westward and later on they started assimilating the survivors. The Europeans in North America, did dispensed the populations of North America, and drove the majority into assimilation by enslavement in various forms, including assimilation by rape. Eventually, they assimilated or killed most of the survivors, after the American Revolution (which was primarily the independence of European colonists from England) and the present United States had been formed.

Native Americans have not been recognized as real humans, or American citizens of the colony, until late in the 19th century, and this assimilation process in itself was quite reminiscent of the gradual absorption on of the Celts in the British Isles by the Germanic invaders. Colonized since the 5th century, some Celts such as the Irish did not become subjects of the United Kingdom until the 19th century, long after the initiated settlement colonization of Ireland in the 17th century, and potato plantations became the major industry. In both cases, the loss of indigenous languages did not start till the assimilation of the Natives to the current socio-economic system.

Noteworthy in all such cases is the fact that absorption of the indigenous population by the colonizers has generally led to the loss of indigenous languages, regardless of whether the Natives are kept in a subordinate position or treated as equal. The critical factor is that of involving them in an economic system in which one must use the language of the new ruler in order to compete in the labor force and function adaptively. This is an aspect of globalization requiring that things work more or less the same way, especially in the exercise of power and control of the working class. Similarities between Germanic influence on the British Isles, the Islamic influences over North Africa and Iberia, and the Roman influences over southwestern Europe can be seen in daily language, architecture, and other social systems.

The impact of linguistic devastation after the Romans left is raising in part the question of why the same thing did not happen in England, as in France, Spain, and Portugal. The question also arises of why what happened linguistically in part of the former western Roman empire, like Italy, did not happen in the eastern empire, where the Romans continued their domination much longer?

The fact that the Romans withdrew from western part of their empire also suggests that their colonization was apparently more on the exploitation model than on the settlement one. The question arises of the conditions under which the language of the former colonizer may be adopted to gradually replace the indigenous languages. One important social ecological factor here is that Roman soldiers and administrators married into the local communities, created a culture of ridicule against the native speakers, and obviously transmitted their language to the children. This is similar to the style or method that has indigenous peoples in the Pacific Islands, the America's, and Africa speaking foreign languages like Arabic, English, etc.

"In so-called Sub-Saharan Africa," segregation was the rule and cross-race unions were relatively rare. Most such unions occurred between the European merchants, those who had no political or administrative power, with African women.

The children had barely more advantages than the more indigenous colonial elite, who had the same kind of colonial education. Overall, as supporting to the colonial rule, the African elite were just intermediaries between, on the one hand, the indigenous populations and, on the other, the European colonizers. They continued to socialize with the less privileged indigenous mass and hardly gave up their ancestral cultures, despite adoption of colonial culture expressions. The people visiting the center must quickly notice, they are hardly westernized, in part because they were hardly acculturated extensively to it.

The conception of wealth is currently, and temporarily tuned to the culture the people collectively allowed to control of lifestyles. Gradual disruption can be corrected with gradual correction, only if the base & supporting elements of the problems are included in the equation. What may have taken centuries to disrupt, may only take decades to fix, if the generations of people are progressively educated. For many peoples, despite their exposure to the languages in control of there economics, they never learned the foundations. Besides linguistic variations, many people are still divided by the Western, Arabic, or other colonial languages.

The usage of colonial languages is highly circumscribed, being limited to interactions with Europeans and less commonly to interactions among indigenous backgrounds, and/or anyone that is different.

CURRENT SLIPPING CONTROL

Even in Post-Independence Nations, the elite maintain the socio-economic structure of colonial control, even though they have become more successful in maintaining linguistic divisions of labor than in sustaining the colonial economic infrastructure. The decline of western economies tend to actually favor the countries of indigenous peoples, since resources are drained away for the western nations favor at times of wealth. In Tanzania, "Swahili" has been promoted as dominant instead of English, and in cities like "Kinshasa," the language called Lingala has gained prestige over French in popular culture, where French is hated.

Former English and French plantation settlement colonies were converted into exploitation colonies after the abolition of slavery, with their administrators appointed from the colonial governance. The economic and educational systems of all-territories remain in these places now called "Third World Nations." Control and founding the educational and spiritual systems renders long-term control abilities. This is why ancient ways have not adapted through the peoples of the world, and technological conceptions are so one sided. Only some medical technologies from struggling Asian cultures seem to be leading the way for others. Haiti, which became independent first, in 1804, shows the highest proportion of speakers of Creole.

Students of sociology, world history, and languages probably should not avoid differences among colonization styles in their studies. Linguistic developments are like natural evolution in population genetics.... Wherever it is absolutely imperative, one should understand what ecological factors bring about consequences. The non-uniform linguistic consequences of colonization over the world make it compelling for linguists to investigate and better understand the socio-economic factors that affect language vitality, favoring colonial languages at times, but indigenous languages at others.

It is also obvious that many of the developments today have foundations in earlier history. In turn, our basic understanding of the past will shed different light on what we thought we already understood well. If you don't know where you come from, you don't know were your going. The New World Order idea must not come from those of descent colonial descent, it must come from the collective will and wisdom from indigenous peoples.

We have to put things in perspective and assess the balance of losses and gains in terms of benefits to the indigenous peoples. There are changes to diversity happening all the time. It is not so much a specific form of diversity that matters, but rather how much can be understood about variation in the architecture of the Universal Grammar based on the diversity that exists.

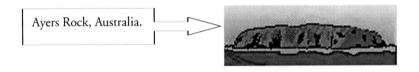

Ayers Rock, Australia.

IMPERIALIST CULTURE LANGUAGES AND LANGUAGE ENDANGERMENT

Globalization is the sense of the emergence of international and regional economic networks with blurred national boundaries, as well as in the sense of economic monopoly over less developed entities for raw materials, and as outlets of one or another's technology have led world languages such as English and French to compete with each other as imperial or hegemonic languages. For example; French is maintained in Haiti only because it is necessary to maintain some economic ties with France, despite the more important fact that the elite need it to isolate the masses.

Taiwan and Hong Kong could do locally with their local Chinese varieties and without English, but they use this language to maintain their global associations at the international level with The United States and the United Kingdom. Malaysia and Singapore could probably also do without English and use Malay only as their national language if their economies did not depend so largely on American and British markets.

The so-called Third World countries, in especially Africa, have become arenas where English, Arabic, and French are competing with each other for monopoly. They connect it with the capitalization of worldwide economies to associate with the spread of foreign movies and other cultural products.

Interestingly, Hollywood films are often translated into local vernaculars (as in Spanish and Arabic), though the music is not. What you may observe in the processes are associations of the spread of imperial languages with their technologies, which are usually exported with their other arts. In many cases, it is the rebellious or revolutionary expressions that are the focus of attention, from African-American artists. Sometimes it is negative images that encourage stereotyping, and copycat negative behavior, that is played intentionally to encourage disassociation, and mistrust between peoples and future relations.

However, in the vast majorities of places where the imperial languages were not already adopted during the colonial period, the languages are being learned in the school systems, or alternatively being abandoned, in terms of costs and benefits to the local population. Those who hope to benefit from dual languages invest the most energy into them.

> "Throughout the world…its agents, client states and satellites are on the defensive—on the moral defensive, the intellectual defensive, and the political and economic defensive. Freedom movements arise and assert themselves. They're doing so on almost every continent populated by man—in the hills of Afghanistan, in Angola, in Kampuchea, in Central America, in Chiapas… [They are] freedom fighters."
>
> Unknown Author (2004)

In places such as India, numbers alone are among the strongest defense weapons against the potential spread of English as a common language. This tends to be one of the factors in the motivation to reproduce in many places around the world. Chinese language varieties like; Bengali, Hindi, Japanese, Javanese, Korean, Vietnamese, and Telugu are alongside recent major colonial languages, viz., English, French, Portuguese, Spanish, Russian, and Arabic.

By record of the United Nations, these are the most common languages spoken at this time: Chinese, English, Hindi, Swahili, Spanish, Russian, Arabic, Portuguese, and French.

There is no doubt that colonization of one style or another in the distant past accounts for the fact that all of these languages are so widely spoken. The history of the world is manifest by regular waves of population movements on small and large scales, with the assumed stronger people assimilating or displacing those that have not yet won challenges against them. This is true of the current distribution of the Indo-European, Bantu, Arabic, and other languages. Asia is no exception, and the current movement for the independence of Tibet from China is blindly accepted by some as an evolution from old expansionist colonization conceptions that brought together populations speaking different languages by force. This is observed through differences among Chinese language varieties like

"Putonghua," (the native name for Mandarin), which is based primarily have Peking, as the unifying language of their history.

The other languages (English, Spanish, French, Arabic, etc.) are recent transfer languages that largely owe the large numbers of their speakers also to their multiple functions. English and French in particular have more non-native than native speakers. While Chinese vernaculars may be a real threat to some Tibetan languages, English, French, Spanish, Portuguese, and Arabic are also dangers to many languages of the so-called Third World, where they are spoken as second language varieties, and for highly restricted functions, but sometimes only by small fractions of the indigenous populations. The concept of "third world" is only a class separation term predicated from those that term others as less significant.

It is also noteworthy that Spanish and Portuguese are widely spoken today mostly thanks to the settlement colonization of several parts of the world by their European speakers during the 17th and 18th centuries. Portugal and Spain have no direct economic or military claims today that would make them threats to other languages outside those same settlement colonies. In more of less the same vein, note that Arabic has become so much associated with Islam that it can hardly stand up to the competition of English and French for the function of an international language, even in those territories of North Africa and the Middle East where Arabic vernaculars are spoken.

Varieties such as African-American English (Ebonics & Geechee), and Appalachian English are not threatened by Standard English. English itself is made up of several languages. Some African words, which come from the descendants of African Americans such as; the Mandingo, Akan, Yoruba, Wolof, etc., are in full-integrated use today.

SOME AFRICAN WORDS IN AMERICAN ENGLISH (MANDINGO, AKAN, TWI, ETC)

Bad—Mandingo word, Banana—Wolof word, Booboo—Bantu, Boody—Bantu, Bug—Mandingo word, Dirt—Akan word, Done—Wolof word, Jazz—Mandingo, Man—Mandingo, Okay—Mandingo, Poop—Wolof word, Rap—Bantu word, Ruckus—Bantu word, Tote—Bantu word, Uh-huh—Bantu word, Coffee—Kaffa word, Cotton—Nubian word, Bronco—Ibibio word, among others.
Ref. (African Heritage of American English.)
By: Joseph E. Halloway—1993, Indiana University Press

INDIGENOUS IDENTITY

Many Mexicans and other Central American natives; in general, believe they are not allowed to speak as Nican Tlaca (Indigenous) people, for fear of social rejection. In many religious, government, and academic organizations, native people are referred to as past tense, insignificant, sub-human, savages, etc. European colonial perceptions spread through so-called education and media have associated the Indigenous People of the America's in that way.

The population of indigenous people in the America's is well over 180 million, but like the census of Africans, the numbers are probably in the 1-billion population mark. It's time for humanity to learn our true histories, which includes over 4,000 years of civilization.

The population of indigenous persons is projected to be over 50% of the North American population of humans over the next 100 years. It has become apparent that media and government officials are trained to take offense and promote the pseudo-ownership idea of their colonial developed nations, like the U.S. when true history is mentioned. Indeed, since the creation of the United Nations, Indigenous People have been categorically denied significant leadership roles for more than short-term roles, by organized assassinations, defamation, etc., if the leadership represents progressive changes for/of the people. They seem to not be allowed to speak of the biological warfare that killed 23 million of indigenous people (95% of the U.S. area population in the 16th century) in general public arenas without persecution, still today. Indigenous peoples, and the African persons related, are practically to speak of the European destruction of the native cities, civilizations, rape of countless women, and neocolonial effects on this part of humanity. Censorship is a popular word for the conservative and liberal person with racial pathology and/or common sense deficiency syndrome.

Many people get advised to stop playing the victim, or to forget about the past. One cannot play a victim, if one is one, and lacks full knowledge of the cause, and skills for the creation of a new way of being. The foreign cultures that oppress others, and control learning resources, do not express interest, or supply true building informational interest materials. It is common that accurate heritage information for adults and children not be available. Cultural assimilation by the people, to adapt to new places, or information, can enforce or enhance ignorance. The false labeling of indigenous people as Hispanic and/or Latino enhances the false perception that they are consciously part of the colonial role.

This is an instigating purpose to decline the true identities of the Indigenous people, and claim that they no longer exist, beyond small pockets called reservations in the U.S., rural areas separated from the main society, or in myths. The Mexica (Meh-shee-kah) Movement has been expressing their perception of measured accounts against native peoples south of the U.S.

The truth is what is desired of the children's potential. They deserve no less than the truth about everything. Just as African American, and Asian Medias in many countries have tended to display programming that benefits the culture of other populations, media known as Latin or Hispanic has tended to promote Spanish & German cultures, counter to the native. Until recently, no media source has responded to the true representation needs of the people.

Value is beginning to be seen in the people learning their heritage, and many that have learned are taking positions to be sure awareness and empowerment are encouraged. Little to none of the children's programming, romance day programming, etc., for either cultures have been for the people, but more for frivolity, and the money tends to come from companies providing interest in encouraging the cycle of corrupt thought.

The conception that European descendants have told their own people and many indigenous people in their own lands, are that non-white people are illegal, foreigners, thieves, uncivilized, immoral ones, and even the oppressors. This concept has taken form in the design of school textbooks on history, political structures, and economic opportunities. Although some specific areas of the world have better designed textbooks for the children, most textbooks; especially those in Africa, the America's, and the Pacific spread an almost worship mode on foreign concepts of world history.

Restoration of an original and more advanced group of indigenous people is completely possible, with the collective intentions/actions of the people. Progressive mass education of the people is usually the best way to initialize change. The people of the world must learn the greatness of themselves from the examination of persons of kinship, the wrongs of current advanced societies, and strategies to attain a better civilization together. From that point, it should be left up to the people to move on the possibilities they feel most comfortable moving towards. The Hispanic/Latino agenda temporarily controls the lives, land, wealth, education, and media of the native peoples. The agenda is different from the Anglo-American agenda only because it uses Spanish instead of English. Neither English nor Spanish are from the America's.

SOME COMMON TRANSFERS OF LANGUAGE

Bantu Words-in-American English Vocabulary		Nahuatl (Aztec Language)-in-Mexican-Spanish Vocabulary	
These words are in general use within U.S. Dialects in Basic language, Gullah, and Ebonics.		Some of the words used in North Central Mexico that were borrowed from Nahuatl (Native/Aztec Language). Some of the words are *not* in use in other Nahuatl speaking regions.	
Banjo	Musical Instrument		
Booboo	An error, mistake		
Boody	Sex		
Bozo	Big & stupid fellow	Zoquete	Mud, a fool
Chance	A guess	Asquel	A small ant
Conga	A group dance	Moyote	Mosquito
Gam	Casual discussion	Petaca	a suitcase
Jiffy	In a moment, quickly	Chiquito	very small
Mooch	To steal info, or stuff	Papalote	kite and windmill
Ruckus	Noisy mayhem	Mecate	rope
Yakking	Excessive talking	tocayo	namesake
Base	Beginning of construct	malacate	winch
Bad	Damn good	itacate	bundle
Bug	Insect, or to annoy.	elote	sweet corn
Cool	Calm and controlled	olote	corn cob
Dig	Appreciative of	popote	drinking straw
Done	To have completed	zenzontle	mocking bird
He	3rd person male ref.	guajolote	turkey
Okay	acknowledgment	molcajete	kitchen mortar
Poop	To defecate	petate	weaved mattress
Rap	To speak, flirt, tease	chocolate,	
Nana	Grandmother	tomate	(same names)
		jocoque	yoghurt
		cacle	shoe
		chante	home
		mexicatl	mexicano

Winifred K. Vass, <u>Bantu Speaking Heritage of the United States</u>. (UCLA: Center for Afro-American Studies, 1979). Pg. 105-122. [Check online Bookstores to purchase]	The Azteca Web Page, **http://www.azteca.net/aztec/**, (09/12/04) [Please visit this site]

Europeans and European descendants have been succeeding in the domination many peoples, either by direct malice, or by acting in trained ways to fulfill expansion and facilitate social control mechanisms. For most, it is not at all the fault of those that are following training/education to collectively focus benefit to finances of England, Portugal, Spain, France, USA, etc. Control of the resources of the land is very high.

They were the first to use mass biological warfare in the form of smallpox, etc. Europeans were not successful against any peoples because they had developed more deadly technology; other peoples, just modified for deadly use, invented indeed most of the technology. Nor did they succeed because of their canons, horses, or because of the European lie that said that, we thought, they were "gods". They succeeded because the leadership passed on immoral, collectively sociopathic thoughts, used biological warfare in savage ways. This is the true genocide & terrorism performed since around 4500 B.C.

CULTURAL RECONSTRUCTION

Among the great re-builders of the world for positive change are those in the Mexica Movement. The Mexica Movement is an educational organization for the people of Mexican, Central American, and North Native American family kinship. They promote the Pre-European history in a positive and constructive Non euro-centric manner, based on the Pre-European books, archeology, anthropology, linguistics, and other sources of the Anahuac Nation and Mexica People.

They research all sources possible, as a base from which we can educate, redefine, reconstruct, and give rebirth and vision to the Children and others.

Progressive people think beyond the 10 years, beyond the next 100 years, to an immanent time when the people have progressively regained their independence and their honorable place in the world, without oppression from the European, Middle Eastern, or others. As with other cultures, Chinese mythical stories are entwined with history. The history is partly based on legend, which is interwoven with mythology, and language development.

When European descendant control of Israel (Jews) is imparted to in the same sentence, why are they given higher attention? Was that over 2,000 years ago? Why is this not asked to be forgotten? Only in the last 10 years, have the knowledge of the most horrific genocidal actions begun to spread to the general public, and be taught about in public school history lessons correctly. The 23 million (95%) natives of the America's who were killed by the Europeans, 100+ Million Africans killed in the east and west Africa slave trades, genocidal actions in the south Pacific peoples, are among the terrific fields of information today's children are learning about in some U.S. schools, contrary to the old Columbus praise along with other murderers.

The post-colonial power nations that rely on the continued exploitation of resources, and programmed reliance, may be reacting afraid that we might begin thinking in our own interests instead of the interests of the foreign occupiers who are now occupying our lands. In all of this we are still innocently, or not so innocently, thinking that all Europeans, and their cultures are justice, a people of morality, and a people of True Faith. Historically they have been a savage people of lies, of theft, of immorality, injustice, and genocide, with the exception of a few that include struggles against that way of being. Prophesy wise, the coming of the destroyers with pale skin, and order for a time has come true. Almost every people of the world have a similar conception of this time, and the future.

OTHER WAR ACTS AGAINST HUMANITY

There has been no period of more than five years that the USA, or another European Colonial nation has had a role in beating on another people/country to create fear and submission for control and subornment. People movements towards regional/continental unity seem to be seen as the greatest threat to current world order-control for decades/centuries. Why? A mass movement cannot defeat an organized force without becoming an organized force, with functions based on knowledge of self.

The monstrous killings were not a matter of accident as written through euro-centric history books. The Genocidal use of biological weapons of mass destruction started as an ad hoc action in a few locations, then once other Europeans learned of this, it turned into a general plan to empty out all lands by killing people with this weapon that Europeans looked at as a sort of "pesticide." The European criminals in this action knew that this biological weapon of mass destruction would allow for the easier establishment of European settlements, and that it would bring about the end to resistance to the theft of land and its resources. This is now a norm in weapons of war.

During the massive invasion of the America's from Spanish Conquistadors to today, the native cities were destroyed; three of the cities were larger than any city in Europe of that time. The libraries were also burned, and most of the books either taken as secret possessions, burned, buried, or tossed into the ocean. A clear majority of the native populations lived in cities and large towns; a very small part of their populations in "North America" actually lived as nomadic tribes. There system of schools and universities were shattered and most teachers and leaders were executed. The destruction could be done because of trickery, superior weapons for death, mass psychotic behavior, and sudden new illnesses from the Europeans. They are the essence of the Pandora's box.

Most Europeans and Islamic based settler/warriors came to foreign lands for the "free land, free slaves, free wealth" under the outrageous pretense of "God's authorization" to kill people, to loot and vandalize cities, and the added bonus of what they saw as the legal right to rape the population. Most indigenous people of the America's that survived the nightmare of European savage biological warfare, and earlier attempts of genocide, were enslaved to serve the interests of Spaniards and the other Europeans who would come to take the land.

As slaves of the Spaniards, those that are called Mexican's were continuously physically raped as a people for generations. Like many natives speaking English, in what is currently the U.S.A., they were forced to take on the Spanish language and Christian/Catholic religion. All have been enforced to have Spanish first names and Spanish surnames.

Denial of true independence is slowly fading away. Like many people's, they have been unable to successfully revolt for the last 500+ years because they are psychologically programmed to accept subservience (slavery). Admission of true heritage and potential is not present among many indigenous peoples of the world, because the adults and children are lacking the information, and accepting servant supporting religions, programming continuous failure. European descendants currently control the land, the wealth, the people, the governance, the education, the media, the economic system, the past, present, and future of Mexico, Central America, South America, and North America.

All of which is completely within the abilities of the natives. Most history books they have written tells Europeans to pretend as if the criminal acts of trespassing and theft were not crimes, as if it wasn't really Genocide but a simple clearing of the land. They looked at the people not as the owners of the land but as wild like bears that had to be killed to make the land safe for Europeans to exploit. Hispania comes from the Latin language of the Romans, referring to the country of Spain [Webster's Encyclopedic Unabridged Dictionary of the English Language (1993) by Thunder Bay Press]. From the word Hispania comes the word "Hispanic" which refers to the people, the language, the culture, and all things related to Spain. Spain is a country in southern Europe.

The people of Mexican and "Central American" descent, are not Spaniards or Europeans, and are not in Europe. They are what are called a Nican Tlaca (Indigenous) people/Anahuac. They are one people who are Mixed-blood (Mestizo People), and the Full-blood Indigenous people.

They are a people under occupation. They are a people who have been subjected to massive rape and cultural castration. They are a people who have been forced into ignorance, self-hate and poverty by the theft of the wealth of resources, and conception that foreign funds are worth more that others.

Language endangerment is a much more complex subject matter than most of the literature has led us to think. The process is far from being new in the history of mankind. It has been a concurrent of language diversification, the hidden aspect that the genetic linguistics has not revealed. This is itself a byproduct of language appropriation, a process during which languages currently spoken by the learners influence the one they target. Such contacts have sometimes caused language shift (instead of sustaining bi- or multilingualism), which is directly related to language loss.

It is also far from being uniform from one territory to another, being in part correlated with variation in different colonization styles and in the communicative functions that the new languages have assumed in various territories relative to their indigenous counterparts. They are largely a function of the new economic systems that have replaced the indigenous ones and the extent to which the Natives have been absorbed, assimilated, or integrated in the current systems.

INTEGRATION

Integration happens when populations coexist in peaceful relations. It also reveals how language loss occurs, and that the stronger language endangers the weakened one(s). While some speakers are happy to be able to communicate (successfully) in the language of their choice and select the same language at all or most such interactions. The procedure is the same even during periods of enslavement, including the ones from the 17th to the 19th centuries in the so-called New World and the Indian Ocean.

Moreover some major languages such as Chinese, Hindi, and Japanese are not hegemonic and constitute threats only to other indigenous languages over which they have prevailed as vernaculars in the present. Aspects of globalization have facilitated expansionism, which is apparently more relevant to the vitality of languages than regional or world-scale aspects of economic globalization. The same is true of Indic languages, with later immigrations having only reinforced communities that developed as separate either by colonial settlement design or due to lack of socioeconomic integration in the host countries. In the Caribbean, the speakers were economically absorbed and their languages have hardly survived. The future of languages in the 21st century partially depends on how individual countries will evolve socio-economically during that time.

It will depend mostly on the changing social structures, relationship to the environment, and knowledge of heritage. In some parts of the world, this globalization is progressing without any serious obstacles that can stop its effects on indigenous languages that do not participate in the economy. There is variation in the way globalization is taking place around the world, which should remind linguists and historians of the danger of over generalizing. Lack of Faith has produced attrition and eventually death for many languages, despite the will of the relevant populations not to give them up.

We should remember that typically speakers do not consciously give up their languages. Languages die gradually and inconspicuously as a consequence of communicative Faiths of their speakers. We can say that speakers kill them by neglect, as they constantly select other language varieties to communicate with speakers of other languages and/or within their own ethno-linguistic group. Speakers typically do this as part of their adaptive response to current socioeconomic ecologies that requires competence in the chosen language for their survival.

We cannot just encourage speakers to maintain their ancestral languages even if only as vernaculars for home, without concurrent actions on the ecologies themselves that prompted them to behave in manners detrimental to their languages. As experts, linguists should consider what particular adaptive alternatives are available for the concerned populations, including whether maintaining their ancestral languages is a realistic alternative.

Except in conditions of slavery and genocide, languages have endangered others typically when tyranny has been insidious. Most cases of language loss and endangerment are late damaging results of post-colonization activities. Grammatical descriptions do not safeguard languages either, they are analyst's interpretations of systems used by speakers, and the interpretations may contain inaccuracies. For the purposes of linguistics, they are of course better than no speakers and no languages to work on.

One new development in the progressive reclamation of Africa by the indigenous people is that they are taking more and more control back. The Masai herdsmen, with a population of about half a million, are one of the smallest tribes in Kenya. When European's had power in the mid-19th century, they dominated most of what is now western Kenya, and upon an old power transfer, the best grazing land was signed to European farmers and consigned themselves to isolated reservations. That treaty, has lapsed with its 100th anniversary, and was also illegal, due to the fact that the Europeans came in as conquerors, not guests.

RECLAMATION

The Masai people claim southern and central Kenya, but the most active dispute has arisen on the western slopes of Mount Kenya, 180 or so miles north of Nairobi. The 38 white landowners unnaturally claim Kenyan citizenship. What most probably should be done is an eradication of the squatting European farmers, along with continuing consistent reclamation of indigenous roles over self-sufficiency, cultural Faiths, and environmental stewardship. Reclamation of a society depends on a total scope of action. "If you only have culture, and you're not hooked into the economics, and it's not related to your politics, then you don't have a system of development, you only have a system of survival.

Economics is the productive capacity in hand with politics as the management capacity. The ecological systems are related to your sociological systems. This duality of economics and politics, ecology and sociology has to be related and then you synthesize them and you have culture, the psychological dimension. Economics, politics and culture relate; as ecological and sociological and psychological dimensions relate." This quote applies to every indigenous people on earth.

PEACE ON EARTH requires knowledge of self & action for the purpose!

Even now in 2005, the miseducation of people to believe the conception that education is and should only be good in the perspective of white American and European governments is predicated on Phillipino, Native Am, African, Australian, etc peoples.

Genocide is not only physical, it is cultural. Ruin, co-option, derailment of scholarship and de-divinity of the spiritual validity of a people are attempts to weaken the self-sustenance of a people. At least 75% of the peoples on earth have developed written languages. African people developed over 10-written languages with active and remnants of the pure state in various places today. Remember, what you are seeing of modern Africa, the America's, and other parts of the world are fragments from wars and other destruction. Mass social centralizing on sports that focus on harm, are as socially destructive as the popularity of games of death & crime. As intellectual growth and unified positive actions are shunned by youth, progressive acceptance of warlike behavior becomes a norm.

"You are who you are, based on your historical reality."
(Dr. Molefi K. Asante)

End of Chapter #3.)
To be continued…

Chapter 4

World Holocausts

The word "holocaust" has been used so much to describe the damage done to one people of the earth, that it is usually not identified with others. The definition of a holocaust is a thorough attempt at genocide of any race or cultural group. This has been attempted and/or successfully accomplished against people, and other life forms, all over this world, especially during European expansions of power in the last 400 years. In order to dispel the conception that the word holocaust should be identified with activities during the misinterpreted war called World War II, I must explain comparisons.

The genocidal actions against the Jewish people by the Hitler era has is currently known as the most significant episode in recent European History, but not in the rest of the world. For example; it has become traditional to ignore the plight of the Native peoples & deny struggles for empowerment. To this day, the European descendant peoples in control of the societies of the America's, deny anyone of native heritage to become a representative in the United Nations, etc. The word holocaust is badly associated only with the Nazi's & Germans in most people educated in Europe and North America.

Hitler and the Nazi Party gained power in Germany in 1933 and lost power in 1945—only 12 years. Yet, by the end of the Hitler regime, the world had been plunged into a global world war, Europe was in shambles and nearly 30 million died. Among the dead were over <u>six million Jews</u> who were systematically slaughtered for no other reason than that they were Jews. This event has come to be called THE HOLOCAUST. In the view of certain writers, the term "Holocaust" must be reserved for this specific time and set of events. Certainly there has been numerous atrocities against humankind throughout history, horrible cases of genocide directed against innocent people—<u>38 million Africans died during the 200+ years of the international slave trade, the decimation of over 18 million Native American Indians in North America between 1600 and the 1870's, due to direct assault, early biological warfare, and corruption of social supports.</u>

The information I gathered generally covers the African Holocaust, Indigenous People's Holocausts, Polynesian Holocausts, and some Holocausts centered on Religious Groups. The motivations for each were racial, economic, and religious. The instigation of the majority of the problems from genocide, to environmental destruction, to cultural changes leading to self-destruction, has been created by the actions of the people of the European Continent. The basis for the conception of destroying other peoples of the world came from a misfortunate series of events, both natural & ego based, for control of the geo-political arena.

To start, I will begin with world history from what is called Pre-History in various civilizations. During this period of so called unrecorded history, virtually all peoples in Africa, and the temperate/tropical zone peoples of Asia, the Pacific Islands, and the America's were advanced in terms of society, way beyond what is currently observed. From this point, I must state a summary of the people's histories, continent by continent.

Africa contains descendants of the original people of the earth. The holocausts that have occurred first were against African people, by people who came from what is now called the Middle East (Syria, Iraq, Iran, and Saudi Arabia), formerly Persia. The conquer of the lands currently called Egypt, Algeria, Morocco, and other places, contained the destruction of scores of people, their civilizations, and recording literature. Throughout the centuries of wars from 4500b.c. to today, descendants of brainwashed slaves, offspring from raped slaves, and other prisoners of war, added to gradual progression into central and West Africa. <u>Entire Cities of people were slaughtered. To date, there are many cities in Africa were little or no Africans exist. This process made for the destruction of over 80-million Africans on the continent.</u>

In current West African Areas, the leadership of the townships, Arabized Africans, other Muslim Exploiters, replaced universities such as Timbuktu, and the cities or they misinformed those they did not replace while including threats and promises. From 4500b.c. to the 1400–1500's, the European Elite had been gaining intentions on controlling Africa. With the advancement of the technologies of weaponry, transportation, home building, and food production, at the same time they were jealous of the profit there past opponents, the Islamic conquerors, were gaining.

All of this was aided by the spread of epidemics from European & their Asian counterparts, and the fact that many African Civilizations were going through golden ages of peace. Within the 1600's, many Nations of Europe engaged in the creation of what we now call the "Middle Passage", or the Atlantic Slave Trade (West African Holocaust). In the main 200 years of this holocaust, a measure of 38 million African people were killed either on the continent resistance wars, in transit across the ocean, or during short lives were they were placed. Results of the attacks on the people have left foreign concepts in play across the continent including, customs like female mutilation, paternal superiority, and poor agricultural practices.

The Polynesians (Hawaiians, others) are Holocaust victims tool. European Invaders were responsible for the Polynesian holocausts. Again, not just weapons and alien fighting techniques, but purposeful infection by spreading there own diseases has been a favorite tool of suppression & genocide. In order to attain the Islands of Hawaii, the European invaders used all available tools at their disposal to take the land from its original inhabitants. Today, only fractions of the 1000's of original inhabitants exist, but are slowly regaining their prominence.

The (Indigenous) Native Americans Peoples of the Caribbean, North, and South America have also endured holocausts. Columbus made four voyages to the continental area called the Americas. Columbus installed himself as Governor of the Caribbean islands, with headquarters on Hispaniola (the large island now shared by Haiti and the Dominican Republic). He described the people, the Arawak (called by some as the Tainos. http://www.hartford-hwp.com/taino/, 3-2-03) to his Psychotic counterparts in leadership of Europe, through his reports.

After Columbus had surveyed the Caribbean region, he returned to Spain to prepare his invasion of the Americas. From accounts of his second voyage, we can begin to understand what the New World represented to Columbus and his men—it offered them life without limits, unbridled freedom. Columbus took the title "Admiral of the Ocean Sea" and proceeded to unleash a reign of terror unlike anything seen before or since. When he was finished, <u>"Eight Million" Arawak—virtually the entire native population of the places we call Hispaniola, Jamaica, Haiti, Puerto Rico, etc.,—had been exterminated by torture, murder, forced labor, starvation, disease and despair. "One day, in front of the Mission called Las Casas, the Spanish dismembered, beheaded, and/or raped 3000 people."</u> The Spanish cut off the legs of children who ran from them. They poured people full of boiling soap. They made bets as to who, with one sweep of his sword, could cut a person in half. They loosed dogs that 'devoured an Indian like a hog, at first sight, in less than a moment.' They used nursing infants for dog food."

This was not occasional violence—it was a systematic, prolonged campaign of brutality and sadism, a policy of torture, mass murder, slavery and forced labor that continued for CENTURIES. "The destruction of the Indians of the Americas was, far and away, the most massive act of genocide in the history of the world."

<u>Eventually more than 100 million natives fell under European rule.</u> Their extermination would follow. As the natives died out, slaves brought from Africa replaced them. To make a long story short, Columbus established a pattern that held for five centuries—a "ruthless, angry search for wealth." "There was no real ending to the conquest of Latin America. It continued in remote forests and on far mountainsides. It is still going on in our day when miners and ranchers invade land belonging to the Amazon Indians and armed thugs occupy Indian villages in the backwoods of Central America."

In the 1980s, under Presidents Ronald Reagan and George Bush, the U.S. government knowingly gave direct aid to genocidal campaigns that murdered tens of thousands Mayan Indian people in Guatemala and others killing indigenous people, including the South African Apartheid regime.

Continuing the gruesome tradition of the 1980s, to terrorize, the U.S. government-funded paramilitaries to mass-murder Indians in Central and South America. The bestial carnage committed by Uncle Sam's armies includes countless disappearances, epidemic rape, starvation, fatal mutilation, and torture. The U.S. trained, Colombian paramilitaries have even made their own gruesome addition to the usual list of horrors; such as public beheadings.

In the U.S., Indians were defined as subhuman, lower than animals. George Washington compared them to wolves, "beasts of prey" and called for their total destruction. Andrew Jackson (whose portrait appears on the U.S. $20 bill today) in 1814 "Supervised the mutilation of 800 or more Creek Indian corpses—the bodies of men, women and children that [his troops] had massacred—cutting off their noses to count and preserve a record of the dead, slicing long strips of flesh from their bodies to tan and turn into bridle reins." The policy of extermination (genocide)—grew more insistent as settlers pushed westward: In 1851, the Governor of California officially called for the extermination of the Indians in his state.

On March 24, 1863, the *Rocky Mountain News* in Denver ran an editorial titled, "Exterminate them." On April 2, 1863, the *Santa Fe New Mexican* advocated "extermination of the Indians." In 1891, Frank L. Baum (gentle author of "The Wizard Of Oz") wrote in the *Aberdeen Saturday Pioneer* (Kansas) that the army should "finish the job" by the "total annihilation" of the few remaining Indians.

The U.S. did not follow through on Baum's demand for there really was no need. By then the native population had been reduced to 2.5% of its original numbers and 97.5% of the aboriginal land base had been expropriated and renamed "The land of the free and the home of the brave." Hundreds upon hundreds of native tribes with unique languages, learning, customs, and cultures had simply been erased from the face of the earth, most often without even the pretense of justice or law. Today we can see the remnant cultural arrogance of Christopher Columbus and Captain John Smith shadowed in the cult of the "global free market" which aims to eradicate indigenous cultures and traditions world-wide, to force all peoples to adopt the ways of the U.S. Today's globalist "Free Trade" is merely yesterday's "Manifest Destiny."

Now, one of the most recent & talked about holocaust efforts was on the Jewish Holocaust. There were little, if any, economic net gains; in fact, one suspects that the Jewish Holocaust brought economic loss to Germany. The victims presented no threat to the German nation, nor to the Nazi regime. Neither national security nor territorial expansions were served by it, though Hitler used anti-Semitism as a rationale for both. The motives tend to be the same in all Holocaust situations around the world, but the methods tend to vary by ethnic region.

"There is nothing more important than the question: 'How do you know?'" (Prof. Manu Ampim)

End of Chapter #4

Chapter 5

Religion & Humanity, —or—Religion vs. Humanism

Religion generates commitment and passion in people. However, this can be a double-edged sword, or a never-ending dance. It has moved countless individuals to lead more spiritual and ethical lives; it has brought feelings of peace and security, it has enhanced connections to the universe, and the inner-self. It has motivated billions to act in a more loving way towards others, and it had motivated others to commit genocide against themselves & other forms of life. It has inspired many to devote their lives to helping others. It has also inspired some to focus solely on material wealth for themselves.

Hatred, based partly in the "so-called organized religions," arranged horrendous crimes affecting billions of people over the centuries, and countless forms of life. A few faiths have no direct relationships to the cause of willful destruction of life, like Buddhism, Toltec, Yoga (Spiritual Form), Yoruba, and the Ausar-Auset. The gods and goddesses of many religions are scientific symbols to analyze the universe. Each element was given a role as a manifestation of the one, which had no name. Only the Europeans and Middle Eastern Asians have believed that the sum total of the universe can be held in a sacred temple, as deemed through specific historical development.

EXPRESSION

The eternal and the revelation of the eternal are attempts to be associated with it, in virtually all forms of prayer. Prayers are expressions of love in Faith. Prayer must not be limited in perspective to praying/reciting/chanting while sitting in a room, or building; it extends to definition to the founding acts of dance, and accord with existing myth. Dance is the Faith of response and connection to rhythm & harmony. A myth is a metaphor of the story told from a religion and/or story telling about existence. A myth is not a lie! Prayers and dances are only a part of the dress of spiritual expression.

The experiences of joy and sorrow are temporal representations of life. Consciousness and the nature of the determination of reality are determined by the historical circumstances of the living group. Virtually all religions lead to the statement that it's deities and prophets are symbolic of the manifestation within yourself, and relationships with all things around you. A deity is the personification of the energy of existence.

As a myth, literal sense should be taken metaphorically but correctly translated from the language of the time it was written. The implications of the lives and symbols represented in the various faiths tend to be more significant than the individuals themselves. God is a projected representation of the entity of all existence, and deification of love. Religions that place physical ego based identity in the form of a supreme being representing a human; tend to grossly express attitudes of conquering and exploitation engrossed within the culture.

The relationships generated have tended to grow capitalistic views, and negatively turn identification of a supreme overseer; lord, or king; or in an attempt to localize a family relationship with the use of the word father, to engage a higher importance in the destructive nature of the male, instead of the constructive. In a crossed perspective in identification of the female as the representation of the universe/god, the feminine powers are expressed as the highest power because they create life from within & birth it. Societies; like the ancient Kemetic, had a balanced relationship of the male/female powers of the order of the universe/nature, by the social and spiritual system.

The female is an equal half of the spiritual representation with the powers of creation, and the male was the physical representation of the universe/god; also sharing with the responsibilities in representation of death time transformation. Each was worshiped with equal respect and prominence as one. Evidence that this and other philosophies of Africa were taught to peoples around the world from approximately 2,000 B.C. to the 1400's A.D.

Various "Primary Researchers" like; Ivan Van Sertima, John Henrik Clark, Runoko Rashidi, Molefi Kete Asante, Manu Ampim, and Leonard Jeffries have irrefutable evidence that many of the civilizations gone and today, have shared trade, and knowledge with ancient African civilizations.

In the three religions of Judaism, Christianity and Islam, whenever the faithful pray, regardless of language, they always end their prayer by saying **Amen**. There is no linguistic translation for Amen, because it is a name and not a word. The origin of *Amen* is Egyptian, for *Amen* was the name of God. The Jews have learned about *Amen* during their sojourn in Egypt, which lasted for four generations. The name of *Amen*, which means the Hidden One, in Ancient Egypt, lives on. True religions inspire the people to achieve greatness, joy, and prosperity for the society. Injustices reign supreme among societies worldwide because of the lack of faith, determination, and true guidance from religions that do not represent to, or for the people.

The people in particular areas specifically dominated by oppressive religions, which call themselves liberating, tend to have multiple, thousands, and in some cases millions of peoples that suffer through decaying progression from foreign religions, outdated ideology, and/or unnatural repression.

Mystic Law is an expressive term that relates to the correcting order/connection to the balance of the universe. Spiritual based religions translate the empowering connection as balancing the order of one's life for the correction of present and future discourses. The operative function of chanting, spiritual dance, and other forms of prayer, are attempts to transcend one's existence into harmony and correction of today and tomorrow, in the view of oneself.

Prayer itself seems to be a natural phase of human evolution, since it has been found to be an expression of our generally undeveloped 7th and/or 8th sense, and/or what is called extra sensory abilities by skeptical cultures, and those taught to think that way. Every high civilization has had terms for this and jobs for those that had professions using those skills. Mystic law is an English transliteration of the Buddhist term, which is identified in different names and extents, within every society past and present. The term is mentioned in different ways in various spiritual orders, but is a part of the general powers/senses expressed through faith and the many types of prayer.

BRIEF OVERVIEW OF CONFLICTS

Author "Carmen Bernand," estimated that the Native population of the place called Mexico was reduced from 30 million to 3 million over four decades. European attacks on Indigenous People's of the America's may have started with the arrival of Christopher Columbus's to San Salvador in 1492. The Indigenous People's of the America's & Caribbean populations dropped dramatically over the next few decades through the psychotic land grab, directly through genocidal tendencies by Europeans. Others died indirectly as a result of contact with introduced diseases; like, bubonic, smallpox, influenza, and the measles; and some directly by the first documented use of germ warfare. The use of unwarranted warfare, terrorism, death march massacres, forced relocation to barren lands, destruction of their main food supplies, fire, and poisoning were favorite methods.

Oppression continues into the 21st century, through actions by governments and religious groups, which systematically place obstacles in the way of Native progress to reclaim culture and religious heritage. A byproduct of this oppression is the high suicide rate, due to encouraged mass depression. Canadian Natives have the highest suicide rate of any group in the world.

The genocide against Indigenous People's of the America's is one of the longest lasting genocidal campaigns in human history. It started, like all useless wars, with the oppressor treating the victims as sub-humans. It continued until almost all Indigenous People's of the America's were wiped of the face of the earth, and/or along with much of their language, culture, historical records, and religions. While the attempt was highly successful in forming current submissive behavior, they did not succeed in destroying all of anything.

It is only in the last 600 years or so, that disruption from corrupted Islamic, Catholic, Judeo-Christians, and Early Capitalists really spread their beliefs through force, manipulation, and false perceptions of power, beyond the corruption of faiths to near perfection against northern Africa. Only those in each of these religions, whether they were a majority under rule by a few that led the people wrong, or the few within the faith that acted in recognition as true followers for humanity can be justified as honorable persons of those faiths. Many religions are expressed outside of their originating areas, so the cultural base of them is usually in a state of continual flux. The Faith of a religion requires Faith of either your own, or a foreign culture, as part of thought. Culture is a combination of language, music, and other factors. Only the mass murder of European Jews by Christians from 306 to 1945 CE, and systematic genocidal contributions made by Syrian, Arab, and Roman descendants on African Peoples since 4500b.c. have been more intent towards evil motivations.

SOME CURRENT RELIGIOUS CONFLICTS AND WARS:

Note: Some conflicts may have ended, expanded, or changed during, or after the publication of this book…

COUNTRIES	MAIN RELIGIOUS GROUPS INVOLVED	TYPE OF CONFLICT
India	Animists, Hindus, Muslims & Sikhs	In late 2002-FEB, a Muslim-Hindu conflict broke out, killing an average of 100 people a day over the first five days. Fringe believers in the peace properties of these faiths are responsible.
Cyprus	Christians & Muslims	The island is partitioned, creating enclaves for ethnic Greeks (Christians) and Turks (Muslims).
Afghanistan	Extreme, radical Fundamentalist Muslim terrorist groups & non-Muslims	Al Queda is generally regarded as having committed many terrorist attacks on U.S. ships, embassies, and buildings. Their goal seems to be to promote a worldwide war between Muslims and non-Muslims.
Kashmir	Hindus & Muslims	A region of the world, claimed by Pakistan and India. The availability of nuclear weapons and the eagerness to use them are destabilizing the region further. Around 70,000 people killed since 1989.

COUNTRIES	MAIN RELIGIOUS GROUPS INVOLVED	TYPE OF CONFLICT
Kurdistan	Christians, Muslims	Assaults on Christians (Protestant, Chaldean Catholic, & Assyrian Orthodox). Bombing campaign underway.
United States & other European dominated nations of the Americas.	Indigenous People	Many tribes forced to live in reservations, or sectors, have been forced to rely on government funds and only have permission to hunt/raise foods at regulated times. Others live by forced suppressive religion, Drug abuse, alcoholism, and forced prostitution. Self-Help is highly discouraged.
Middle East	Jews, Muslims, & Christians	The peace process between Israel and Palestine suffered a complete breakdown. Prejudice against others is encouraged and feeds both to hate and have desire to harm the other. Doctrine or Culture?
Nigeria	Christians, Animists, & Muslims	Yoruba's and Christians in the south of the country are battling Muslims in the north. Country is struggling towards democracy after centuries of Muslim or Christian military dictatorships.
Northern Ireland	Protestants, Catholics	Over 5,000 killings and assassinations between them, since 1961.

COUNTRIES	MAIN RELIGIOUS GROUPS INVOLVED	TYPE OF CONFLICT
World Bank & Others	Indigenous Peoples of Africa & the America's.	Educated representative leadership, education systems, various governing leaderships, and full U.N. representation are prevented by the organization of Neo-Colonial, U.S., E.U., and Worldwide capitalist interest groups to maintain supremacy of tri-lateral commission nations.
Philippines	Christians & Muslims	Centuries old conflict between the mainly Christian central government and Muslims in the south of the country. All is due to neo-colonial influences.
Russia, Chechnya	Russian Orthodox Christians, Muslims	The Russian army attacked the breakaway region. Muslims had allegedly blown up buildings in Moscow, and similar attacks by the Orthodox. Why?
Australia	British & Aboriginal People	Colonization, Genocide, and Intent Cultural Degradation of the Aboriginal people.
Serbia, province of Vojvodina	Serbian Orthodox & Roman Catholics	Serb Ethnic cleansing programs have "encouraged" 50,000 ethnic Hungarians (almost all Roman Catholics) to exit the northern provinces of Yugoslavia.
South Africa	Indigenous & Christians	Hundreds of persons, suspected and accused of black magic, are murdered each year. This a form of covert religious war and cultural suppression.

COUNTRIES	MAIN RELIGIOUS GROUPS INVOLVED	TYPE OF CONFLICT
Sri Lanka	Buddhists & Hindus	Tamils (a mainly Hindu 18% minority) were involved in a war for independence since 1983 with the rest of the country (70% Buddhist). About 75,000 killed.
Sudan	Animists, Christians & Muslims	Victimization of Indigenous faiths, and Euro-Christians in the South of the country. Slavery, crucifixion, rape, child mutilation, etc., for genocide.
Tibet	Buddhists & Communists	Chinese Communists annexed the country in the late 1950's. Suppression of religion continues with attempted capitalization via traditional privacy loss, youth redirection, and mass tourism.
Bangladesh	Muslim, Hindu, Buddhists	Muslim-Hindu (Bengalis) intent on destroying Buddhists (Chakmas)
Thailand	Buddhists, Muslims	Pattani province: Buddhists defending against Muslims. Muslims attempting to destroy Buddhist temples, etc.
Middle East	Hasidic Jews & Muslims	Religious doctrine misinterpretation, Zionism, and other political motives created the current country called Israel. The formation of that nation is not seen as valid by many peoples in the region.

COUNTRIES	MAIN RELIGIOUS GROUPS INVOLVED	TYPE OF CONFLICT
Uganda	Animists, Christians, & Muslims	Christian rebels of the "Lord's Resistance Army" conducted a civil war in the north. Their goal is a Christian theocracy whose laws are based on the Ten Commandments. They abduct about 2,000 children a year who are enslaved and/or raped.

-Secret Societies

- Round Table, Order of Skull & Bones, Mensur, The Club of Rome, Bilderberg Group.
- Subversive and coordinated activities to alter worldwide activities against humanistic purposes.

ORIGINALITY

Many problems of conflict within several societies stem from conflict of religious identity. Due to the after-effects of colonization, and historically recent changes in global residence relocation, several belief systems have spread. This directly effect global politics, as most places are fragments of the original way, which can only become whole when knowledge of self, from and about self, is accepted, and attained. For example; until an African leader publicly acknowledges, honors and prays to an African God, the people accept true heritage information, the Africans there will continue to be viewed as pathetic imitators of others, never having believed in themselves.

To embrace a foreign religion and heritage, about self, means to embrace a foreign culture and order. Again, remember most indigenous peoples have learned false heritage, to encourage long-term suppression and advantages for the former colonial powers. Sociologically, the same can be mentioned about descendants in the Diaspora, and other peoples in Asia and the America's.

To criticize myself & other African Americans that are Buddhists, Muslims, Christians, Catholics, etc., many of the traditions in these religions are not centered from our ancestry. In order to defend one's character and balance from betrayal of one's own culture, the integration of one or more elements, or thoughts from one's personal relationship with the universe must be added, or replace a portion of a faith from another culture. Integration of the purity of culture into a philosophy may be impossible, but it is completely possible to make a personal addition prayer.

It is entirely true that the base of many religions stem and/or have direct similarities to African spirituality, ancient history, and that may be enough of a natural connection, at this time in civilization. Nationalism is not a form of true identity, nor is it a form of spirituality. This is often confused in materialist societies, and those trying to integrate limitations of thought into faith. The concept of religion is virtually always in connection with a civilization. To deny the viability of one's religion as valid is to suggest that the person is uncivilized. This is a serious problem especially among fanatic groups of European and Arabic speaking religions.

In order to build both true connections and maintain connections with an appealing element in the residing culture, many people are willingly adopt a faith and modify the expression or Faith individually/or as a group for maximum perceived self-enlightenment. Indigenous peoples of the America's, Australia, Pacific, Asia, Europe, and Africa have a crisis in civilization because most of humanity has a crisis of myths. Even in the reading of prophesies, many so-called leaders deny accurate telling of the coming Messiah/Mishra/Thisna, or any other names. The throne of David in the Bible may be best translated as the African Union. The new Roman Empire is best translated as the European Union.

Expressions of ignorance, insecurity, and over-zealous pride are stated when people and/or the text of a religion states that what they have created is the best and only important thing that has ever been done, over others. The expression of this can be heard and read in various Christian, Islamic, recently among some Buddhists, and others. This way of thinking discounts the eons of people in the past and the future. It also severely limits the scope of world-view and personal growth of the members and leaders, and the minds of the developing children. The individual, or collective ego, are what is desired to be fed when this is done.

MYTHOLOGY OF TODAY-TOMORROW

Myths are mystic stories in fantasy and spirituality meant to help explain the realities of the past, reflection to the improvement of self, and suggested wisdom to enhance the happiness of the future. Most old myths; such as those designed of old civilizations (Hebrew, Islamic, etc.,) do not have the relevance to present historical reality for the current or future needs of civilizations. As each are designed from the nature, history, and spiritual consciousness of the people of the particular geographic region of origin, particular intentions to employ other cultures to popularize foreign spiritual expressions has never fully benefited any foreign society. Evidence of this can be seen in the lack of true social progress of various people's engrossed on foreign religions, especially those that engage in continual conflict of self, contradiction of reality, defiance of nature, and/or defiance of attempts to claim happiness of the soul, mind, and body.

Myth is not simply a story of life, or living, myths are clues to the experience of life. God is a thought, and a name; but its reference is beyond all categories of thought. In essence and reality, the names given by peoples of many cultures to acknowledge the universe, recognition of existence, and attempt to understand time. The tranquility that all living beings are connected too, has never called itself a name, so humans have given names in order to contain it in an identifiable form. What this does is marginalize and limit the natural ability to understand the whole of existence to a personality. This is not expressive of respect to the dynamic powers that we have had, since the near time of birth, and for most, not until the moments of death.

If you really want to help this world, what you really have to do is teach people how to live in it (Messege of the Myth, Joseph Campbell,—1986). Life is a journey to understand the experience of being alive. Myths are clues to the spiritual potentiality of the human life. (Message of the Myth, Joseph Campbell,—1986). Since about 5,000 B.C., to the time of colonization, the ancient advanced civilizations of Africa, Asia, India, the America's, the Pacific, and to a much smaller extent, the Norse peoples of Europe, were progressively engaged in inter-continental trade of technology, commerce, other forms of inter-action.

The interaction was not violence-based as is the foundation of the transformations we have today. Acknowledgement of the development of this existence; in full, is a needed step towards developing the best future for humanity. Sometimes the knowledge of how to develop peace may ironically come from the story of a fighting style such as "Kwa Asilia Avita Sanaa."

Religion is supposed to help you change the world from the difficulties and problems of today, to the way they should be. Those that sit-back, only pray, only give money, and/or only go to service, are as guilty as those that do the evils to our world. The order of faith, study and practice are an equal and necessary balance worthy of respect, because it shows respect to the living, dead, unborn, and builds strength of self.

The paternalistic story of the Garden of Eden exemplifies the notion of Nature being an evil corrupt wild force, and humans being superior to all. Nature, you, god, death, are not separate elements. Everything is everything! God could best be understood as a non-entity form of all existence and non-existence, with and without consciousness. Personalization of the universe can lean towards identification, but cannot be limited in perception to a single identity. Each and all are meant to be perceived as God, Goddess, Buddha, Element, Gaia, Pecacweenan, Ma-apus, or of All. Each and all are meant to be perceived as God, Goddess, Buddha, Element, or Being of the All. Aramaic & Hebrew texts are required reading for those that wish to understand the Bible.

Allah (All-Law) is probably the most perfect term or definition that could be the future definition of a unified spiritual name for the universe. "This does not mean Islamification of anyone." Allah and Islam are "Arabic" words and not "Muslim" words. Islam means peace. The word "Islam" is not "owned" by the "religion" of Islam. Parts of virtually every faith have complete relevance for a potential world spiritual faith order, or spiritual consciousness. This respects all foundations, and/or elements relevant for the development of a supporting future. Now that world societies are in gradual progression to become interconnected the changes can be seen. This cannot be successful without total social acknowledgment of the correct histories, and moving forward from there. No society can advance into being a civilization, without full acknowledgment of its foundations. The life principles of Buddhism, Toltec, and Ifa seem to be the correct paths that can cease the current problems of humanity.

The acknowledgement of the world's societies relatedness is only a part of the equation. We as humans in our various societies must disregard species-ism in the notion that humans are the only important and advanced beings on Earth. As the first chapter explains, "Disrespect of Nature" has been a prime factor in the degradation of us. Acceptance of our place in the balance of life is the primary acknowledgement of the importance of the stories of all people, and the image of the Earth itself may need to become primary.

As societies and civilizations change, the spiritual order must change to fill the morals needed. Most people flock away from the old religions present today; in part, because they do not relate to the wisdom, cosmological, balance, or guidance needs of now. The metaphors within the old religions must change to reflect today, not civilization centuries ago. To live from the lessons of peace, wisdom, and commonality learned from the past is more likely beneficial, to live from the lessons of harm, sorrow, and greed from the past is perpetually self-destructive.

> "Absorb what is useful, discard what is not. Add what is uniquely your own"
>
> Bruce Lee.

TRADITIONS

There are no people without traditions and traditions are the lifeblood of a people. A people who refuse to express its love and appreciation for its ancestors will die because in traditions, if you are not expressing your own, you are most likely participating in the expression of someone else's. No person is completely separate from an attachment to some culture. Those who speak of Christian or Islamic morals; especially the fundamentalists & extremists, have often been the very ones; in conception, who have defiled the ancestral memories, called others sacred rites evil, then participated with various forms of destruction for superiority under the guise of holiness, etc. Most peoples that have those religions engrained into there societies have made their traditions a part of the enforced religion.

"Malcolm X," once said that the world pushes the African around because we give the impression that we are chumps, not champs; but chumps, weaklings, falling over ourselves to follow other people rather than our own traditions." This is true of several peoples around the world. The causal purpose of the missionary is to spread a foreign perception of existence on the native people. In some places, the introduction of a foreign culture has provided a clearer perspective on the establishment of other foreign traditions. Excellent examples are the humanistic views against female genital mutilation, slavery, and various forms of degrading trade. Neither type of trade was a long-term norm in ancient advanced societies in Africa, Asia, Pacific, or the America's.

The distribution of many religions, represent the distribution of power & attempted control. Nature and ancestral awareness, and spirituality among the peoples of the world are minimal but growing. The religions that people Faith are based on the influences that have captured their imaginations. Among, African American's, the Caribbean, and South America, one will often find Yoruba, or other elements of West African ancestral spirituality integrated into the faith of the region. Unlike religions centralized to other continents, Yoruba is Africa's most powerful religious export to the Americas, but has none of the oppression history similar to most others, and embraces traditional leaders. Traditional religious leaders of Christianity and Islam, have often stated other philosophies as less significant, and unproven.

The individual practicing it, and what is expressed determines the affects, and effects, on one's life from philosophy. This action can be qualified to a level of peer pressure on the civilization level.

In the Philippines, the indigenous traditions present, prior to Spanish colonization, are historically stated to have beliefs in a Supreme Creator God. They held a common belief structure that every civilization has developed while in relation with the ancient worldwide trade from African civilizations. The name of their god varied depending on what region of the islands. Among some of the names are: *Bathala, Diwata, Kabunian, Mansilatan, Makaptan, Laon, Lumauig, Mamarsua, Tuhan, etc.*

COSMOLOGY OF CREATION OF THE INDIGENOUS PHILIPPINES

The Supreme God was invisible, or without form, and no images of the supreme one were ever made, beyond a period of time. The name was considered

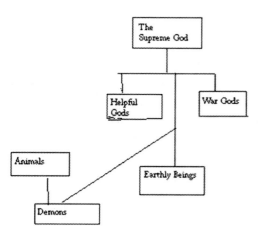

too sacred, and seldom spoken, with the exception of sacred rituals by special initiates. The Supreme God was professed as too involved in higher matters for direct worship. Only the lower deities were the principle objects of prayer, plea, and ritual. The basic gods/prophets/angels were known by names like *diwa, diwata, tuhan* and *anito*. As in other spiritualist cultures, the deities were divided into beneficial and malicious categories. As in nature, this is a dualistic role of sorts. Unlike western European and Arabic theologies, the malicious deities were not seen as enemies and were often praying to the supreme one too. Their roles in death and injury to earthly beings are seen as having a special worth to the universe. While a sort of battle between good and evil did exist, this was primarily between the beings of earth and the lower realms.

AFRICAN AND CHINESE SPIRITUAL STORIES

Some traditional Chinese religions like others; have common themes to the African deities taught to the ancient civilization founders, like those of the Shang Dynasty.

CHU JUNG is the God of fire. Chu Jung punishes those who break the laws of heaven. **KUAN TI** is the God of war. The Great Judge who protects the people from injustice and evil spirits. A red-faced god dressed always in green.

An oracle. Kuan Ti was an actual historical figure, a general of the Han dynasty renowned for his skill as a warrior and his justness as a ruler. There were more than 1600 temples dedicated to Kuan Ti. **KWAN YIN** is the Goddess of mercy and compassion. A lady dressed in white seated on a lotus and holding an infant. Murdered by her father, she recited the holy books when she arrived in Hell, and the ruler of the underworld could not make the dead souls suffer. The disgruntled god sent her back to the world of the living, where Kwan Yin attained great spiritual insight and was rewarded with immortality by the Buddha.

"IFA" is a religion of the Yoruba people of Nigeria-West Africa. This is also one of the best examples of high civilization religions in the world. According to record, it is the oldest monotheistic religion of humanity. It does not separate body, mind, or spirit; linear & non-linear, logic against intuition, material pursuits and pride, male & female, birth & death, spiritual and material gain, empty & full, because all of existence is equal. It is the integration of Arabic and European cultural expressions that allot forms of male/female dualistic conception in current ways of life & alterations of expressed history.

Like Buddhism, "IFA" leads and shows the one that engages in the ritual & prayers that it is fully permitted and imperative that we use our spiritual capacities to favorably influence our everyday lives. "IFA" may be one of the worlds great somewhat untapped sources of spiritual power, that should be acquired by the African American, and others in the Diaspora, that search for such a philosophy of life. This faith recognizes the universal need for secure and fulfilling lives, and gives lessons of life, and rituals for tapping into our nature, and energetic connection to the universe we are a part of.

Kinship and ancestor recognition is one key part of the ritual, in no way should be considered primitive. The use of the word "primitive" is of course used to denigrate the relevance of another. "IFA" is a faith that is as equal in relevance to Faith as is Buddhism, Islam, Christianity, etc. In comparison to some, many people may believe it is more personally beneficial. This religion is over 8,000 years old, and elements of it have been integrated into the religious Faiths of many African American's, just as many African dance, speech, and singing styles are prevalent throughout the cultural expressions of descendants throughout the Diaspora.

THE SIXTEEN TRUTHS OF THE IFA

1.) There is a Single God.

2.) There is no Devil.

3.) All events in life can be forecasted for change, with the exception of birth and day of death.

4.) It is your birthright live with happiness, prosperity, knowledge, and health.

5.) All beings have resided to grow to obtain wisdom from the elders and experiences of life.

6.) You are born through your blood relatives.

7.) Heaven is home, and the Earth is the marketplace of the living and dead. We are in constant passage between the two.

8.) You and all are a part of the Universe, and flow of energies.

9.) You must never initiate harm to another human being, and kill nothing without use and thanks.

10.) You must never harm the nurturer of your existence.

11.) Your terrestrial and spiritual capacities must work together.

12.) All beings are born with a specific path and intention. Humans are given the ability to choose the paths of continued happiness in life, and self-corruption.

13.) Our ancestors are to be honored every day of life.

14.) The choice to sacrifice guarantees success.

15.) The Orisa (deities) live within us.

16.) Fear is not a need.

DEITIES

Next after the Supreme Being is the EARTH DEITY. In most African societies, the earth is given a feminine image. The Akan of Ghana and the Igbo of Nigeria regard the earth as a goddess. Among the Akan, she ranks next after the Supreme Being and the second deity to be offered a drink during worship. Her day of rest is Thursday and severe punishment was meted out in the past to those who infringed this taboo. Although there are no temples, shrines or priests dedicated to her, because her bounty is accessible to all, She nonetheless receives offerings and sacrifices at the planting season. The land generally cannot be farmed without asking for her permission. When a grave is about to be dug the Spirit of the earth is offered sacrifice. The Igbo of Nigeria, unlike the Akan, dedicate shrines and priestesses to the Mother goddess, the Queen of the underworld who is responsible for public morality.

Homicide, kidnapping, stealing farm products, adultery and giving birth to twins or abnormal children are all offenses against her. Laws are made and oaths sworn in her name.

The most-loved deity is the one who is closest to the people. She helps them if they are in trouble with other divinities, but punishes hardened criminals. Also the most important festival, the yam [harvest] festival is held in her honor receives offerings during the planting season, also when the first fruits are harvested. "Temporary houses [Mbari] are made to accommodate sacred sculptures and other statues representing deities always contain the statue of Ani, which stands in the middle. Here, she is depicted as a mother with a child in her arms or knees and a sword in her hand. Facing Ala is the storm god a subordinate counterpart of the goddess.

The Mende of Sierra Leone also regard Mother earth as a goddess, the common mother of mankind, and the wife of God [Maa-ndoo]. Like the Akan, the Mende do not worship the Spirit of the earth, although she is invoked together with God [NGEWO] during important occasions. Laws are made to protect her sanctity; for example, sexual intercourse in the bush is a violation of her sacredness and offenders are severely punished. Apart from the Earth goddess, several other deities are found residing in bodies of water."
http://members.aol.com/akbsankofa/Akan1.html, (09/02/2004)

THE HERO

Praise and worship of the hero in social order and mythologies are a key part of every society. Individuals and groups have been defined as heroes throughout civilizations years. Roles that have been cast through the life of the worlds heroes are; Prophets, Organization Leaders, Teachers, Farmers, Hunters, Librarians, Politicians, Law Enforcement, Gangsters, Cartoon Characters, Soldiers, Writers, Revolutionaries, Lovers, Thugs, etc., etc, and at times, the very organizations they represent are noted as the hero. A hero is typically identified as someone that has given his or her life to something bigger than self. The physical deed of sacrifice and/or the spiritual deed of learning to teach others are basic elements of heroes. Morality towards a basic set of principles is the general objective in most stories.

The act of saving a person, saving a people, holding an ideal, and sacrificing him/herself for something is the most important statement of a heroes actions. The Buddha, Muhammad, Jesus, Quetzalcoatl, Isis, Heru, Shaka, Brahman, and others, symbolize creation of a new and better state of consciousness. Each has legends of trials and revelations that brought greater wisdom to the native society, but not meant to be related towards dominance of other societies. Followers of the stories told of; and/or with them, are intended to tell a story of local, or personal revolution, starting with self, not to be misconstrued as notice to advance on other societies. Interpretation of the story must be understood for the time it was written, because such temporal stories can only be copied for there positive principles in the present.

The current created heroes of society are collectively the same as many mentioned in ancient stories. It is the role in a society, and identity of the character, that continually changes. Myths deal with transformation of consciousness, within them, heroes deal with benefit of social order. As stated earlier, "Roles that have been cast through the life of the worlds heroes are; Prophets, Organization Leaders, Teachers, Farmers, Hunters, Librarians, Politicians, Law Enforcement, Gangsters, Cartoon Characters, Soldiers, Writers, Revolutionaries, Lovers, etc., etc, and at times, the very organizations they represent are noted as the hero."

Humans generally have the same natural instincts as many other forms of life, but more cognitively realized needs for ideals, characters, materials, and faith. From the 17th century to today, the industrializing societies have gradually shifted the role of hero from the sustainers of existence; such as, the farmer, the hunter, and the traveler; to the gangster, the law enforcer, the entertainment artist, and the cartoon character. One should understand the hero role of these particular characters, as the spiritual/religious leaders of social law, in comparison to the stories of their counterparts in the past. Even more important are the actions, and rites of passage each role is given respect for.

For example; "how and why is a gangster in the year 2005, etc., seen as a hero to youth in current society?" The answers are the absence of correct historical knowledge, tainted aspirations towards becoming successful, and an opportunity to join an organization with relevant guidelines of faith. Youth naturally strive to learn about life through observations, lessons, and active experimentation. I mentioned earlier that the concept of a "Hero" is a paramount figure in the stability, transformation, and story of a society.

The image of the hero has been the image of the foreign individual; or foreign religious example, for several centuries. Indemnity or identification to being Asiatic, Hispanic, or any of the other alien identification tags enforced by foreign faiths are self-denigrating, and genocidal. Emulation of others is a natural action in play, and some celebrations, but becomes negative when used in disrespect to self and/or others.

The answers are in the expressions of the children, especially since true innocence, and aspirations for playing are inappropriately weaned out as people gain in age. Full disclosure of ancient and modern heritage from each family of people involved is extremely essential towards the recreation of justice, peace, and equality.

IDENTITY

The <u>Wolof</u> of Senegal-West Africa say, "Wood may remain in water for ten years but it will not become a crocodile." The idea of Christian names or Muslim names promotes and advances those cultures. Why must you change your name even if you chose to buy into a foreign religion? What is wrong with your name? Any religion that asks you to do what others do not have to do is asking you to abandon something. You probably should check several perspectives, and history first. An old book by author.—Samuel Huntington, called "The Clash of Civilizations," claimed that there are six major civilizations: Chinese, Japanese, Hebrew, Hindu, Western Christianity/Catholic, and Islamic.

This opinion denies the existence of the African, the Indigenous Peoples of the Americas, the Australian, and others as significant in the human family. He believed that each one of them has a nation that is deeply committed to its religion and history. Africa has no nation, and neither do the true American's. Of 53+ nations on the African continent, only one is more African in religion than either Christian or Muslim. That nation is small Benin. The fact that no Native Americans are recognized in the U.N. should be self-explanatory on how much control the Christian, Catholic, and Capitalist world power structures still have here in 2004.

SPIRITUAL ORDER

The process of thought or conception, and natural energy we share, according to various healing sciences, states that faith is a powerful factor in healing. We as Humans may have a greater ability to control the subtle electromagnetic fields and directed energy we are connected too, than any other mammal on Earth. While some might consider the power "love," today's western science is recognizing what is called Ayurvedic/Quantum Healing. In part, it say's that the force responsible for healing is within you, and that each person is a combination of the mind and body, under watch by the soul.

Spiritual, and mental health, are almost the same. Inner-Stability is attained partially through creativity. Solitude is not loneliness; it is interconnectedness with everything else. Creative people like leaders, have the ability to recognize that life is a field of opportunities and stay in balance with nature within and around them. Spiritual health is dependant upon maintaining and practicing prayer, dance, and/or chanting, for balance with nature, the universe, and the power we feel and call love (the all). When this is done in a sheltered place alone he/she tends to center on the self, when this is done in a group a bond in prayer is shared, but when this is done without walls, the harmony in prayer truly connects with nature in & out.

It is contradictory to conceive of oneself as a separate being from nature, when all elements of your existence from conception to death are in-kind with all other forms around you. Each civilization falls in the path with their beliefs and place in nature. Religions based from people in nomadic, survivalist, patriarchal systems, have tended to develop challenge over nature conceptions, instead of acceptance and order with it. Condemnation of nature is inherit as part of the prophesies of indigenous people's in the telling of the time of evil. Reading scriptures in the position of denotations instead of the connotation of the poetry, is not the way to read them. This is because they were written in poetic form for the time.

Through Christianity, Jesus said that he who drinks from my mouth will become as I am, and I shall be he; In essence, this is the same as becoming a Buddha. A Buddha is to become enlightened in all ways. The functions of the 'Devil' and the 'Buddha' exist within our lives. Ultimately, our battle is with ourselves. In your spirituality, daily activities, or just sleeping, everything boils down to a struggle to attain, or retain the natural balance of positive and negative forces of life." (Here is a portion of my religions scripture)

THE WRITINGS OF NICHIREN DAISHONIN DEFINE THE 3-OBSTACLES AND 4-DEVILS OF LIFE:

The obstacle of earthly desires;

The obstacle of karma; and

The obstacle of retribution (also obstacles caused by one's superiors, such as rulers or parents).

THE FOUR DEVILS ARE:

1.) The hindrance of the five components;

2.) The hindrance of earthly desires;

3.) The hindrance of death (because untimely death obstructs one's Faith of Buddhism, or because the premature death of another practitioner causes doubts); and

4.) The hindrance of the devil king.

The Buddhist concept of the Ten Worlds is used to describe the range of potential states or conditions that a person can manifest and experience in his or her environment. Individually, they are:

1) The world of hell: a totally limited condition in which living itself is misery, and anger and rage become a source of further self-destruction.

2) The world of hungry spirits (also called hunger): endless desire in which one is never truly satisfied.

3) The world of animals (also called animality): a totally instinctual condition, without reason, morality or wisdom.

4) The world of asuras, or warlike demons in Indian mythology (also called anger): persistent, though not necessarily overt, aggressiveness and excessive pride, which prevents one from seeing oneself or others as they truly are.

5) The world of human beings (also called humanity): control of desires and impulses with reason and desire to harmonize with one's surroundings.

6) The world of heavenly beings (also called heaven or rapture): contentment and joy caused by release from suffering or satisfaction of desire.

7) The world of voice-hearers (also called learning): self-development through learning the ideas, knowledge and experience of others.

8) The world of cause-awakened ones (also called-realization): seeking self-development and lasting truth through the observation of natural phenomena.

9) The world of bodhisattvas: working toward enlightenment both for oneself and others.

10) The world of Buddha's (also called Buddha hood): a state of perfect and absolute freedom in which one realizes the true nature of life.

PRINCIPLES OF PRAYER:

• To give thanks to all elements in your life, the earth, and for the joy of all you love.

• To engage balance with the universe, whether directly, or through the term of a god/goddess.

• To call for an envisioned reality of a better future, of your choice.

• To thank love, for itself.

• To inspire action in intended participation of the environment you desire.

Your actions are a part of your prayers. You are what you eat, drink, speak, pray, and act.

REACH FOR CORRECTNESS

There is an obvious qualitative progression from the bottom, hell, to the top, Buddha. Because of that, one might be led to think that the point of Buddhist Faith is to eradicate the lower worlds and maximize the higher ones. It is to facilitate balance and order of self, and to attain the highest level of being and potential. This is a basic desire to reach for correctness, which is articulated differently in various religions. Indeed no philosophy is without negative points when it is not written from the present day language, & and calls to improve the future.

As humans, mistakes are made, and individuals within each religion form to develop understanding and connection with the world around them at the time of there physical existence. Acceptance of faults, and/or some individuals that direct faults as representatives, betray the reasoning of the faith, unless faults are encouraged. Many religious leaders and members have denied conclusive evidence of ancient relations and foundations with other peoples. They have also tended to ignore basic evils expressed within the texts they read.

PASSAGES FOR DESTRUCTION

> The Prejudice Apostle Peter; Devalued all other Religious Faith Groups; *He is quoted as preaching that salvation is only available through Jesus.*
> *Acts 4:10-12* "Be it known unto you all, and to all the people of Israel, that by the name of Jesus Christ of Nazareth, whom ye crucified, whom God raised from the dead, even by him doth this man stand here before you whole…Neither is there salvation in any other: for there is none other name under heaven given among men, whereby we must be saved." *There are varieties of interpretations of this, and other passages:*

Many Christians take that passage as fact, instead of it in the metaphor that it is. They believe all non-Christians will remain unsaved, and will be eternally tormented in Hell after death. These verses have inspired many missionaries to go into the non-Christian societies, and coerce religious conversions. The punishment of all non-Christians implies a belief that they believe God is profoundly intolerant of others, so the people should act the same way.

Corinthians 10:20-21: He wrote that Gentiles worship devils. In modern terms, they would be considered Satanists: "*But I say, that the things which the Gentiles sacrifice, they sacrifice to devils, and not to God: and I would not that ye should have* *fellowship with devils. Ye cannot drink the cup of the Lord, and the cup of devils: ye cannot be partakers of the Lord's table, and of the table of devils.*" Here, Paul writes that the Gods and Goddesses of other religions are actually demons. Christians are to completely isolate themselves from non-Christians.

2 Corinthians 6:14: Paul requires that his followers separate from "*unbelievers:*" "*Be ye not unequally yoked together with unbelievers: for what fellowship hath righteousness with unrighteousness? and what communion hath light with darkness?*"
The author of this biblical passage recommends that Christians avoid close relationships with non-Christians. He implies that non-Christians are automatically unrighteous. He associates Christianity with "*light*" and other religions with "*darkness.*" Because this passage from 6:14 to 7:1
Some theologians believe that the passage was written by some other author and later added to Paul's writing, during the Council of Nicea.
The groups that he condemns presumably include the other two competing movements within Christianity at the time—Gnostic Christianity and Jewish Christianity. It would also include Roman Paganism, Greek Paganism, the Mystery Religions, Mithraism, etc.

1 Thessalonians 2:14-16: Paul directs a blast of religious propaganda against all Jews, blaming all of them for the murder of Jesus. "*...Ye also have suffered like things of your own countrymen, even as they have of the Jews: Who both killed the Lord Jesus, and their own prophets, and have persecuted us; and they please not God, and are contrary to all men: Forbidding us to speak to the Gentiles that they might be saved, to fill up their sins always: for the wrath is come upon them to the uttermost.*"
Some theologians believe that "the Jews" had little to do with Jesus' execution. His aggravated assaults in the Jerusalem temple would have been considered an insurrectionist act by the Roman occupying army, and make him eligible for crucifixion.

Christians rejecting Jewish converts: Peter delivered a sermon to a mixed group of Jewish Christians and interested Gentiles. Many of the latter were converted, filled with the Holy Spirit. The Jewish Christians were surprised because they felt that Jesus' message was only for the Jews. They viewed the teachings of Jesus as a reform movement within Judaism, and assumed that Jesus' message was not intended for non-Jews.

Acts 10:44-45: "*While Peter yet spoke these words, the Holy Ghost fell on all them which heard the word. And they of the circumcision which believed [i.e. the Jewish Christians] were astonished, as many as came with Peter, because that on the Gentiles also was poured out the gift of the Holy Ghost.*"

Jewish Christians rejecting other Christians: Some Jewish Christians criticized Peter for being in the company with non-Jews and even eating with them. They viewed the teachings of Jesus as being for the Jewish people only. Peter convinces them that it is the will of the Holy Spirit to also teach the gospel to the Gentiles.

Acts 11:1-3: *"And the apostles and brethren that were in Judea heard that the Gentiles had also received the word of God. And when Peter was come up to Jerusalem, they that were of the circumcision contended with him, Saying, Thou went in to men uncircumcised, and didst eat with them."*

Islam: In the Holy Quran, there are also several claims stating that those that do not believe in the god named "Allah", or the teachings of the Prophet Muhammad are doomed to hell, shall be destroyed, or should not be considered on a honorable level with humanity serving Allah.
Surah 3-Ali 'Imran…section-2: #10. *"Those who reject faith-neither their possessions, nor their numerous progeny will avail them, aught against Allah; they are themselves but fuel for the fire".*

Deuteronomy 7:1-2, NIV *"When the Lord your God brings you into the land you are entering to possess and drives out before you may nations…then you must destroy them totally. Make no treaty with them and show them no mercy."*

Deuteronomy 20:16, NIV *"…do not leave alive anything that breaths. Completely destroy them…as the Lord your God has commanded you…"* The Qur'an tells us: *"not to make friendship with Jews and Christians" (5:51), "kill the disbelievers wherever we find them" (2:191), "murder them and treat them harshly" (9:123), "fight and slay the Pagans, seize them, beleaguer them, and lie in wait for them in every stratagem" (9:5).* The Qur'an demands that we fight the unbelievers, and promises "If there are twenty amongst you, you will vanquish two hundred: if a hundred, you will vanquish a thousand of them" (8:65).

Christianity & Islam came mainly from patriarchal social influence, which was transformed by force away from the matriarchal social structures, and betrayal of the base philosophical & historical origins from Ethiopia and Kemet. The Celtic is historically the most popular of the ancient matriarchal cultures of Europe. Many cultures around the world that became patriarchal, such as; the Middle East nations, have problems like "Honor Killings, female mutilations, and child abuse." An example of this is when parents will punish or kill

their own daughter if she offers a simple friendship to an eligible but UN approved member of the opposite sex for marriage.

The Roman process of execution called the crucifixion is the most sadistic figures in the worship towards self-degradation, killing, and social suppression. Like many quotes in certain termed "organized religion texts," the actions historically mentioned and destructive principles; have often been emulated by the average person, missionaries, and other followers. A religion becomes destructive when the people serve the religion, and productive when the religion serves the people. Sadly, the peoples of the America's, Phillipines, Africa, etc., are pray to the servitude structure of financial, physical, and mental abuse that is maintaining the average short-term repression, over lifelong times.

Many leaders in each of the religions that have taken part in enslavement, have inspired self-suppressing traditions in several societies they invaded. Early stories of leaders from Persia like "Abdullah," and Assyria like "Esarhaddon" led the way for mis-education of conquered peoples of Africa, by selective perception of rule through Islamic expansionism, mainly through extremists. One of the major crimes inspired was female genital mutilation. This comes from patriarchal beliefs that women should not have natural pleasurable sensations involved in creation. Like many lying myths, made by conquerors, the story propagated on this subject is that the people made the Faith of mutilation a part of the traditions before the conquerors came to civilize them.

To some extent, women are measured as a sin, liability, of lower value than boys, beings that exist just to please men, and vehicles that make babies through patriarchal supremacist cultures. This is taught, and expressed, to lesser and lesser extents, only in recent times. The focus on any portion of religious tenets, depends on the culture and/or leader(s) in charge. Not all persons of any particular religion commit negative actions against all of another group.

Some groups and individuals have acted against particular negative expressions based on certain personal perspectives, in favor of humanistic perspectives based in the same spiritual texts. The problems we see, seem to be coming from many misinterpretations of the humanistic goals written by the entities of each text based philosophy, as well as from those denied correct information by choice.

AN END-TIME SCENARIO IS SPREAD OUT OVER
THE FOLLOWING BOOKS OF THE BIBLE:

1-Corinthians 15:51, Revelation, Revelation 9:13-16, Isaiah, Jeremiah, Daniel, Daniel 11:40, Ezekiel, the Gospels, Zechariah, Zephaniah, Joel, 1-Thessalonians 4:13, Ezekiel 39: 1-6, Joel 3:14-15, Matthew 24:29, Mark 13:24.—Several cultures around the world have similar for-telling stories.

DOMINANCE OF THE WRONG MASCULINE PRINCIPLE

The dominance of the masculine principle has also resulted in the control of power as a much appreciated value. This can be seen in the fact that nations, religions and classes have often thought that it was good to have power over others by thinking of themselves as superior in some way. The high value given to control of others, under patriarchal lessons have the sexes regarded as unequal. It is disputed that as long as power remains a principal value, there can be no hope for world peace. For society to become more balanced, relationships based on power and domination, which are the main causes of antagonism and divisiveness, have to be discarded in favor of cooperation and equality. The connections of world peace, gender equality, and control terminology should be understood.

The imbalance of the masculine and feminine principle is directly related to the history of strife and conflict spread from the post-colonial, paternal structured, and dis-affected societies of the world. It should also be stressed that problems such as weapons trade, environmental pollution, depletion of natural resources, poaching, war, poverty, hunger, drug trade, and population explosion cannot be divorced from the result of the dominance of values such as power, aggression and competition which are closely tied to the existence of patriarchal societies; products of the imbalance of value given to the masculine and feminine principle in history. Worldwide, societies presently are experiencing the crisis that has resulted from the domination of natural but super-imposed male attributes (i.e., expanse of control, territoriality, materialism, exploitation acquisitiveness, aggression, racism, nationalism, phallic symbol weapons (ex: missiles, etc.)

There are over one billion Muslims in the world, but nearly none of them, or the other people of the world know the true historical development. To be more accurate, many are counted children between faiths. Allah is a restructure of the moon goddess, which was worshiped prior to the paternalization of the regional societies, by the spread of Islam. In a small way, some Muslims respect, acknowledge, and attribute the origins of some of their prophets in correct historical order, unlike most of Christianity.

Islamic paternalizing of the Arabian Goddess named, Al-Lat, Al-Ilat, the Allatu of the Babylonians, was formerly worshipped in the Kaaba of Mecca. Allah was a male transformation of the lunar female deity of Arabia. Muhammad the prophet was historically known to have forced sex with pre-pubescent girls, but these facts do not defy the great positive attributes of most Moslems of today.

The ancient female symbol the crescent moon now appears on Islamic flags, but most current Muslims do not longer admit or recognize any feminine symbolism connected with patriarchal Allah. The Holy Quran verifies Allah's lunar, or night-sky status: "the name of our Lord morning and evening; in the night-time worship Him: praise Him all night long."

(Q 76:23) and at (Q 2:189): "They question you about the phases of the moon. Say: 'They are seasons fixed for mankind and for the pilgrimage." When Mohammed ordered the over-through of the old religion of Arabia, he did not dare get rid of the moon cult. In a late time of Islamic development his religion became powerful enough to forbid prostration before the moon (Koran Surah 4:37). Before Islam was created, the Moon Deity was the most prominent object of faith groups in Ancient Arabia, and considered the parent of mankind.

The desire for power has encouraged beliefs in capitalism, enslavement, and social corruption. Through worldwide mis-education, this effects how many of the people that participated as students in those schools over the last 150 or so years, the perception of ourselves, our relationship to others, and our relationship to the society we live in. The natural "nurturing" values such as cooperation, concern and love need to be given priority in the education of young men and young women. World peace implies first and foremost the attainment of unity in thought and actions among the people of the world. This is contrary to the popular belief that peace must be attained before unity of thought, and action can be achieved without goal.

ECCLESIASTES

The man called Jesus, created the Nazarean Party. Ecclesia means a place of gathering for political reasons. The Nazarean party organized to form a union against the invading Roman empire on the land called Israel today. They were a group of black unions under the leadership of Yeshua Ben-Joseph (Jesus) determined to fight against the Romans, as a revolutionary action. Like most of humanity, politics and religion were not separate entities. As a more spiritual people, this mix was not seen as a division, it was felt to be enter-twined and a part of the whole of the society motivating true civilization and true advancements.

All peoples on earth that have a literature have books, art, and dance that explain their history, founding of there nation, descriptions of religious Faith, etc., that are set apart as sacred or holy to them. These things are meant to be symbols of relationships to the divine intelligence of the universe. This is what is meant as the action of a holy existence. Predication of ones religion over and against another's culture is prejudicial to the point of religious racism.

OUR LADY OF GUADALUPE/VIRGIN MARY OF THE AMERICA'S IS: TONANTZIN

When the Spaniards came to the continents now called the America's, the Aztec Indians, who called themselves the Mexica, recognized that they were barbaric in there actions of conquering the more ancient civilization of the Toltecs, who existed in the valley of Aztlan. A principal deity worshipped by the Mexica and by other tribes of Mesoamerica was Tonantzin ("Our Lady"), the mother goddess, identified with the moon. The modern Basilica de Guadalupe in Mexico City is the principal shrine to the patron saint of Mexico, the Virgin of Guadalupe, located in the former location of the pyramid of Tonantzin.

By cultural translation, the Virgin of Guadalupe and Tonantzin are the same. This is a prime example of cultural survival, resistance and potentiality of full recovery from damage done to the people. It is a proud example of the power of the native people of the America's. Catholic rituals have only served to blur the heredity of the spiritual and cultural region.

The spiritual entities, or saints are reincarnations of the more ancient gods, and breath life into the believers, perpetuating a living tradition, which is gradually progressing to acceptance.

THE WOMAN IN THE STORY

Adopting the new mindset means to fully and sincerely appreciates the intrinsic worth of both the masculine and feminine principles. The balancing of the masculine and feminine principles is a fundamental base for the alteration of the entire value base, and social structure of society, and is ultimately crucial to the advancement of world peace. It rejects rigid role delineation, patterns of domination and arbitrary decision-making. It implies changes in both men and women, each acquiring traits formerly assigned to the other. It must necessarily entail a change in many traditional habits and spirituality.

Such a worldview liberates not only girls, but also boys. While men have overt social power, they also experience oppression. For example, most men's capacities for being compassionate, loving, and nurturing, are trained out of them as boys. This is just as derogatory as the character fashioning of a girl becoming a woman, while reducing her ability to attain professional competence. A particularly damaging form of oppression occurs because men are viewed as the sex that does not feel emotional pain, or damage; the machismo complex.

This conception is not in tune with the natural facts of childhood. When boys and men cry, they often experience humiliation, rejection, threats, and isolation at the hands of their peers, fathers, mothers, or potential mate. A certain level of this for motivation to mature is needed, but by far this is put to an extreme in many societies. This issue goes into the factors that can end the needs for sexual harassment, and other laws related to relationships between adult men and women. When each are taught to accept themselves, and the other in full nature, respect for all, and resistance to oppressive motivations are socially rejected as a culture.

Cultural rules are stronger than government laws. Rituals and prayers that include motivation of equality help to solidify this way of thinking. Like the misconception of many religions, prejudice has been created with false accusations against "Wicca" have been passed through generations.

> "By the earth it is her body, by the air that is her breath, by the fire of her bright spirit, by the waters of her living womb," the circle is open, but unbroken, may the peace of the goddess go in your hearts, merry meet and merry part, and merry meet again....

Wicca is one of a few growing current religions that is a religion of the goddess. It is a female centered, nature guided spirituality, that has no relation to devil worship, praise, justification, or acknowledgment, unlike the prejudicial perceptions placed on it from paternal religious leaders.

It is a corrected religion with the people leading their religion, instead of the followers following leadership of their religion. In addition; I suggest reading the story of the "wheel of the year."

THE DREAM CATCHER LEGEND....

Many years ago, grandmother found a spider in her home. It was building a web above her bed, and she spent many days watching it work and marveled at its beauty. One day, as the web was nearing completion, her grandson came to visit and he saw the spider and immediately went to kill it. Grandmother stopped him, and said that the spider had been there for several days, working hard on the web. It had not bothered her, and she had enjoyed watching it.

The spider thanked Grandmother for saving its life and told her that in return for her kindness, it would give her a gift. The spider said that the web above her bed would make sure she only had good dreams—the bad dreams would get caught in the web, and would burn up when the sun rose. Only the good and important dreams would pass through this Dream Catcher.

A VISION QUEST PRAYER

I pray to the four directions....
I pray to the West, which gives us rest and reflection.
I thank you for these gifts for without them we could not live.
I pray to the North, which gives us patience and purity.
I thank you for these gifts for without them we could not live.
I pray to the East, which gives us energy and emotions.
I thank you for these gifts for without them we could not live.
I pray to the South, which gives us discipline and direction.
I thank you for these gifts for without them we could not live.
Grandmother, share with me your wisdom, and I thank you for this gift.
Grandfather, share with me your strength, and I thank you for this gift.
Grand entity, grant me the serenity to accept the things I cannot change,
I ask for the courage to change the things I can, and the wisdom to know the difference.

PART OF THE MAORI STORY OF LIFE

From the conception, the increase...
From the increase, the thought...
From the thought, the remembrance...
From the consciousness, the desire...

End of Chapter #5.)
To be continued...

Chapter 6

Organized Crime

THE TRANSNATIONAL MAFIA

Among the most influential global organized crime groups, are the money worshiping medical companies, typical mafias, and corrupt local, state, and federal government officials. The Mafias are both complex and intriguing in their cozy associations with crime. The main groups based in Italy are the Sicilian Mafia or "Cosa Nostra," the Neapolitan Camorra, the Calabrian 'Ndrangheta, and the Sacra Corona Unita.

The Cosa Nostra is generally perceived to be the largest and most important of these groups, and is organized around a law of silence and close associations. Relationships are partly functional, partly personal and familial, and partly based on fear, a constant within other Italian Mafia groups as well. Although the Cosa Nostra retains many of its traditional ways, it has proved to be both dynamic and adaptive.

The power of the Cosa Nostra is primarily concentrated in southern Italy where it has sought to nullify competition between businesses through coercion and other illegal activities. However, the Cosa Nostra has increasingly evolved into a transnational enterprise. The group has successfully moved much of its organized criminal activities from rural to industrial and business cultures, and from a local and national network to an international one. This global focus has been facilitated by migration flows, particularly to the United States, which contributed to the establishment of a Sicilian share of the U.S. heroin market in the early 20th century. The expansion of links to other criminal organizations remains a major challenge to law enforcement. The legalization and gradual social disapproval influences of the society are among the few and only ways to reduce or eradicate this problem, after and during a real humanistic attack on the prevalence of poverty.

The Colombian, El Salvadoran, and Mexican cartels have begun diversifying their efforts for profit on drugs, sex-slavery, political manipulation, and human transportation of various foreign born persons into neighboring countries. These cartels have merged corporate and criminal cultures more successfully than other groups that developed an industry that is based on sound management principles that include specialization and division of labor. The main Colombian cartels have been centered towards various tight knit families in Medellin and Cali. The main drug trafficking families in Columbia control large production and distribution networks with vast agricultural enterprises dispersed throughout the Andes mountain range.

This includes multiple laboratories and production facilities that generate over nine hundred metric tons of cocaine per year and a distribution network that move the raw products by plane, ship, and every other means imaginable to destinations to five continents.

The cartels also manage an extensive marketing operation that focuses on the United States, Canada, Europe, and other places. These groups maintain a sophisticated financial and accounting system to keep track of thousands of tons of drugs and billions of dollars in profit. They launder the proceeds in the financial and banking networks and repatriate some of the laundered funds. Much of these funds are then invested in the U.S., Europe, Africa, and elsewhere. A 2,000 mile border with the United States provides Mexican organized crime groups with a unique geographic advantage, allowing for access to the world's largest consumer of drugs. Somewhere between 50 and 70 percent of the South American cocaine that enters the U.S., as well as 80 percent of the foreign grown marijuana that is consumed, is transported through Mexico. The Mexican cartels have also become involved in opium poppy cultivation and heroin production, currently producing 20 to 30 percent of the heroin consumed in the U.S. further, these criminal organizations are increasingly dominating the manufacturing, sale, and distribution of amphetamines, ecstasy, steroids, and experimental drugs.

The Russian Mafia has emerged to become among the largest networks of organized crime in the world. It feeds off the political and economic transitions taking place in Russia, undermining objectives of national reform policies. A gray area between criminal and legal business activity has allowed Mafia groups to penetrate most areas of the Russian economy and has provided them with a disproportionate amount of influence. Between 5,000 and 6,000 gangs operate within the boundaries of Russia, including several hundred organizations whose activities span the territory of the Commonwealth of Independent States, Central and Western Europe and the United States. These transnational groups are regarded as very sophisticated and are believed to be operating in approximately 29 countries.

What makes the Russian Mafia unique is its infiltration of key sections of the government bureaucracy. According to government investigators, more than half of the country's criminal groups have ties to the government. A number of Mafia organizations are fronts for the former Soviet party elites (nomenklatura capitalists) who have engaged in illegal activities, including bank fraud, to become wealthy monopoly owners. Since 1993, successive corruption scandals have been hitting the government; for example, senior commanders of the Red Army were caught in smuggling rings while cabinet ministers and police officials were discovered working for shady commercial firms and the pornography industry. In the early 21st century, the mafia groups of Russia gained a considerable amount of control over the functions of the government.

Some tactics such as bombing schools, religious institutions, and government buildings demonstrated the reasoning behind some decisions for the people and leadership to have strong consideration for turning into a socialist economy, under more strict communist type political structure.

A major group based in Russia is the Georgian Mafia, which controlled much of the black market under the Communist system and has now extended its range of activities. Two other ethnically oriented organizations include the Chechens and the Azerbaijani groups, who have contributed to a major upsurge in the illegal trafficking of drugs, metals, weapons, sex slaves, nuclear materials, and even body organs. Several of the Mafia groups have infiltrated the Russian banking system and have used tactics of intimidation and violence against bankers and businessmen that do not cooperate. Among the most influential Mafia groups in the United States are the Odessa Mafia, based in Brighton Beach, NJ, the

Chechens, who tend to concentrate on contract killings and extortion, and the Malina Organization, a multi-ethnic group also in Brighton Beach that maintains extensive international connections and is active in a variety of areas including drug trafficking, credit card and tax fraud and extortion.

The Asian Triads are based primarily in Hong Kong while also active in Taiwan and Mainland China. They are highly structured organizations that work through criminal networks where their members organize various enterprises. The Triads have primarily based themselves through rituals, oaths, secret ceremonies and incentives to secure personal loyalty. Family affiliation is important within the Triads and individual membership provides credibility and influence. These groups engage in a broad range of criminal activities, including drug trafficking (almost exclusively heroin), alien smuggling, theft, murder, extortion, credit card fraud, prostitution, sex slave trade, and illegal gambling.

There are over 160,000 Triad members in Hong Kong alone belonging to around 50 different organizations. Hong Kong is the home base for the Sun Yee On, the 14K, and the Woo Group while the United Bamboo originate their operations out of Taiwan. The Triads also have extensive overseas networks, which allow them to prosper in transnational criminal activities. The Triad groups are assumed to have close ties with "tongs" or chambers of commerce, and the youth gangs that exist in many Chinese communities throughout the United States. It is these relationships that provide for the major importation of heroin from Southeast Asia into the U.S.

Nigerian organized crime has become influential in transnational illegal activities only recently. It can be traced to the collapse of oil prices in the early 1980s and the subsequent problems that this caused for an economy that relied on oil exports for 95 percent of its earnings. This resulted in a number of well-educated Nigerians, many living in other countries, to be deprived of their primary source of income. This in turn created a wave of individuals turning to crime as a means of supplementing their income.

Nigerian Criminal Enterprises have developed large-scale drug trafficking operations that are second only to the Asian triads in their import of heroin into the United States. This has been facilitated by a relatively secure home base, characterized by lack of legislation and law enforcement capacity, as well as political instability, corruption and few sources to devote to fighting organized crime. Further, Nigerian organizations have engaged in extensive fraud and extortion activities, including credit card fraud, and fraudulent activities through commercial banks and government assistance programs.

GOVERNMENTS

The U.S. Government itself is a key factor of the subject. Organized Crime is about 80% of the foundation and workings of the U.S. Practically every natural resource in the development and maintenance of the U.S. is taken from the continent, through annexation, or without true right from the indigenous peoples.

Since the publicized 09/11/01 attack on the U.S., the sense of paranoia by agents of U.S. Federal Investigation Bureaus & mainly the European American Population has increased for caution, and uncertainties of world control. The same and more horrific actions have been committed by the descendents of colonial and neo-colonial national culture and education structures. It was told to the general public that the U.S. Government had been involved in teaching just about every person and group they now consider dangers, like the Taliban, in various U.S. media reports throughout the since the 80's. This is an issue that is felt as justified by some, but fearful by others. The media and many people quickly disregarded those facts due to the annual rise in nationalistic attitudes. Racial profiling, and other measures that increase racism, are not normally publicized now, or discouraged.

World-view thinking is needed to understand and begin to solve problems that big. Nationalism in cases like this, inspire class discrimination, racism, and religious persecution. The unknown "Street Terrorism Enforcement Prevention Act" is a special domestic suppression law that subversively aims at "minority organizations & youth," for observance of potential social uprisings against domestic and foreign government actions (new age cointelpro). Just like in the early 70's, the government is looking to have federal monitors over those with the ability to create social change, especially students. Racial pathology in the military and police of a nation can harbor the worst behaviors, especially among the older members and brand new recruits. The older ones protect their racial comments and anti-humanist actions, and the young ones may not know any better. Many times the workers are just following orders that they do not know the long-term effects of.

In the contemporary level, a percentage of this is that exceedingly more social justice, spiritual, music/movie artists, environmental rights, and cultural enrichment organizations in the U.S. have noted that they have either suddenly received unusual harassing questions on business Faith and about associations during the years of mainly Republican U.S. Presidents. The main targets of lawful and unlawful investigations have been mainly on any person or organization with an Arabic name or physical similarity. This problem has even affected elementary kids in the U.S.

The problem of negative stereotyping and racism is a serious infection throughout humanity & damages everyone when it is used.

Several agreements have been made over the past few decades with countries noted to actively be participating in acts of racial suppression and genocide. During the Reagan years, the U.S. was involved in fund & military/police training assistance of nations such as South Africa, Ecuador, and Israel. The Israeli Government (not the Jewish or Hebrew religion) had adopted a policy called Zionism. This policy has effected the perception of all Israeli's in various negative ways, because it inspires racism and exclusionism. On a historical note, most people there are descendants of Rome are Europeans. The actual definition of a Semite is a person equally of African and another geographic heritage. The same goes for the biblical and Torah definition, with correct interpretations.

It is a "criminal government policy, not a religious policy" that calls for exclusionist policies and repression of other races & persons not supporting the state. This is similar to virtually every location where persons from a colonial heritage like the Roman Jews, Assyrian Muslims, and others from neighboring cultures have developed elsewhere through time. The historical evidence of this cannot be proven wrong, with the exception of false recordings of a people's history. There are a few societies in the America's and other places that did similar things to others, but the scale of damage to humanity and nature is less than a ¼ of what those from the Middle East and Europe have done since about 4500bc, according to the late. Dr. Chancellor Williams.

Former U.S. Presidents, European Government Leaders, the former Prime Minister of England—Margaret Thatcher, and many other pro-neocolonial world leaders supported the Apartheid policies of the European Colonial offspring in Southern Africa. The National leaders of Ecuador and Mexico; like many other Latin American Nations; still emulate their European counterparts, actively suppress the empowerment of Indigenous People, hesitate true education, and encourage emulation of foreign economic and social structures.

NATIONALISTIC OPPRESSION

As mentioned in the chapter representing linguistics, "settlement colonies, exploitation, and trade colonies, it is also important to know that current globalization is a by-product of earlier Islamic expansionism, and European colonization since the 11th century." Recently, it has been found that chemical weapons tests followed a joint military exercise between Syria and Sudan. The test targets were/are the indigenous Africans of Sudan, by members of the Arab Alliance of States, which have illegal residence in Africa to expand colonial control; as well as force and manipulate population statistics of religion popularity.

Millions of Muslims, Christians, and a few other religions, have a high percentage of peoples that entered the religion through attrition of force, or other coercive means. Another example of what is going on around the world today (2004) is what has been going on for centuries to indigenous Africans. A woman that tried to escape enslavement in the Sudan by "Arab & Arabized African soldiers" was attacked with guns aimed. Most of the men in the village were killed. The story mentioned that the women ran towards a nearby lake and tried to hide under the water but were caught.

Each woman was raped by up to six invaders. One of the woman refused to have sex with them, so they split her head into pieces with an axe in front of them in a sadistic rage. After the women and girls were taken to Khartoum, the soldiers were paid and offered praise to Allah. The Dunfar tribe has the potential for creating a formidable resistance extension against Islamic and Euro-Christian expansionism.

Pledges of allegiance to a nation are territorially, culturally, and in many instances historically limiting. The existence of nations is among the most unnatural, and anti-indigenous creations of the colonial powers. The underlying goal of inspiring goal-setting perspectives on life, are lost in the mandatory state type education of school children, and others to a belief in an eternal conception of anti-indigenous/foreign created allegiance. It is up to the people to learn and act on revolutionary reformation of the world around them in order to ensure permanence of people-centered governmental change, in harmony with the world around it. The USA Constitution is based through information from various cultures and is an excellent partial base for the creation of a worldwide constitution. In many ways the U.S. is designed as a supreme achievement of governmental process, as many other nations. The bad elements must be removed, and the good elements must be replicated from each, for all.

THE HOMELESS

The concept of homelessness in a society was virtually unacceptable before the advent of the European Industrialization. In many countries, capitalistic intentioned persons take advantage of the homeless and troubled. Anti-homeless people behavior can be observed in many places around the world. Sadly, instead of supporting the life enhancement, and life sustaining systems that anyone could be in one day; including themselves, many societies that claim justice and prosperity as base elements of the society, pass laws to hurt, and ban homeless people from attempts to survive. A common example of the exploitation of homeless working families is grouping many of them in small homes to pay exuberant rents, then kicking them out if one payment is late. This is a milking tactic that is strictly slated for profiting against the weak. Most people in this situation are caught in violent or simply constraining cycles of dependence, or hit a short rough time in their life.

At anytime at least 80% of a population can find themselves at risk for not having an income, at any time. In the U.S., and many other countries, striving to gain a higher status is encourage socially, but discouraged financially by taxation decided by the governing bodies, not the people. The best example is the disparity of cost for higher education vs. contracted government service. If an individual is selected to be a servant of the government, they are rewarded for following the guideline plans of the agency or military. They get partially paid or government sponsored homes, vehicles, etc. If the person has higher aspirations of creating a world for her/himself, by reaching for higher education, they are hit with increasing debts.

Many students that attend Junior Colleges or Universities are on the edge of bankruptcy and/or are homeless. Many are just on the verge of homelessness, and would be if there were not so many that they are forced to live in groups to afford a place to sleep. Disrespect for the importance of the student in the society is incredibly high and self evident if you as an individual observe students in mainly non-elite colleges/universities. General populations of homeless men, women, and children become homeless for several reasons. Misconceptions of wealth and/or a lack of education towards assuring financial stability are prevalent among most of the poor worldwide. It is most common that men become homeless due to financial mismanagement, inadequate skill training or education for more stable occupations.

Homeless women tend to become homeless more due to the same reasons as men, but also are victim to trained codependence on employed men. There are not as many older homeless women as there are younger ones. As with some younger men, each may learn self-destructive habits that lead them to negative situations. Some have been homeless since they were children and become comfortable in maintaining the condition or tendency throughout life. The state of life of a homeless person differs from persons to families.

Most of the time the striving goals are stifled by prejudice portrayed against them by more financially successful persons. The thing many don't realize is that anyone can become homeless due to reasons like natural disaster, accidents, financial crisis of the employer, etc., etc., too.

IGNORANCE AGAINST YOUTH

A multitude of psychological changes happen through the development of a youth. Depression, sexual interest, and thoughts on metaphysics are common experiences throughout the teen years. Conservative and western European based cultures tend to have degrading perspectives towards older youth as a group. Perspectives in this manner have existed against older youth (teens) for centuries. A part of social interaction skill development needs are expressed through expression of sexual interests. Ignorant thoughts; such as, the theory stating, "To be young is to be mischievous," permeate the pre-conceptions of many adults on teens.

While some of the adults may be correct in there perspective on some teens, the thought is well over generalized. The U.S. did, not recognize Children's Rights, until 1966, with constitutional rights, and also by the United Nations with the in-adequate "Declaration of Rights of the Child." Ratification of the declaration has still not been given by all nations of the world.

As most people that may be reading this book are likely to exist in such a society, this part of the book is directed specifically to you. The "Webster's 9th New Collegiate Dictionary" was among the first to define the term "Juvenile Delinquency" coming from 1816. It is juvenile conduct characterized as an anti-social behavior beyond parental control, subject to legal action. Throughout the years, knowledge of several issues has steadily been weaned away from acceptance in various societies. Among the issues are ways to raise children from mid-elementary to the late teen years. These issues have been dealt with in the ancient developed civilizations, through parental councils, elder relations, mentoring, and rites of passage programs.

THE GREATEST PROBLEMS IN TODAY'S SOCIETIES ABOUT YOUTH TEND TO BE THE FOLLOWING:

- How to nourish children properly
- How to educate them
- How to Discipline them

- How to impart values
- How to prepare them to live a happy life
  *No established mythical hero stories.

Today children are given less consideration in budgetary, and planning interests for the future. Treatment of the environment, construction of living spaces, industrial management, and religion-based prejudices are among the constraints children have faced through the centuries.

For example; during Europe's middle ages, and renaissance periods, children used and learned to use obscenities as common language as soon as they could talk.

This type of social behavior is in its middle development stage throughout American society, and others. Children in England that were not raised properly tend to have been imprisoned on floating ships off shore in the 18th century.

This was one of the many punishments these types of societies placed on children. Currently, the U.S., and some other societies believe it is civilized to raise children improperly, under fund beneficial programs, under fund education, glorify self-destructive behavior, and imprison children for the problems they are responsible for leading, or allowing children to do. Mostly as acceptable means of gaining needed attention.

Gang behavior should not be seen as a totally evil. The root causes for the creation of gangs are mostly positive. Older children, like adults, are emulating elements of social grouping, social intention, and self-defense they have observed in general society, the news, school lessons, and to a lesser extent, lyrics from music. The achievement of attention by force, participation in a popular group that has committed crimes against humanity, and gain of financial wealth by any means, is among the lessons taught to be the most important within societies gangs flourish in.

COLONIAL APTITUDE IN HISTORY LESSONS

The European invasion of Australia started in 1788. The indigenous population of Australia was approximately 800,000. By 1911, over 700,000 innocent people had become victims of another European Genocidal Campaign for expansion of their populations. Diseases introduced by the invaders decimated most indigenous people. The Aboriginals had no natural defense against the measles & other contagious diseases they spread. Aboriginals were finally granted citizenship in 1967. They still await an apology from the Government of Australia.

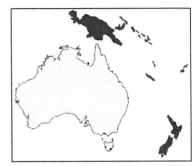

Certain Europeans and other people that have been mis-educated, praise people like Christopher Columbus. On his psychotically motivated second voyage to the eroded first trip to the Caribbean, he was given the title of Admiral of the Sea, and reigned terror unlike anything seen before. When he was finished, over eight-million Arawak people, (the native population of what they call Hispaniola/Haiti) had been the victims of genocidal homicide by torture, murder, forced labor, rape, child abuse, starvation, disease, and suicide.

His friends & evil kin like Hernan Cortez and other European Christian/Catholic invaders systematically murdered tens of millions of Indigenous people, from the Canadian Arctic to South America. Since then, natives have been murdered by warfare, forced death marches, forced relocation to barren lands, intentional and accidental spread of disease, poisoning, the promotion of suicide through the destruction of their cultural and religious heritage, suppressed from any representation of governmental leadership recognized through there United Nations.

Estimates of the overall Genocide in the Western Hemisphere are between 100 and 300 million humans killed by biological warfare, forced labor beyond living tolerance, execution, massacre, suicide to avoid torture and mutilation. Canadian Natives have the highest suicide of any population group in the world. This genocide has been the longest lasting genocidal agenda in European designed world domination.

BAD EDUCATION

Before you are a race, religion or occupation you are a human. If you wish to exist as a pig, bitch, cat, chicken, or any other animal, which could be a problem, you must give up your right to be considered a human, by your peers. But, if you are constantly going to take pride in calling yourself a human being, remember that you are not superior, or a superior being. We are as much a part of this world as the ant, or tree, we just developed different than other forms of life. Anglo-Saxon/Euro-centric educational systems tend to teach anti-humanism and make you believe that you can have human rights without responsibilities. The current general educational system tampers with the process of thinking by the use of foreign selected labels, symbols, letters, numbers and false histories.

True civilization is never achieved; because the human being must act for survival, not think as an element of support.

It is a crime against the future that children are being taught memorization for tests, instead of thinking. If you go through your whole life by the simple use of memory and not intellect, any problem that you confront, and you don't remember how to deal with, you will be deal with. This is demonstrated daily by people that join a military force out of reaction to memorization to be patriotic, the school system that financially relies on results of a politically motivated test system, individual aspirations for low-level achievement by social gatherings around liquor stores, worshipping without questions non-supportive systems, etc.

For any group of people to progress they must be in touch with the teachings of their ancestors. If all you see are your ancestors in chains as slaves, drinking poisons, wasting money, eating wrong, etc., you'll most likely follow that pattern of behavior. When a race of people can't refer to the wisdom of their ancestors they repeat the same mistakes, thus hindering any progression to civilization. We must have history to move forward. To be civilized, a person must learn and naturally act in manners of maturity, self-sufficiency, support, and responsibility. Virtually every society of humans have been becoming swayed from traditional civilized behavior of their own culture, to imitation of technocratic societies, in the illusion of true advancement.

From the top down, many schools around the world are operating in a criminal fashion against the future of the children. The created excuses from a lack of funds which happen to be re-directed to other places by those making the claim, to purposefully assigning insufficient staff to manage and facilitate education is a serious epidemic. This is directed by either wealthy individual's directing the decisions from the top-down, some by so-called leaders that perceive education to be less important than fancy weapons, religious/secret society organizations, foreign government control, or any mixture. In most cases the commitment of parents in collaborative education, stops once the child either reaches or passes Kindergarten, 3rd, 4th, or, 6th grade.

Sorrowfully, schools that contain minority students are coercively, directed to be mismanaged, under-funded, and targeted for low success. Social structures involving the parent's lives in the chosen areas tend to involve inundation of poor environment mainte-nance. Poor environment maintenance is the process of continuing a stable, or radical stage, of social degradation. Adults that believe in inadequacy, tend to teach inadequacy to the children around them. The con-sequences of these factors, peer interaction that emulates maintenance of degraded social status, do not appropriately set punishments & boundaries, or involve themselves as a parental council for the school(s) of their children, get what they pay for.

In all, the combination processes of bad education, and bad parenting, create unfavorable children. There are a few examples of children that progress no mat-ter what, but a majority in trouble are not being treated or developed correctly from either both, or one of the main two sources affecting their lives. Teachers get certificates and many are great, what about parents that parent with bad founda-tions, divorce, etc.?

FOR WORLD PEACE

Everyone should understand that when others extend their values, religion and institutions unto others by force, or through exploitive measures at times of social weakness, they are penetrating traditions, which may be supportive of the native society. In this way the action; intentional or not, is a tendency to poison, teach hate of self, love of the oppressor, or to favor the other culture more than one's own. The conception of economic prosperity needs an immediate alteration too. Most of the ancient perspectives on money did not place separate value of the money from different places, only equal number of funds for equal numbers of funds. Inequality of funds, through the ranking of the colonial financial con-trol centers (World Bank, etc.,) help to maintain the system conception of 1st world, and 3rd world.

The struggles for equality of financial resources, belief in placement in poverty, foreign conceptions of wealth and prosperity, control of knowledge expression, control of political rule, police and military powers are all elements of unbalanced humanity. Patriarchy generally means rule by the male only. A part of the antagonization towards war and resisted social transformations is due to problems males are trained to exemplify for protection of the male centered system. Many of the world's religions and cultures are highly patriarchal, and some of them are getting worse.

IMBALANCE OF POWERS EQUALS IMBALANCE IN STRUCTURE.

While some religions and cultures now have more modern versions that are gracious to the idea of equality between the sexes, in their fundamental, or orthodox versions they adhere firmly to patriarchal beliefs which attempt, through their customs and ideology, to maximize men's control over women, and everything else. This are can best be explained as a formation and side effect of organized crime expanded through history. A part of the repairs of the world require the full academic acceptance of the significance of full-disclosure from all peoples.

Patriarchal societies; like the U.S.A., have a set of typical values. Values are stated "masculine" priorities such as, ownership, authority, law, power, control, victory, courage, and strength. The main interactions are the power struggle and the competition. Inclinations towards centralization of authority are common ways of thinking to achieve greater and greater power can be seen in daily life. One group of examples, are the attempts of male Governors to centralize control of the state to the masses. It is very rare when female Governors do the same thing. It is a social condition whereby the end justifies the means. "Winning" and "Losing" or being "first" and "last" are important results in a patriarchy. Societies like this are much more common around the world, as previously colonized societies attempt to emulate the traditions, institutions, civilization, and control over the natural world. The concept of superiority, arrogance, and aggression is of absolute importance. All of this is a learned property of in-adequate lessons of life.

Of all values, "power" is the one which is most prized. In international relations, the assessment of ego, strength, the building of enormous offensive weapons, are extremely important themes, since World War III cannot be won by any, but those reaching for peace. The instigation that one group has a bigger package seems to be the leading concept. Desire for power as a need is a main reason for the countless conflicts in the history of humanity. It seems to now be a struggle of technocracies against civilization.

For example, if Group "1" holds power as the supreme value, and Group "3" does not, then everything that "3" does would not have any value. If "3" sticks to its own value and refuses to compete for power with "1" it is dominated, and "1's" value will be ever increasing and will be imposed over "3." However, if "3" decides to compete with "2", and this inevitably means a power-struggle, this would mean that "3" would have adopted power as a value and then loses "3's" own values. In both situations, "3's" values have been effectively under enemy control by "1."

Simply replacing men with women is not the answer to restoring effective social balance. The principles would still be there! The answer is radical principle, status, and leadership changes, during the time of similar educational shifts. Slow changes leave too much time for counteractions to be fed into changes. Enforcement of changes may be needed for a short time, the human nature of the majority populations of the world, currently called minorities, are generally more inclined to accept the changes 80–100%, than the countries with colonization and genocide, as a support system in there history. If someone instigates gender equality in male dominated institutions to allot equal access of advancement for women, they must realize that if the institutions are fundamentally flawed, if they mirror patriarchal values, terminologies, and/or relationships.

The inclusion of women in positions of influence is a not a balancing victory. If a multinational corporation routinely exploits female labor, pollute the environment, then integrates the women into the management of the corporations, the same conditions may still exist, and be related as vital to the corporations success and micro-culture. Without that, fundamental beliefs are the same, as the actions tend to remain the same, or get worse. Principles are the base of social structure.

In contrast of patriarchal society, the highest values in a matriarchal society are more towards nurturing, empathetic compassion, sensitivity, creativity, working with nature and giving support to others. The principles are towards mutual cooperation. The means are as important as the end, and the process is just as important as the product. Victory and success are judged by the condition that everyone's life is improved, and not who has obtained power over whom. There are logical problems with this, due to balance needs. A New World Order where balance in the values attributed to the masculine, and feminine principles, are what will make a perfect worldwide set of civilizations.

It is counterproductive to coagulate the world's cultures without 100% conscious agreement of each society, and/or desire by needs of reconstruction. Structures of authority and power would have to change in all areas of government; including fundamental principles.

Structures do not rest on individual(s). The significantly important activities of life are not just trade, finance, buying, and selling, but also nurturing the community, promotion of civic consciousness, etc. The more immediate and important goal in a society is to change the values that matter in our society right now. Civilization is an advanced stage in social development. Technology, is the science of mechanical and industrial arts, it is not civilization. Just because you have fast cars, boats, planes, you could go to the moon, we have medicine, does not make you civilized. Being civilized implies being human. The true purpose of the human is to serve humanity. If you are not working for the advancement of humanity, you are anti-human.

Implantation of humans with microchips to track and, in the future, control the activities of people, is currently underway worldwide. The E.U., Mexico, and many other places are encouraging the implantation of the chips into babies, prisoners, the poor, and others now. Educational systems that administer false history and psychologically degrading history, are teaching anti-humanism.

In order to assist the colonial control, and suppress liberation movements, many leaders of the United States have supported dictators, ordered assassinations, and funded subversive movements through these and other places/actions:

- Tiananmen Square—China. (1989).
- General Suharto in Indonesia was brought to power with the help of the CIA and overthrown with the help of the Pentagon's Defense Intelligence Agency.
- Chilean Socialist President. "Salvador Allende" assassinated. (09/11/1973)
- Malaya against the British and Indonesia against the Dutch.
- Guatemala, 1953–1990s: A CIA-organized coup overthrew the democratically-elected and progressive government of Jacobo Arbenz, initiating 40 years of death-squads, torture, disappearances, mass executions, and unimaginable cruelty, totaling well over 100,000 victims—indisputably one of the most inhuman chapters of the 20th century.
- Philippine guerillas against American puppet, Ferdinand Marcos
- 1981: U.S. launched Vietnam-style operations in Central America, supporting insurgency against a Sandinista government in Nicaragua sympathetic to

Castro's Cuba; U.S. supported cocaine trade of Nicaraguan counterrevolutionaries, the "Contras"

- 1960: Koreans overthrew Rhee—Americans put in Park Chung-hee, first of 3 army generals who would rule from 1961 to 1993. South Korea against American puppet dictator, Syngman Rhee

- Americans tolerated a coup d'etat by General Chun Doo-hwan in 1979 and covertly supported his orders that led to the killing of several hundred, maybe several thousand, Korean civilians at Kwangju in 1980 (probably far more people than the Chinese Communists killed, Chiang Kai-shek and his son Chiang Ching-kuo in Taiwan.

- Ngo Dinh Diem (assassinated on American orders), General Nguyen Khanh, General Nguyen Cao Ky, and General Mguyen Van Thieu in Vietnam.

- The Congo/Zaire, 1960–65 (Patrice Lumumba)

- East Timor, 1975 to present

- Grenada, 1979–84

- Haiti, 1987–94

The Foreign Policy of the U.S.A. has mostly been determined by devotion to the necessity to serve imperatives, which can be <u>summarized as follows:</u>

- Preventing the rise of any society that might serve as a successful example of an alternative to the capitalist model supporting the white world order;

- Making the world safe for American corporations;

- Enhancing the financial statements of military, small arms, textile, agriculture, and drug cartels at home who have contributed generously to members of congress;

- Extending political, social, and economic supremacy over as wide an area as possible.

Similar actions are continually taken by other nations. The most important theme to underline is that we are facing a period-when we look back in five or ten years that we will consider to be a defining period of U.S. imperialism. The U.S. ruling class has been trying to redefine the world to take advantage of the collapse of the USSR, in an attempt to alter the international terms of trade, and perpetuate the cause of creating a "Uni-Polar World." In the 1990s the United Nations UNICEF agency stated that over 100 million children under the age of five died of unnecessary causes: diarrhea, whooping cough, tetanus, pneumonia, and measles-diseases easily preventable through cheap vaccines or simply clean water.

UNICEF estimates that up to 30,000 children under the age of five die of easily preventable diseases every day. The old USSR government is speculated to have exterminated millions of its citizens. Over 100 million people over 70 years are estimated to have died from being worked to death in the camps of the gulag, terrorizing the public by random executions, purges, show trials, mass exterminations, and induced famines.

Kofi Annan declared in 2001 that as many as 24,000 people starved to death every day. Altogether one billion people are chronically malnourished while barren measures imposed by the IMF (A European controlled agency) have resulted in a drop in real wages in the "so-called third world." Anywhere from 70–80% of the world's wealth is in the hands of 20 percent of the people. 1-out of—10 humans suffer from severe starvation and malnutrition, while 7-out of—10 are insufficiently nourished. The U.S. has been the preeminent military and economic power in the world, and it wants to ensure that the future, over the next 40 to 50 years and longer, keeps looking the same way.

The European Union has been in self-development to become a military force equal to the 20th century U.S., and has retained several levels of political control around the world, since initial colonial actions. Irregardless to this, evil is evil. Imperialism describes a world economic, financial, and military system in which the key great powers compete to dominate the world and to divide it between themselves. That's the classical theory of imperialism. Economic competition leads into military competition. The industrialized World War I showed this in detailed expression.

The termed, Second World War was a repetition of the First in a number of key respects, or really the conclusion of the unsettled items from the First World War. From the Second World War onward, there was a change. Instead of a struggle among several key imperialist powers—notably the conflict between the European powers and the rising American and Japanese superpowers, the system of imperialism characterized by that competition emerged as being between the USSR and the United States.

The concept of "World War" negates the significance of previous real world wars. The continual attack on Africa by Islamic and European Imperialists since around 4500b.c., Islamic Imperialists wars across Indonesia & Asia, and European Imperialism across the America's, over the past centuries concise the true World Wars. The war commonly known as World War II, more accurately should be considered WWXIII. The battles of the colonial countries between each other, to maintain control of themselves in a particular way is less significant in full retrospect, to the significance and respective intents towards defensive and offensive measures.

In a simile to the learned behavior of the historical figures, the hero/challenger role is emulated in the practice of many sporting events. Soccer, Basketball, Football, Hockey, and the various types of boxing are among the top pro-violence sports, with only a few persons in all in recognition of the positive benefits. As a social control and sub-development tool, many countries feed on the maintenance of clan-like rivalries within their own societies to inspire distraction from collective positive awareness & actions in the society. It is also used as a justification towards frivolity, which is of enormous benefit to the capitalistic institutions that have little or no interest in the health of the people.

MORE WEAPONS OF EGO & STUPIDITY

Airborne High-Power Microwave Weapon A pulsed power airborne high power microwave (HPM) system. This medium range weapons system constitutes the primary payload of the host escort defense aircraft. The system generates variable magnitude HPM fields that disrupt or destroy electrical components in the target region. It can engage both air and ground targets.

Hybrid High-energy Laser System (HHELS) A system consisting of several ground-based, multi-megawatt high-energy chemical lasers and an assemblage of space-based mirrors. HHELS can be used in several modes of operation. In its weapons mode, the laser engages air, space, and ground targets by reflecting a laser beam off one or more of the mirrors to the intended target. An example of this can be seen in the movie: Spies Like Us.

Space-Based Kinetic Energy Weapon (KEW) A general class of low earth orbit (LEO) based weapons that include a variety of warhead types from pellets to large and small high density rods. The KEW may be directed at air, space, and ground targets; it achieves its destructive effect by penetrating the target at hypervelocity.

Solar Energy Optical Weapon (SEOW) A constellation of space-based mirrors, which allow solar radiation to be focused on specific ground, air, or space targets. The lethality of this system is limited, due to optical diffusion; however, it may prove useful for disruption or perhaps weather control.

Space-Based High-energy Laser (HEL) System A multi-megawatt high-energy chemical laser constellation that can be used in several modes of operation. In its weapons mode with the laser at high power, it can attack ground, air, and space targets. In its surveillance mode, it can operate using the laser at low power levels for active illumination imaging or with the laser inoperative for passive imaging.

Solar-Powered High-energy Laser System A space-based, multi-megawatt, high-energy solar-powered laser constellation that can be used in several modes of operation. In its weapons mode with the laser at high power, it can attack ground, air, and space targets. In its surveillance mode, it can operate using the laser at low power levels for active illumination imaging, or with the laser inoperative for passive imaging.

Space-Based High Power Microwave Weapon (HPM) A weapon system capable of engaging ground, air, and space targets with a varying degree of lethality. It consists of a group of satellites deployed into low orbit that can direct an ultra-wideband of microwave energy at ground, air, and space targets. Its effect is to generate high electric fields to disrupt or destroy any electronic components present.

Subliminal Social Convey: The basics of subliminal social manipulation are in the purpose of control of thought. Early in the year 2000–01, more and more safeguards against the use of this, and lobbied support for the use of this as passive domestic and select foreign social control.

Elecro-Magnetic Pulse Bomb: The essentials of the workings of an E-bomb are grounded in a basic understanding of electro-magnetic physics theory. The technology relies on an electromagnetic pulse that may be conceptualized as an electric shockwave created when a stream of highly energetic photons collides with atoms of low atomic numbers to cause them to eject a 'pulse' of electrons. This is called the Compton effect; and was first observed in open-air tests of nuclear bombs when the immense detonation energy interacted with the oxygen and nitrogen atoms in the atmosphere to shoot mass quantities of electrons radically outwards from the explosion. Though these pulses diminish in strength over distance, electric lights hundreds of miles away get overloaded. They would be an assistance measure in urban warfare.

<u>Ebola</u> A very fast reproducing virus, Ebola and its relatives Lassa and Marburg kill by hemorrhagic fevers (VHFs), which cause internal bleeding. Bleeding out of the eyes, mouth, ears, nose, and other body orifices occurs uncontrollably. The nervous system and organs degenerate as patients suffer grandma-seizures and delirium. Some suffer shock or go into comas. Relatively 50% to 90% of those infected die in extreme pain. Death tends to happen within a week of becoming infected, as the victim dies, they become convulsive, splashing in their own pool

of infected blood, and highly contagious. It is a class-4 biological warfare agent that was released, and spreading beyond control.

Anthrax 100kg of anthrax can kill about 3-million people. Anthrax can create similar casualty numbers to that of a hydrogen bomb, at a tiny fraction of development cost.

BIO-TECHNOLOGY

It is interesting to realize the fact that AIDS, Ebola, and several other super-viruses, and infectious agents began in areas were the people are considered expendable by certain racist colonial/imperialistic wealthy nations. Those nations have been the only ones capable of producing such agents, with recorded intent. Stealth viruses are unique cell-destroying viruses that are not recognized by the human immune system. These viruses cause persistent infections because they are missing specific genes, which initiate particular immune responses. Several viruses are circulating throughout the human populations, and a few may only be awaiting a trigger agent.

The establishment that AIDS and Ebola are byproducts of genetic engineering, comes from records classified by corporate labs like Merck, Bionetics, Hazelton, and other government funded labs to develop and test effects of bio-war viruses, since the 1950's. During the late 1960's, typical racist white male researchers created a theory of evolution that stated developments of future research of viral evolution and retroviruses a "genetically superior race of humans could be synthetically evolved."

Many of the same companies and agencies that are secretly noted as responsible for the initial development and spread of the HIV Virus, are now partially covering themselves from claim, by pretending to be fully engaged in making cures. Funds are channeled inappropriately, and the only acceptable research and production done is for the creation of symptom suppressors, not solutions to the problems they caused. A gradual flow of customers for the symptoms means a constant flow of income. What may have taken $10 million dollars to make should not require $100 billion dollars to cure.

The World Health Organization (WHO), or World Death Organization as it probably could be called, is usually a central conduit that becomes a blaming agent. This organization is supposed to help the people's struck down from the legacy of colonialism, under the powers of the previous dominators.

The currently economically advantaged countries establish biological control laboratories; set standards for development, manufacture, distribution, and administration of over 95% of the worlds pharmaceuticals. In 1969 the U.S. Department of Defense requested $10 million from Congress to perform studies on immune-system-destroying agents for germ warfare defense. According to WHO records, in 1970 studies were conducted on viruses that were capable of altering the immunologic response capacity of T-Lymphocytes (immunity T-cells) Prior to that, WHO had issued a 5-year research report on advances in virology experimentation relating primarily to the causal relationship between viruses, and cancer.

During the 60's and 70's, Russian, American, and other European researchers had learned how the human immune system could be "boosted or destroyed by old and newly developed germs." The WHO also applied administrative leadership and funding for several programs designed to evaluate specific disease vulnerabilities of minority groups from American Indians to African natives through collection and analysis of gene pools and blood supplies.

In 1970 the WHO and the Vaccine Development Committee endorsed an African smallpox immunization program with a budget of $14 million for use in Zaire and neighboring countries. This has been found to be the shield for the practice of HIV testing and population control experimentation. HIV and AIDS were non-existent anywhere prior to 1975, and the same goes for Ebola. Both originate from the same area in Zaire. Furthermore, the U.S. Army, USAID, Merck Laboratories, the National Cancer Institute and Litton Bionetics were all focused on "vaccines and studies in which cancer-causing retro-viruses were isolated and transported from Africa to the U.S. and visa versa."

In February 1999, a Dr. Boyd Graves discovered indisputable evidence, of the experiments that led to the development of what the world now knows as the AIDS virus. That document is called the "1971 Flow Chart of the Special Virus Program of the United States." The Flow Chart is the blueprint for the development of Auto-Immune Deficiency Syndrome (AIDS). It is located in one of the 15 progress reports of the federal program entitled "The U.S. Special Virus Cancer Program." It is proof of the U.S. origin of HIV as a synthetic biological agent.

The scientific evidence shows that HIV seeks out the receptor site in the blood of specifically African genomes. According to genetics, the receptor site is called the CCR5 Delta 32+ (positive) gene that all people of color have. Transversely, the 15 % world population of Caucasians carries the CCR5 Delta 32-(negative) gene. That means the people of Northern Europe by design are immune from getting this illness, unless it somehow mutated to get them too. Over 90% of the world's populations are in danger from this designer virus, and other synthetic biological agents.

Over the years, both treatments and cures for HIV have been made. Due to geo-politics of certain nations and peoples of the world, cures have continually been repressed. There have been drugs made from nature that have curative abilities for virtually every human ailment found in the rainforests, etc. In Kenya, a scientist created a potential cure called Kemron, and another has recently been created in the U.S., called "Imusil." Like many businesses, etc., that harbor the creation of cures for various chronic ailments, regulations and corporation demands acquire the abilities to suppress, discredit, and destroy many cures as they are repeatedly re-created throughout the world.

WAR AGAINST YOUTH

Anti-Social Senator Charles Schumer (D-NY) is offering Senate Bill "S-1735," the "Criminal Street Gang Abatement Act of 2004" as the answer to gang violence, to be enacted on by his kind. This bill would make it a federal crime to participate in a "criminal street gang"-defined as three or more people who cooperate to commit, or are merely suspected individuals of "gang crimes." Harsh laws don't solve criminal activities of organized groups. Anyone involved with youth should be able to tell you that problems of mental, physical, and spiritual abuse are not addressed in jailing a teenager. A clear majority of youth involved in gangs, organize as a result of the effects of poverty and persecution that injure their families. "Obviously, this is open warfare on children, especially those that may simply be acting proportionately in a society that encourages distrust of teenagers." If the issue is simply gun control, bullet pricing, and bullet control should be a much higher priority.

What is happening is that the mindsets that built the prisons, envies youth, and fears change of the status quo; no matter how corrupt, has decided that children shall guarantee the success of the prison industrial complex, sanctity of corrupt thought through bad socialization of the average boy/girl, and discouragement towards leadership to run the world around them, in ways different from previous generations. Like the three-strikes law, this mandatory sentencing does not work; it causes a negative impact on city and state budgets. True positive changes in any society begin with the conception(s) held by the people. A life based on principle, is 10x better than a life based on legal law.

The bill will force the gangs to reinvent themselves, as the need for the creation of gangs is based on desires to create a unified secure family/clan for support the society refuses to them. In defense of there security, people may get hurt if gang members think they are being ratted on-in order to protect themselves from the onslaught that will come if this bill. The average streets will get more dangerous within cities that have exceedingly less support & prevention elements in place, from people representing their needs. This is one of the many violence—directing plans on issue that are meant to help stock the prison-industrial complex.

The bill's sponsors are calling for $663 million in federal funding over five years, from 2005 to 2009, mostly for the Department of Justice, with $250 million for grants to state and local governments to "combat" gang activity through community-based programs. Grants are extremely likely to contain subversive conditions, or be very difficult to obtain. A street gang expert named Dr. Malcolm Klein, Ph.D. of the University of Southern California-based Social Science Research Center, woefully disagreed with S-1735. Like every law created to suppress an element of humanity, it is met with equal or superior resistance. Only agreed upon principles shared by and from all can change the direction of any segment of society.

Gangs are a part of every industrialized capitalist nations history. They can be traced back to the 1700s and early 1800s, when gangs were usually comprised of members of the same race and ethnic background. According to the website: www.knowgangs.com, they band together for protection, support, recreation and financial gain. Those are many of the reasons youth come together today, and are natural desires. "The United States was started by several peoples that formed gangs; the English, the Italians, the Missionaries, the Jews, and the Irish." Movies like Scarface, Gangs of New York, Civil War, Alexander, National Treasure, The good-the bad-and the ugly, Indiana Jones, among many others, show that there is a war between themselves, and untamed instinctual desires to control others. The English maintained government control, Irish gang members went into law enforcement, the missionaries melded into various areas including health care and education, some Italian gangs improved in organized crime, many Jewish gang members went into entertainment, education, finance and other ventures", to in-all create white-collar crime, etc., original organized crime skills.

"Instead of bills from the Senate, we need programs for intervention and prevention that gang members can trust, not more jail cells or laws that add another layer of criminality. An extremely successful example of gang reformation was celebrated in April 2003, on the 10th anniversary of the historic signing of the gang truce initiated among four of L.A.'s housing projects. In 1992, when the city was on fire with riots and racial tensions, gang warfare had reached an unprecedented high, claiming approximately 1,900 lives. While a large faction of the city took to the streets rioting in the wake of the Rodney King verdict, former gang members were marching for peace through the volatile housing projects. The peace treaty designed by a Mr. Ralph Bunche between Egypt and Israel in 1949 was used as a model.

Former gang members and chosen representatives from each housing project redrafted the language of that peace agreement to fit the terms of their gang truce. It partly included the "United Black Community Code"-a list of do's and don'ts for gang members with the stated purpose of "taking the necessary steps towards the renewal of peace in Watts and Los Angeles as a whole." The code explains that, "No conflict of the land, that is, drive-by shootings and random slaying or any community representative organizations shall commit any warlike or hostile act against the other parties or against innocent civilians in the neighborhoods under the influence of that community representative (gang)." For the African American population, one of the initiating solutions could dwell in the creation of Africa-Towns, just as there are China Towns, instead of projects. The best bet is a spread of knowledge, with inspiration towards actions that benefit all.

In recent years, taser guns have become a weapon of choice to control minority and other students deemed to be dangerous elements. Adult creations of schools; such as the dilapidated one represented in the movie called "Lean on Me", constitute the will of the complacent and ignorant in various places. M26 Tasers are the most popular weapon with so-called law enforcement on the streets and, more recently, in schools nationwide.

The M26 and X26 tasers are used as equipment school officers. The guns fire electrified barbs that can shoot up to 21 feet and hit with a disabling charge. More and more money is invested in these types of measures, instead of positive reinforcement, counseling, and after-school programs. The same officials make it more and more difficult to attain, retain, and want to be a public school teacher. Here in 2004, laws like the so-called "No-Child Left Behind Act," are designed without the consultation of any common-sense commission including the people that matter the most in education, the teachers.

If required extra classes and or tests are actually needed to help the children be more successful, they should be free or at least ½ of the extra-ordinary costs, and available over the summertime. During such time, substitute teachers and special educational enrichment programs should be available for all students.

"Our government has kept us in a perpetual state of fear-kept us in a continuous stampede of patriotic fervor-with the cry of grave national emergency. Always there has been some terrible evil at home or some monstrous foreign power that was going to gobble us up if we did not blindly rally behind it..."

General Douglas MacArthur, 1957—U.S.A.

SLAVERY TODAY

The enslavement of women and children for free/low cost labor or sex for the patriarchal worldwide systems has been a very powerful business since the advent of colonialism, and even longer in some societies. From Spain to Sudan, India to Indiana, Russia to Rome, Botswana to Brazil, Thailand to El Salvador; more people are enslaved today than ever before because of evil principles, faulty senses of maturity, and desires for patriarchal capitalistic superiority. Several thousand poor people a day send their children to work, many not knowing what they are really forced to do. Thousands of poor Phillipino, Haitians, Brazilians, etc., send their children to work for the Elite class of people, and certain companies to help support their families back home.

It has been documented that the girls are sent to stock houses of prostitution, sold as disposable sex toys; the boys are used a free labor and disposable sex toys; and besides the system of false information, and economic strife perpetrated on the people, many children worldwide are kidnapped for these purposes into this billion dollar industry.

Sadly, most people believe slavery no longer exists, sorry! Indeed, there may be more slaves in the world than ever before (www.iabolish.com, 2004.) Modern slavery includes up to date forms of human bondage; forced labor, servile marriage, debt bondage, child labor, concubines, camel jockeys, cane cutters, fabric makers, road construction, weapon transporters, forests cutters/burners, drug smugglers, and forced prostitution. Modern slaves can be aged between a newborn, to a person about to die. What is needed is mass revolutionary change, inspired by revolution, not subtle reform, inspired by alterable changes, not so much from a bad harvest but due to a drinking or drug problem. Some have been filled by European American, and European capitalistic and materialistic corruption, and simply must have a car, television, or CD-Player, etc.

Sex slavery is now so entrenched in Thailand, that many girls accept their fate as just another way of life. The fear of AIDS has spawned an intense demand for girls who are supposedly disease-free. Thai-based sex slavers now seek out the very young and girls from other countries. Tens of thousands of girls from Burma, China, Africa, Eastern Europe, the Americas, and Cambodia are being lured and kidnapped into this system. An organization called "ECPAT," is waging an international campaign for Western countries to criminalize the sexual abuse of children by their own citizens in foreign countries.

For example, on March 1, 1995, the CPCR organized a raid on a brothel in Chiang Mai, Thailand's second-largest city, to free foreign girls who were held against their will. The girls were from the Akha hill tribe and were trafficked from Hong Kong, Darwin, Burma, and Thailand. The CPCR called in the CSD. The raid worked, the girls were rescued, and the pimps and mama-san were arrested. They were immediately released on bail, and after they disappeared, local Thai police were "too busy" to search and re-arrest them. The brothel is now functioning as before. Revolution is more effective than reform. The people must be organized with knowledge of the foundation, current status, and potential future they can create, before changing the world around them.

In the Sudan of 1988, one automatic weapon could be traded for six or seven child slaves. In 1989, a woman or child from the Dinka tribe of the Nile could be bought for $90. Some of the children have been trucked into Libya, according to the U.S. Embassy in Khartoum. They are stripped of their cultural, religious, and personal identities by Arab nomads; just like what they have done for centuries against Africans to take over Egypt, etc. The boys and men can be found staggering around on their tendons, which were cut because they refused to become Muslims. Just like in the Christian chattel slavery methods of the United States of its early years, those caught trying to escape are castrated; branded like cattle, loose a limb, or a publicly murdered.

Mauritania may have the world's largest concentration of chattel slaves. In 1993, the U.S. State Department estimated that up to 90,000 blacks live as the property of North African Arabs (known as Beydanes, or white Moors). Other sources add 300,000 part-time and ex-slaves, known as Haratins, and many continue to serve their owners out of fear or need. Local anti-slavery group El Hor ("The Free") estimated that as many as one million Haratins existed at any given time. Chattel slavery is the type of slavery most known through the study of U.S. history against the descendants of the African peoples in the Americas.

Africans in Mauritania that were converted to Islam over 100 years ago, in this way although the Koran forbids the enslavement of fellow Muslims. In this case race outranks religious doctrine. The Black Muslim slaves of Mauritania are forbidden to share the basic rights of Muslims in even the poorest of countries: They may not marry, attend school, or go to mosque. All of this is a part of the orchestrated attempts to suppress and default the African Peoples of the world to insignificance and destruction.

Over 20,000 sex slaves are trafficked into and throughout the U.S. in cities like San Francisco, Santa Fe, New York, Miami, Portland, etc., through an international cartel.

In some cases the prostitutes are rotated from one U.S. city to another to work as part of an avoidance of good law officials, and contractual service whether by force, or false aspiration of business. These types of actions were reported in an excellent article within the 2004, San Francisco Chronicle. As with many businesses, the multi-million dollar cartel exercises control of officials, media, and others when it can to prevent profit loss, discovery, and defamation.

Several countries have officials responsible for these and other crimes against humanity. Sad-fully, in the 3rd U.S. presidential debate of 2004, incumbent President—George Bush stated that he would not sign over the government officials under the review of the World Court, with a smirked statement of refusing accused government agents for trial. Aspects of the world court also have leniency towards calling the U.S. to pay reparations to the generation of Native Americans, and descendants of enslaved Africans. The recent situation with Iraq and governmental allowances, have been reported to have allowed 1000's of jobs to be offered to recruit corrupt police, military, mercenaries, and others that engaged in human rights abuses such as; torture, mass murder, apartheid, and other evil deeds through S. Africa, Israel, Augusto Pinochet of Chile, Slobodan Milosevic of Yugoslavia, etc.

How did a political assassin end up working for the U.S. government in Iraq? The answer illuminates an ominous aspect of what can happen when the business of war is handed over to the private sector. The United States and its allies have turned to private companies to fill tens of thousands of jobs once performed only by soldiers, from prison interrogators to bodyguards for high-ranking officials. To Iraqis, the corporate guards are indistinguishable from U.S. troops, with whom they often cooperate. Barely 2 out of 3 pre-employment screenings, disallow bad background persons to become employed. Media reports of killed soldiers may be as a result of the corrupt corporate soldiers actions, and increased instability could be coming. E.U. activities during this time tend to be somewhat ignored by worldwide media.

End of Chapter #7.)
To be continued…

Chapter 7

The Children

Several issues surround my causes for concern for children worldwide. In my opinion, there are four issues that can address just about every hindering factor of their success.
#1) Trained conceptions of positive and negative. #2) Parental Misunderstanding of their roles in reinforcing guidance. #3) Inappropriate Nourishment. #4.) Old & Better "Children's Rights"

#1) TRAINED CONCEPTIONS OF POSITIVE AND NEGATIVE:

The public school system of the United States, and various post-colonial schools today, teach kids how to steal, kill, make war, and the schoolyards tend to become Faith grounds. Most teachers and administrators either do not realize, or they do not have the ability to make realistic changes. The curriculum is partially controlled by the businesses that supply the materials, and officials in the various government agencies over the school districts. The general educational systems of the world do not satisfy the human consciousness needs of today for tomorrow.

The school systems that have been noted to be reaching to this goal, suddenly find themselves in budget cuts, and officials transfer funds away.

Politicians damage education by damaging budgets and creating over-testing of educators & students, without teacher participation in the decisions. The people involved and encouraging these ways should literally be considered white-collar criminals. In fact, they do more damage to the future of humanity than any government entity, including a military occupation. For any group of people to progress they must be in touch with the wisdom and history teachings of their ancestors. If all you see is your ancestors in chains as slaves, working only as servants to other peoples, requiring drugs for happiness, etc., 9–10 of those persons will follow that pattern of behavior subconsciously. When a race of people can't refer to pro-creative wisdom of their ancestors to adapt the world around them, they repeat the same mistakes, thus hindering any progress to becoming a true civilization.

Multiple interventions by parents with the help of school, community, and religious leaders can make a difference in stemming unwanted behavior. Families are the core group that has to address the root problems of mental, physical, spiritual neglect, and abuse. Allocation of the peoples tax funds into community/teacher, not administrator controlled education has been proven to be more beneficial to a society than any dollar amount spent on a war, creation of war, or intentional damage to the environment for multimillion dollar buildings. Research motivated, spiritually confident families and communities tend to be the ones that address societal problems that cause poverty, family destabilization, and other problems.

The formation of beliefs that older children (teens) are all wrong, and approaching those that express inappropriate emotional development with persecution is a part of the self-fulfilling prophecy which makes more and more juveniles unwitting candidates for the fast growing, government & private prison industrial-complex and its growing slave-labor populations. At best, the U.S. and other places are only striving to be better technocracies, not civilizations. Civilization is an advanced stage in social development that fully supports the educational, spiritual, and physical development of its people, with technological advancements for the enhancement of the society, in accordance with the needs of the people.

Technology; is the science of mechanical and industrial arts. A technocracy focuses the progression of the society on the tools it has, and the control measures it has on the access and education about the tools; it is not civilization. Computers, televisions, cars, missiles, planes, do not make a civilization. America has become an "imperialistic, semi-democracy, technocratic republic." The same is true for most European based societies.

According to many philosophers, the true purpose of the human is to serve humanity. Educational systems that administer false and psychologically degrading lessons, teach anti-humanism. Like other social structures by higher forms of life, human beings must think in order to survive. When you interfere with a bird's wings you may mess up its daily life, likewise for the human; when you tamper with a human's mind you muddle its daily life. Whose idea was it to start inducing mind-altering drugs to children and minorities now?

Difficulties we see today with children start both at home, and on the institutional level, from the top down, with the help of a few at the direct instruction level. It is not the fault of all teachers, some teachers that may or may not see this, challenge the process with their own styles, but overall there are not enough of them to effect true humanistic knowledge the right way for today. Certain people that love the status quo, or just poorly educated are in positions of power over education. They are the ones that truly control policy, funding, and direction, since the majority of parents are not unified, educated, and have beliefs that it is the teacher's fault.

The so-called educational system tells students the answers to questions on average, a few weeks or so before a test, and later they test your memory for the answer; this is not thinking, this is only memorizing. People that go through life relying solely on memory and not intellect don't do well. Any problem not remembered, cannot be dealt with. The current educational system is based on the memorization of lies, and planned behavior.

There are some that are embracing of this tactic, but like most people in these societies, teachers are trained to continue the currently established system of non-civilization.

The teacher may be trained to ask you, "What is American History, or how is European History remarkable?" If you do, and you told the teacher kidnapping, genocide, and theft, in addition to a few good things, the teacher may feel an emotional need to give you a lower grade, if the teacher has not been trained to truly teach, and/or is deficient in historical information. The same answer could be given with the question about patriotism. The female of a culture has always been the center of the society, even in the current patriarchal systems. Music is a key part of the expression and current tendency gauge of a society.

The lyrics of songs are no different that the telling of mythical tales to teach a way of life. The lyrics are meant to tell of a way of living, a condition of an object, or suggested way of behavior. People go to concerts in the thousands as developing girls are called bitches, sluts, hoes, etc., and developing boys are called pimps, gangsta's, Macs, playas, G's, and hustlers. At least 70% do not place a priority in the existence of themselves or the other, to challenge, or have the conscious foresight of positive ways of existence.

Again, many of the artists are also products of the systems structure to maintain and guide social structure, only a few realize how, and pursue wisdom-based lyrics. The people that purchase the lyrics are usually those integrated into the negative structures of life, but some are actually thinking people that study the problem in there own way to participate in the production of the world they want to live in.

Every form of African American music and dance is an extension of traditional African music and dance. As social struggles and advancements are called, the expressions created by the people change, to enhance the development. Gospel, Hip Hop, Jazz, etc., contain storytelling, as well as dances are a part of the generational transformations of African Culture, in the United States and other places around the world.

A relative of mine was Ma' Rainey, the mother of the Blues. The expression of her skills is responsible for much of the foundation of African American music today. Tony Joe White, Shirley Ellis, Sonya Sanchez, Cab Calloway, Isaac Hayes, are essentially rap artists too. Rap is a rhythmic music style based on poetic storytelling with direct influences from ancestral African Griots. Griots travel from village to village, carrying a message about life, or a situation, in rhythmic form to an audience, usually with compliments of music.

CONSUMER MANIPULATION

To actually produce and be a consumer of children's games that teach the process of murder, theft, rape, and other structures of destruction, symbolizes aspiration to the lower elements of existence, and social suicidal ambitions. This notion towards humanity and life in general is also prevalent for explanation in movies, and television, as some excuse for entertainment, usually based on the Roman cultural theme. Popularization of the theft of ancient places they call archeological sites, how to destroy a family, steal cars, etc., and how to be a hero protecting the same structure, are funded the most by the power groups over the display. The only proper place for this type of behavior in a civilization has been as an instruction of how bad societies work, history of corruption classes, rights and wrongs stories of life, and mental disability institutions.

Students should be minimally guided in their research of humanity worldwide, with all information present and at a level proper for comprehension. Poor excuses of examples for civilization like Ancient Rome, and the post-colonial nations of today, are improper role models for the creation of civilized peoples. Only the masses can change society; if they are guided to destruction, they will destroy; if they have the will, guidance, and thoughts for creation, they will create.

Memory is a good tool of the intellect, and intellect is a good tool of common sense. If a recording artist is violent, someone had to teach them, or allow them to develop into violence. You must be introduced to obscenity to even know it exists. Then you must be taught obscenity, to truly express obscenity. The same concept applies to being nationalist, having a human superiority complex (specieist), racist, etc. Learning can be defined as an experiential process resulting in a relatively permanent change in behavior, which cannot be explained by temporal states, maturation, or innate responses to tendencies. Without common sense, correct thinking is impossible. And when correct thinking turns into incorrect thinking, actions based on them lead to mistakes. If you don't know the history of the author of a book, you don't know what your reading. People write books, not gods. You're only reading 50% of the book when you don't have history of the author.

#2) PARENTAL MISUNDERSTANDING OF THEIR ROLES IN REINFORCING GUIDANCE.

Here I have an example of parenting by an Ancient Anahuac People;
The Mexicas (Indians) were especially interested in education. Boys and girls were carefully educated from birth. During the first years of life, fathers educated boys, while mothers took care of girls. Once family education was over, the children of the nobles and priests went to the calmecac, and all others went to the *tepochcalli*. The Aztecs believed that education was extremely valuable and insisted that boys, girls and young people attend school. Parents took active roles in the in school and at home educational process, throughout the age of the child. There were two main types of school, the so-called tepochcalli and the calm*cac. Boys and girls went to both, but were kept separate from each other.

The Tepochcalli was for the children of common families and there was one in each neighborhood. Here, children learned history, writing, myths, math, religion, family life, and Aztec ceremonial songs. Boys received intensive physical training, learned about agriculture, respect for women, and the community trades. Girls were educated to form a family, and learned the arts, writing, myths, mathematics, and economics. Everyone was to learn several languages. The calmecac were specialize schools for the children of the nobility, and served to form new military and religious leaders. Teachers were greatly admired throughout the society and given great benefits.

#3) INAPPROPRIATE NOURISHMENT

This is so simple that to write much more would be ridiculous! Besides what was mentioned earlier in the health chapter, the good foods in natural balance, supplementation with love, and interaction with appropriate friends & family lead to healthy children. Problems come from deficiencies, wisdom comes from knowledge, and relationship's comes from communication. Children learn nearly 80% of life from what they see and/or touch. What is around you, what you say, and what you do, may be three different things, but actions-to-life are what children naturally emulate. The arts are the skill area that over 85% of the youth participating in illegal activities have as their strongest area of thought. Engagement in relevant arts, benefit these types of children the most.

Remember that in the U.S. and many other countries, many people ingest entirely too much fluoride. Fluoride is one nutrient that if taken in large enough doses like in tap water and most brands of toothpaste, inhibit the already deficient absorption and use of magnesium, and other nutrients. This is another source of the medical problems of today. Persons with Diabetes Type II, Hypertension, Fatigue Syndromes, and some other problems tend to be severely deficient in the nutrient magnesium. This is one of many elements that have effective usages in the body that control the functions in the body preventing the development of the above health problems. A high amount of today's children ingest entirely too much sodium, salt, carbohydrates, and toxins in the USA and elsewhere, added with lower intake of fresh water.

The so-called lunch pre-made packages, kid juices, packaged noodles, and federally directed health codes for U.S. schools and other places are inappropriate poor quality nourishment sources. Children tend to get high doses of chemical pesticides, MSG, low grade or insufficient nutrients in daily diets. Along with the increasing prevalence of improper discipline measures by more and more parents, the mind and body of a child becomes out of form with the normal behaviors needed in a social support society.

The behavior on a mass level steadily degenerates to struggles for survival, hysteria, and growth in servitude behavior in institutions of violence. This also results in the multitude of directed, and calculated medications set out for children, benefiting the financial gains of the pharmaceutical cartel. In measure only a 1/16th of the children, at most, that are getting medicines for ADHD are actually true candidates in need of a little extra help. The rest are victims of deficits.

Humans are social animals. We learn from observation, much more than from words. Children record and emulate the behavior of those they are connected with, towards self-development. If a child observes and/or is encouraged to be a liar, lazy, or cheat, beyond a 1–2 time possible experimentation for attention, maybe he/she sees the behavior in you? All adults that participate in the lives of children, whether as a parent, sibling, relative, neighbor, or even just as a passing by person, should realize that learning eyes and ears are observing you. The old statement saying, "you have two eyes, two ears, two nostrils, two hands, two feet, and one mouth," mean a lot. I cannot describe the other senses here besides intuition. We as humans tend to learn more from one or a combination with other senses, than just talking.

Like most mammals, the human brain needs multiple types of academic, sensory, and physical learning stimulation. The ages from 3 months to 6 years are the most basic and critical time frame to stimulate mental aptitude towards advanced conceptions. The most basic stimulatory actions for children of virtually all ages includes co-reading with teenagers; whether they like it or not, it helps to enhance academic and other mental abilities in a positive manner with time. There is almost no reason that students should require special-day classes, with the exception of an actual medically diagnosed damage in development or processing ability. The minds of children around the world are drastically becoming less stimulated with inadequate learning factors; therefore reducing the potential for the advancement of humanity.

It should be common knowledge that positive parental involvement enhances student motivation, raised graduation rates, lowered and/or ends drug and alcohol use, absence of the need for gang development/involvement, higher enrollment into colleges and universities. Today's main problem is that the children of children are attending today's schools.

**Stop the Spread of Germs in Schools, etc.,
Fast Facts**

- Approximately 1/5 of the U.S. population attends or works in schools. (U.S. Dept of Ed, 1999).

- Some viruses and bacteria can live from 20 minutes up to 2 hours or more on surfaces like cafeteria tables, doorknobs, and desks. (Ansari, 1988; Scott and Bloomfield, 1989)

- Nearly 22 million school days are lost annually due to the common cold alone. (CDC, 1996)

- Addressing the spread of germs in schools is essential to the health of our youth, our schools, and our nation.

- Students need to get plenty of sleep and physical activity, drink water, and eat good food to help them stay healthy in the winter and all year.

- U.S. Center for Disease Control, 2004.

U.S. Center for Disease Control, 2004.

BULLYING

Bullying: The act of repeated and systematic harassment and/or attacks on others by individuals or groups. When done through children, it is an area of behavior that if stopped, can make a big difference in how peace on earth is made, in their future.

Forms of this behavior include:

* Physical Violence, and Attacks

* Verbal taunts, Name-calling, and Put-downs

* Threats and Intimidation

* Extortion, Stealing of Money, and/or Possessions

* Cheating through Intimidation

* Exclusion from the Peer Group

Racial and sex based verbal abuse are general basics of bullying too. This behavior is seen throughout all societies as examples of the poor parentage and weak social structure.

An average of 20% of the worlds students from Pre-School through College are involved. The lack of traditional structures leading to peaceful resolution, sharing, and knowledge of self, exacerbate the problem. A developing bully is a student who is aggressive, swindling, or taught to use confidence over timid persons for personal gain to dominate those deemed not to be able to retaliate, or act in an assertive manner. This can be a girl or a boy. Cuteness on the outside is limited to the outside. Beauty from the inside must be nurtured.

If you went or go to current K-12 schools, you probably realized that older students tend to bully younger ones, or wealthier students tend to bully those from less financially secure situation. As with other interpersonal violence; such as dating violence, child abuse, and domestic abuse, the power imbalance conception of supremacy tends to be a main factor in understanding. This is a cycled behavior in many people that learned these ways as acceptable through academic lessons of colonial history, parental structures allowing child dominance and/or consistent subversion to child wants, trained/or modeled behavior of parent/guardian conflict resolution methods, or through a medical problem.

Rates of bullying are the same or higher in England, the United States, Japan, Ireland, Australia, and the Netherlands, Brazil, among other countries learning from the Euro-centric model of education. Patterns of bullying and victimization are very different for boys and girls. Boys are much more likely to report being bullies, and perpetrating violent acts on others than are girls, at each age. Girls are less likely than boys to be the victims of physical bullying, but that fact is quickly changing. Girls are more likely to use indirect, subtle, social means to harass other girls; like social exclusion, manipulation of friendship relationships, spreading rumors, etc.

A lack of attention and affection toward the child, together with modeling of aggressive behavior at home, and poor supervision of the child, provide the perfect conditions for aggressive and bullying behavior to develop. Parental teaching of aggressive behavior may include use of physical and verbal hostility toward the child by parents, or use of physical and verbal aggression by parents toward each other. Children who are impulsive in temperament may be more inclined to develop into bullies. Bullying problems can be greatly reduced in severity by appropriate supervision, intervention and climate in a school. Just as low levels of supervision in the home are associated with the development of a bully in individual children; as well as low levels of mass control in schools, particularly on the playground, or schoolyard, and in the hallways. Also, the appropriateness of interventions by adults when they see bullying, or are made aware of it are extremely important.

The act of fund misappropriation and fund cutting for character education and school staffing is another prime reason for the problems of today's children and loss of teachers.

The social climate in the school needs to be one where there is warmth and acceptance of all students, and one where there are high standards for student, teacher, and administrator behaviors. Teacher attitudes toward aggression, and skills with regard to supervision and intervention, partly determine how teachers will react to bullying situations.

Curriculum, administrative policies, and parental support are integral for student success. Sometimes the placement of inadequate administrators is the sole cause and facilitator of a school, or college's problems. Most times it is the inaction of the parents rightful place to contribute.

PARENTING

Currently, more than 200 million children worldwide now live apart from their father or mother. In a typical year, well over one-third of the children of the U.S. will not see their dad. Well over half of all European-American children and three-quarters of African-American children born since 1975 have or will live some portion of their shaping years with only one parent, usually without dad, by social design. Children with little or no contact with stable/correct fathers, or father role persons, are more likely to drop out of school, become involved in drug and/or alcohol abuse, engage in criminal activities; while girls are more likely to become pregnant as teens, focus on inappropriate mate choices, and other self-destructive behaviors. Training and allowance of corporal punishment could be one of greatest benefits to the future, as discipline is a factor of fear most parents have

The greatest problems exist because of the lack of faith traditions, communication, and relationship building in the family. In many cases, the average of the late twentieth to mid twenty-first century parent exhibits the need for some sort of parent certification, or rite of passage. An added problem is that songs praising and motivating good fathers have tended to not be accepted by the current music control agencies. Traditionally, the act of raising a child has not been limited to one or two parents, in any culture. The old African Proverb stating: "It takes a village to raise a child," refers to the role of the uncles, aunts, grandparents, and other persons in a society, playing a direct and indirect role in the development and protection of the child.

Parenting is a complex lifestyle that includes the benefit of several adults and should naturally include elders. At virtually any age, and any moment, a child can lock you in their thoughts as the role model at that moment in time. Emulation is one of the greatest factors in repetitive learning, and can be the greatest compliment to the confident expression of awareness. The ability to form decisions are among the highest levels of world conception that must be enhanced through information and experiences the child should develop, so she/he will not develop into a sole-servant of others.

Being able to live in a supportive father-mother relationship through absolute involvement provides excellent social learning opportunities for all children. When the male and female role models, usually father and mother, are truly partners in parenting, developmental challenges of the children and each other are normally constructive. Even with and after disputes, the individuals tend to become enhanced persons and a better group through the learning stages, and progression through life. There has been a traditional overemphasis in women's lives on the mother's role and a corresponding under-emphasis in men's lives on the father's role within the western European social structure. This structure is self-destructive when absorbed in action by other cultures.

The high divorce, and poor socialization structures of various populations of African Americans, and other peoples in the U.S. are an excellent example of internal family struggle. The female, even as a young girl, has the importance of motherhood consistently brought to her attention. On the other hand, the male, usually hears little about his potential responsibilities until he is just about to become a father. This gender double standard has contributed to the frequent and unfortunate one-sided responsibility of mothers, high divorce rates, poor family structures, growing needs for orphanage type institutions, and confusion throughout societies.

Neither gender has tended to be educated about the socialization needs to be in a relationship during the late half of the 20ᵗʰ century, in any mass level. Children have and are using role models they see in the media, and from any sporadically observed individual that they may believe is an acceptable role model. Sadly enough, nearly 60% of the children in the world have no-stable positive adult role model.

TYPES OF DOMESTIC ABUSE CHILDREN EMULATE FROM ADULT ACTIONS

Sexual
The treatment of women/girls as sex objects, using dress codes that make them uncomfortable—under threat, having affairs with other women/man, forcing sex for the purpose of non-consensual pleasure,(rape) leading to harm, (sometimes in the opposite sex role, the woman does this to the man)

Physical
The pushing, slapping, punching, biting, home restricting, throwing of objects, purposeful abandonment in a dangerous situation, rape, refusal to assist the other during illness, threatening or injuring with or without a weapon.

Verbal/Emotional
Purposely ignoring the other person's feelings continuously over long time periods, ridiculing, or insulting women as a group (or men as a group), ridiculing or insulting a person's most valued beliefs, withholding approval, keeping a person from working, abusing pets, threatening to kidnap children.

Financial
This includes the lack of providing financial resources to support the victim and/or children, denying access to joint financial information, denial of income earnings, taking earnings away in the desire to control. (This does not include loving assistance in spending control in joint, or habitual spending resistance help)

> *Children learn more from the seen, heard, and felt, than just what is told.*
> *The role model is you!*

BASIC EDUCATION

In addition to the earlier chapter on education, this is a condensed focus on some applied education methods.

To tell a student to study hard, that math is hard, athletes are not suppose to be academically inclined, or to encourage more failure from a low esteem, or struggling student is an attack on them. Everyone knows that students need to be re-assured towards writing in-line, making certain math is written in column order, and that double-checking information should be encouraged.

THINGS TEND TO BE REMEMBERED IN THE FOLLOWING SCALE:

- Reading only 10 %

- Hearing 20%

- Seeing 30%

- Seeing & Hearing 50%

- Talking 70%

- And: Talking & Handling by 90%

Low nutrition, and/or abstract teaching of many subject's leaves a lot of learning to be boring, and irrelevant to the average student. Next to the statements saying math is hard, and low parental involvement in homework assistance, this is a main factor in the status of academic deficiencies. The computer is not the best tool for math, or other academic encouragement tools, but it is a good one. Whether you, or a student that is a visual, auditory, mobile, collective, operative, or informal learner, a combination of learning style practices for any combination group of learners will enhance comprehension of almost any subject.

Actions come with positive motivation and expectation. The separation of the average student group, per general education ability, can help focus identification of abilities.

If the separated groups are gradually integrated in accordance with general adaptability to specific peer-assistance, over time the general group of student will grow to the expectations that should be reinforced as a mass group. Active reading is among the best methods of reading.

Students should have the opportunity to engage in short discussion groups, and create questions through the reading they do. This is a group of ways that a student can go from remembering 25% of a reading, to at least 80% of a reading. Studying smart is better than studying hard. The best processes for studying must be researched in available videos, books, and through personal style development as the person recognizes what works for them.

THE GREATEST PROBLEMS IN TODAY'S SOCIETIES ABOUT YOUTH TEND TO BE THE FOLLOWING:

- How to nourish children properly
- How to educate them
- How to Discipline them
- How to impart values
- Disengagement from games of living for good, to those of killing and theft.
- How to prepare them to live a happy life
  *Sporadic positive myth/real hero's.
- Children raised by undisciplined youth inundated the schools, forcing teachers to spend more time focusing on disruptive and rude behavior, instead of teaching.

"3/4 of the time it is the fault of the general society, 1/8 health, 1/8 bad schools."

Every race of human has a certain characteristic that is natural. Some of the African-American student attributes are that they have been found to naturally be more empathetic and insightful than their European American counterparts in general. This type of finding can partially be attributed to those in stable positive families. Resistance from students of various cultures in classrooms today is due to the failure to recognize that they are being asked to replace one communication style with another or rather, or one world-view with another placing them unequal or lower. Everyone has a different cognitive style. The main problem with the most known school systems is that the teachers are not allowed, or taught to teach.

Many are trained to give answers to questions, train students to memorize statements, and test based on set testing times to guide the student towards serving the institutions of society. As students in this system develop maturity of thought, or have the developed cognitive reasoning to question the knowledge they have gained, they attempt to search for accurate information, or information counter to what has been told to them in natural rebellious aptitudes for self-discovery, and untold aspects of wisdom not taught but hungered for. Is it dangerous to be right, when the government is wrong?

Education and other parts of life rely partly on the information given by symbols. Intentional and unintentional symbols and images; must be examined by every people with children in foreign schools, and schools focused for the children of other races. A curriculum of universal inclusion of all can be created for multi-cultural societies, but some level of centralization per the relevance to the cultures of the area is generally required to make a fully successful system.

The curriculum must not only include the classical civilizations in the social studies of the various peoples in a population, it must include math, science, metaphysics, and arts in the various forms from throughout the world.

PRESENT (OLD VERSION NEEDING IMPROVEMENTS) UNITED NATIONS HIGH COMMISSIONER FOR HUMAN RIGHTS
Declaration of the Rights of the Child Proclaimed By: General Assembly Resolution 1386 (XIV) of November 20, 1959

Whereas the peoples of the United Nations have, in the Charter, reaffirmed their faith in fundamental human rights, and in the dignity and worth of the human person, and have determined to promote social progress and better standards of life in larger freedom,
Whereas the United Nations has, in the Universal Declaration of Human Rights, proclaimed that everyone is entitled to all the rights and freedoms set forth therein, without distinction of any kind, such as race, color, sex, language, religion, political or other opinion, national or social origin, property, birth or other status,
Whereas the child, By: reason of his physical and mental immaturity, needs special safeguards and care, including appropriate legal protection, before as well as after birth.
Whereas the need for such special safeguards has been stated in the Geneva Declaration of the Rights of the Child of 1924, and recognized in the Universal Declaration of Human Rights and in the statutes of specialized agencies and international organizations concerned with the welfare o f children, statues of specialized agencies and international organizations concerned with the welfare of children,
Whereas mankind owes to the child the best it has to give, Now therefore, The General Assembly Proclaims this Declaration of the Rights of the Child to the end that he may have a happy childhood and enjoy for his own good and for the good of society the rights and freedoms herein set forth, and calls upon parents, upon men and women as individuals and upon voluntary organizations, local authorities and national Governments to recognize these rights and strive for their observance By: legislative and other measures progressively taken in accordance with the following principles:

Principle 1
The child shall enjoy all the rights set forth in this Declaration. All children, without any exception whatsoever, shall be entitled to these rights, without distinction or discrimination on account of race color, sex, language, religion, political or

other opinion, national or social origin, property, birth or other status, whether of himself or of his family.

Principle 2
The child shall enjoy special protection, and shall be given opportunities and facilities, By: law and By: other means, to enable him to develop physically, mentally, morally, spiritually and socially in a healthy and normal manner and in conditions of freedom and dignity. In the enactment of laws for this purpose the best interests of the child shall be the paramount consideration.

Principle 3
The child shall be entitled from his birth to a name and nationality.

Principle 4
The child shall enjoy the benefits of social security. He shall be entitled to grow and develop in health; to this end special care and protection shall be provided both to him and to his mother, including adequate prenatal and postnatal care. The child shall have the right to adequate nutrition, housing, recreation and medial services.

Principle 5
The child who is physically, mentally or socially handicapped shall be given the special treatment, education and care required By: his particular condition.

Principle 6
The child, for the full and harmonious development of his personality, needs love and understanding. He shall, wherever possible, grow up in the care and under the responsibility of his parents, and in any case in an atmosphere of affection and of moral and material security; a child of tender years shall not, save in exceptional circumstances, be separated from his mother. Society and the public authorities shall have the duty to extend particular care to children without a family and those without adequate means of support. Payment of state and other assistance toward the maintenance of children of large families is desirable

Principle 7
The child is entitled to receive education, which shall be free and compulsory, at least in the elementary stages. He shall be given an education, which will promote his general culture, and enable him on a basis of equal opportunity to develop his abilities, his individual judgment, and his sense of moral and social responsibility, and to become a useful member of society. The best interests of the child shall be the guiding principle of those responsible for his education and guidance; that responsibility lies in the first place with his parents. The child shall have full

opportunity for play and recreation, which should be directed to the same purpose, as education; society and the public authorities shall endeavor to promote the enjoyment of this right.

Principle 8
The child shall in all circumstances be among the first to receive protection and relief

Principle 9
The child shall be protected against all forms of neglect, cruelty and exploitation. He shall not be the subject of traffic in any form. The child shall not be admitted to employment before an appropriate minimum age; he shall in no case be caused or permitted to engage in any occupation or employment that would prejudice his health or education, or interfere with his physical, metal or moral development.

Principle 10
The child shall be protected from faiths, which may foster racial, religious and any other form of discrimination. He shall be brought up in a spirit of understanding, tolerance, friendship among peoples, peace and universal brotherhood and in full consciousness that his energy and talents should be devoted to the service of his fellow men.

AUTHORS IMPROVED VERSION
FOR THE UNITED NATIONS HIGH COMMISSIONER
FOR HUMAN RIGHTS
A DECLARATION OF CHILDREN'S RIGHTS

This version contains universal directed principles, recognition of girls, caregivers for parentless children, acknowledgement of nature, and acknowledgement of true heritage.

Principle 1
All children, without exception, shall be entitled to these rights, without distinction or discrimination on account of race, color, sex, language, religion, political status, or social origin.

Principle 2
All children shall enjoy special protection, given self-productive opportunities and facilities, by: law, cultural change, and By: other means, to enable her/him to develop physically, mentally, morally, spiritually and socially in a healthy and

normal manner and in conditions of freedom and dignity for the benefit of self, the environment, society, and future children. In the enactment of laws for this purpose the best interests of the child shall be the paramount consideration.

Principle 3
The child shall be entitled from his/her birth to a name, nationality, and education with central focus on the child's true ancestral heritage.

Principle 4
The child shall enjoy the benefits of social security. She/He shall be entitled to grow and develop in health; to this end special care and protection shall be provided both to her/him and to proper parents/caregivers, including adequate prenatal and postnatal care. The child shall have the right to correct nutrition, safe housing, adequate recreation and medical services.

Principle 5
The child who is physically, mentally or socially handicapped shall be given the special treatment, education and care required By: her/his particular condition.

Principle 6
The child, for the full and harmonious development of her/his personality, needs love and understanding. She/He shall, wherever possible, grow up in the care and under the responsibility of the parents/caregivers, and in any case in an atmosphere of affection and of moral and material security; a child of tender years shall not, save in exceptional circumstances of torturous abuse, terminal danger, or supervising caregiver/parent request, be separated from the caregiver/parent. Society and the public authorities shall have the duty to extend particular care to children without a family and those without adequate means of support. Employment assistance, and entrepreneurial opportunities, and all accessible forms of self-improvement education shall be primary offers to all families & potential families.

Principle 7
All Children are entitled to receive true education, which shall be free, required, and contain the most accurate historical lessons (history, science, art, and math) of the world, from the perspectives of the indigenous and colonial peoples, without inspiration of bias. She/He shall be given an education, which will promote his general culture, respect of nature, and enable her/him on a basis of equal opportunity, to develop her/his full abilities, her/his individual judgment & creativity, and her/his sense of moral and social responsibility to become a useful member of society, to inspire the future that is collectively desired among there generation.

The best interests of the child shall be the guiding principle of those responsible for her/his education and guidance; that responsibility lies in the first place with her/his parents/caregivers/guardian(s). The child shall have full opportunity for play and recreation, which should be directed to the same purpose, as education; society and the public authorities shall endeavor to promote the enjoyment of this right, under full security and protection.

Principle 8
The child shall in all circumstances be among the first to receive protection and relief, in the case of disaster, or accident.

Principle 9
The child shall be protected against all forms of neglect, cruelty and exploitation. She/He shall not be the coerced to become the subject of illegal activities in any form. The child shall not be admitted to employment before an appropriate minimum age decided By: country vote; she/he shall in no case be caused or permitted to engage in any occupation or employment which would prejudice her/his health, or education, or interfere with her/his physical, mental, or moral development. Financial benefit to the minor shall only be given as earned benefit for benefit of family, self-gratitude, legal child-controlled business, or a motivational lesson/tool for understanding social purpose.

Principle 10
The child shall be protected from Faiths, which may foster racial, human supremacy, religious and all other forms of destructive prejudice. She/He shall be brought up in a spirit of understanding, tolerance, and friendship among peoples, peace and universal consciousness that her/his energy and talents should be devoted to the service of our world.

Principle 11.
Each student is to receive development for the ability to understand, respect and accept people of different races; sexes; cultural heritage; national origins; religions; political, economic, social backgrounds, values, beliefs, and attitudes."

Principle 12.
Each child shall be given accurate knowledge, skills training, and behavior education which enables development of self-esteem;" as well as "the ability to maintain physical, mental, and emotional health."

Chapter 8

Extra Knowledge

HISTORY/HERSTORY USE OF THE COWRIE SHELL

Cowrie shells originally were obtained from East Africa's Coasts & the Ivory Coast of West Africa. In ancient history, the Cowrie was one measure of currency much like the dollar—in fact they are still in use in some parts of the world (such as Nigeria). This was used from the east coast to the west coast as currency, and even in ancient intercontinental trade in Asia and the America's by Nubians, Kushites, Mali's, Yoruba, etc., etc.

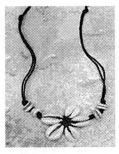

Though it has become one of the symbols of the African continent, it is fact that the Cowrie played such an important role as money in ancient China that its pictograph was adopted in their written language for money. Thus it is not surprising that among the earliest countable metallic money or coins were cowries made of bronze or copper, in Ancient Southern Africa and China.

The Cowrie Speaks...through divination, patakies (sacred stories of the Yoruba) in which the Orisa (prophet) relate proper moral, spiritual as well as everyday methods to solve conflicts, through Ebo's (sacrifice), the Cowrie speaks! The cowrie is the mouth of the Orisas since it is used in divination. There are related stories about the cowrie that teach about being humble and respectful to your elders, that help the cowrie to have the attributes it has historically as well as today.

If you are attracted to cowries it could mean that you are a son/daughter of Yemaya, a Yoruba ocean spirit associated with wealth and mother earth. **It is a powerful symbol about Africa,** which people generally associate with Africans in America or Africans on the Continent wearing it. It is said to raise the energy and bless those that wear them.

SOME ANCIENT TECHNOLOGIES

Ancient Kemet (Egypt) developed many of the scientific technologies we use today, with many found as three dimension diagrams. Reflections of scientific knowledge and achievement can be found throughout the world in various ancient civilizations. Some centered on the formation of electromagnetic energies. Pictures and tangible evidence show work in the fields of biology, chemistry, dentistry, ship building, aeronautics, geometry, algebra, physics, electromagnetic energies, surgical technologies, etc.

Much of the interpretation is left to those in our timeline to decipher, as creations and theories are based on the observational perspective of the environment at the time. Every sacred symbol of to the gods had esoteric, and scientific purposes. An assumed cathode-ray tube from the "Temple of Hathor" depicts a source of heavy ions, powered by a battery. The walls are decorated with human figures next to bulb-like objects reminiscent of oversized light bulbs. Inside these "bulbs" there are snakes in wavy lines.

The use of electrochemical processes in Kemet, and in ancient Babylonia, cut-crystal lenses have been found. That process can only be done by the use of the element cesium oxide, which is only produced with an electrochemical process. Crystal cut lenses were used to create astronomical lenses. The info on this may be available in the book called "Chariot of the Gods". Archeological pictographs may interpret this activity as the snakes pointed tails from a lotus flower, interpreted as the socket of the bulb. This could be seen as similar to wires leading to a small box. Adjacent to it stands a two-armed djed pillar as a symbol of power, which is connected to the snake. This scene might not be the accurate interpretation.

Some of the common architectural structures around the world are the arch, dome, and pyramids. The origins of the ability to create these structures started from the Shona Civilization of what is now called Zimbabwe. Through the centuries, the creation of these structures and other technologies were enhanced in Africa, and further developed in different ways after they were taught to other peoples around the world. Among the most commonly represented structures known in today's educational system are the proliferation of pyramids.

Within China, the "Great White Pyramid" of "Xian, China" is about 300 meters high. It is found in the official place called Tibet, in the Qin Ling Shan Mountains. There are over 100 pyramids, made of clay, that have become nearly stone hard over the centuries. Many are damaged by erosion or farming. One pyramid is as large as the Pyramid of the Sun of Teotihuacan in Mexico. The Burma Tibetan Pyramid is called—The Pyramid of Gathering. In the Bhutan Province the preserved limestone white pyramid is said to glow under starlight.

> "A great revolution of character in just a single individual will help achieve a change in the destiny of a society, and further, will enable a change in the destiny of humankind."
>
> Dr. Daisaku Ikeda, The Human Revolution

> Thought without action is empty. Just as action without thought is blind. If you are not involved in actions for the people, you are working against the people. One cannot simply think of creating peace, you must act for it. There is no gray area here. If you are not involved for the benefit of the masses of the oppressed, by your inactivity, you are against the people, and for the enemy!
>
> (The Late Honorable) Dr. Kwame Ture

Azteca Pyramid

Pyramid in Xian, China.

A Kemetic (Egyptian) Pyramid

This is an element of proof: Global Trade, Civilizations, and Peace existed before what we have at this time.

The names given to everything in the Universe vary from culture to culture. With respect to our Solar System, the myths of the Egyptian Gods may describe the history of our Solar System:

Amen-Ra = Sun,
Tefenet = Comets
Hathor = Super Nova,
Geb = Earth,
Nut= Moon,
Heh Twins= Venus + Mercury,
Isis = Jupiter,
Nephthys = Saturn,
Seth/Horus = Mars, and
Osiris = Asteroids

These are only a few of the entities that represent other elements of the universe.

"The process of *initiation* concerns undergoing a fundamental set of rites to start a new phase or beginning in life. It marks the passing from one phase in life to the next more mature phase. *Initiation* fundamentally has to do with transformation, and has been a central component of traditional African cultures since time immemorial. The details of the rites vary among the different societies, but these rites are nevertheless basic components of the society as they help guide the person from one stage in life into the next stage of one's life and development, that is, from birth to death and beyond." "A rite is a fundamental act (or set of rituals) performed according to pre-scribed social rules and customs."

(http://www.manuampim.com, 10/16/04)

The learning of these processes and modernized applications can create a perfect society.

The life stories of these, and other peoples in world history can provide excellent character base for people around the world: *MOCTEZUMA, BUDDHA, MUHAMMAD, SHIVA, SOLOMAN, ISIS, SHAKA, NZINGA, SITTING BULL, ADONIS, HERCULES, KALAUKA, among a few others.*

TRANSLATED EXCERPT OF
HUMAN LIFE DEVELOPMENT

The following is a generalizing compilation of the rites of passage of
various cultures around the world.

RITE OF BIRTH—When a person's name reflects their life's purpose, this can help keep focus on life's work.

RITE OF ADULTHOOD—"One who learns, Teaches." A person not only must have a level of aged wisdom, he/she must also be systematically initiated into adulthood. Social and moral responsibilities must be clarified and recited in clear actions in order to be regarded as an adult, in respect to other.

RITE OF MARRIAGE—Marriages formed between individuals that don't have birth or adulthood rites accomplished, do not work. If both individuals have clear focus in life, or at least one that does not and the other has a need to care take for the other, they would also know how to best support the other partner's purpose. You marry the person, the purpose, and needs. Sometimes one, or both are in progress towards the purpose.

RITE OF ELDERSHIP—Persons that have the ability to recite progressive lives can provide organization, direction, and effective leadership, for a society in a collective manner. This is the true role of the elder in virtually every ancient advanced civilization. There is no reason that the last few hundred years or less over-ride the primary and advanced needs for any societies balance by its elders.

RITE OF ANCESTORSHIP—A society, and each individual should select an ancestor in there prayers. This level of respect for one or more relatives that have passed on, or another individual or group of people of kinship is healthy for the spiritual empowerment of each person. Many people pass on not knowing that they have served as a hero model to anyone.

SOCIALIZATION

Fundamental human growth and development depends of the processes of social development. In the basic establishment of family orientation for the child, and progression through life, a system of a rite of passage has been developed in virtually every human family. Each action for life enhances the potential of each involved. The processes of this can be observed through study of the overall society, during casual situations involving children, and very likely can be remembered in your own family situations through childhood.

PARANORMAL

Abilities like those many call Psychic, Clairvoyant, Empathic, Telepathic, etc., or other abilities are only examples of person that have stronger, or accepted natural abilities. There is nothing supernatural, because everything is natural. Less advanced civilizations tend to deny translations and self-understood intrinsic knowledge of the powers of prayer and life energy. Spiritual Science is a term used by the Ausar Auset Society, an Afro centric level spiritual organization. It is an objective, and subjective term, used for the description of ancient wisdom teachings of all of the now called "special abilities" of such people. The abilities are evident in dogs, cats, and some other mammals according to historical tales, and modern day scientists in the European (including the U.S.) and Asian countries. Gordon-Michael Scallion is a futurist, teacher of consciousness studies and author of the best selling book Notes from the Cosmos: A Futurist's Insights into the World of Dream Prophecy and Intuition. His texts are among the best in this field of research.

Prophesies in virtually every religion, have been written or said in the language of the day, but translations into modern language shows most of them to be accurate to today. Most for the future is told as potentials that can be altered for positive or negative outcomes. Nostradamus is a very famous psychic of a few centuries ago that is most known about in the United States. Many like John Edwards, Astara, Nancy Matz, Cynthia Sue Larson, Monique Chapman PhD., and others, are only a few examples of the growing natural abilities of the human species. There are of almost always few pretenders out of any group examined for ability. If you announce a talent show, at least 60% people will either be very talented, and 40% just want the attention, or the opposite. Sometimes only 5–10% will truly have the abilities.

Mediums, Psychics, Empaths, are only examples of people born with a part of our natural evolutionary abilities. The abilities to do these, and other things may be observed to an extent by other life forms, but humans have a unique natural ability to train and focus there abilities, if there body chemistry allows for its active use. ESP (extra-sensory perception) may not be a proper term. With the number of people having either a minuscule, or major controllable aware ability, exact premonition dreams, remote event awareness, etc., in the general population, the abilities cannot be described simply as an extra ability. They can only be defined as a natural ability, of which, a percentage of the population is not aware of, or is deficient in the ability to express.

Late 2001 to 2012 seems to hold the basic elements of initiating WWIII, and other events of devastation, crowning the achievements of the colonial era. Like many people, I am also aware that the orientation of the future is alterable. The future is a constant path with many directions on the subsistence of the circle of existence. The region from Poland to Turkey will see great turmoil. A great Holy War will be born in this region, ending with the purification of the land by fire and water.

Unclear health conditions leading to the death of a key Islamic Cleric, help to elevate to the beginning of WWIII. The Non-Hebrew leaders of Israel choose to use nuclear weapons to protect themselves. A group of former Soviet Union states, China, North Korea, and the Arab League will take a part in the initiating what is called Armageddon. A measure of 80% of the human population will perish in the first three hours of nuclear exchange. Many national capitals, military instillations, and economic center cities in the U.S., E.U. Russian Federation, Arab League State, and some other places are targets of nuclear annihilation. In the U.S. Los Angeles, Dallas, Miami, New York, and Travis AFB; in Europe: London, Madrid, Paris, Hamburg, Venice, Rome, and Liverpool, among other places around the world.

Sorry, I cannot post the "Future Map of the Earth"
http://www.matrixinstitute.com/futuremap.html
(Purchase of the map is recommended)

POTENTIAL NEGATIVE FUTURES

<u>Potential Year 2000—2070 Developments:</u>

(a) More major biological warfare agents made by either the E.U. or U.S. spread worldwide.
This is to be seen as another effort to retain control of others.

(b) Radical environmental damage from certain humans becomes realized, and retribution is begins.

(c) Major astronomical event will inspire worldwide changes in behavior.

(d) The African Union and other indigenous peoples regain sustaining and supportive control of lands and life.

(e) Nuclear exchange between Russia, and others. United States hit in early A.M. and late P.M. Targets are military, metropolitan, and trade cities. (Year-) Due to changing aspects of our present, the exact dates repeatedly change.

(f) Dictatorship of China orders troops to circle Japan, assist actions in the westernmost nations of Asia.

(g) United States collapses due to economic, social, and natural disasters.

The beginning of the return of the guidance to civilization has begun to return to the charge of the indigenous Africans, Asians, Islanders, and peoples of the America's, as knowledge of self is spread. It is written in virtually every holy book of the worlds civilizations, that there is to be damage to the earth, a plague of a people representing evil & worshiping destruction, a great cleansing, and a rejuvenation by those that deserve the honor of care-taking the earth, and building harmony. The ancestors of those that have committed mass crimes against the world, are developing to destroy themselves, as part of the great transformation to a positive world leadership of humanity, based on consciousness, not colonialism.

ALIENS

Now, this topic is usually coincided with the area of Paranormal, and many people have misgivings towards the existence of other forms of life, outside of our planet. This is another example of closed-minded specie-ist behavior.

Throughout human history in every continent, the story; usually metaphoric, tells of a message, visit, or examination type abduction. Stories can be found in the spiritual stories around the world, particularly those that state a mystical light, or special unnatural event from the sky. Implanted odd metal chips that give off a mildly detectable signal, and scars are among the few physical evidence markers that thousands of people have provided along with physical descriptions.

Crop circles are among the many particulars of suggestive evidence. One of the most recent news broadcasts were of a multiple sighting of an alien spacecraft in Mexico, near an ancient city, during Spring-2004. What are projects Blue Book & the Majestic-12? There are 46 known stars in this galaxy that are sun-like stars. This is a map of the 11-known nearby life-sustaining stars, as of 1987.

Fear of more advanced species is as dumb as fear of greeting your friends great-grand parents. Such behavior is genetically endemic to one species of human, and is learned behavior by others.

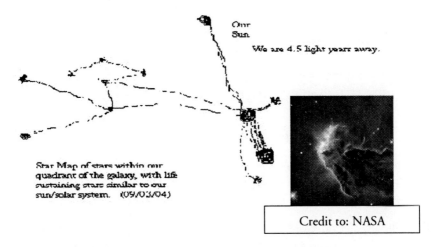

Our Sun

We are 4.5 light years away.

Star Map of stars within our quadrant of the galaxy, with life sustaining stars similar to our sun/solar system. (09/03/04)

Credit to: NASA

SOME BENEFICIAL WAR TECHNOLOGY

Science in harmony with nature, for the good of all, can harvest incredible future & present benefits. Author and genius Margaret Cheney—published "Tesla" a book that advanced public knowledge of energy, gravity, and matter conversion. Scientist. John Hatcherson is one person that has made great strides in the understanding of electromagnetic forces, changing of molecular structure of materials, anti-gravity, and the alteration of molecular structures like metals by the use of electromagnetic force. It has been discovered that anti-matter is created by the forced integration of a proton into element with the atomic number of 115, to create element 116. When this occurs, the element decays rapidly, exuding the energy "anti-matter." An antimatter explosion could damage a 1/3 of a continent the size of Asia, or be a beneficial energy source, and fuel.

Spoken Language Translator: A hand-held or worn device that translates oral communications in near real-time. It enhances multinational operational effectiveness in all areas, including training, diplomacy, special operations, and conventional ground operations. It is capable of one-for-one word substitution in a wide variety of languages, and it provides two-way communications between the owner and another person. The system has a limited ability to compensate for differences in sentence syntactic structures, cultures, dialects, and idioms/slang, and a limited ability to select words according to context. Careful placement of both microphones and both speakers is required for decoding (not having to hear both languages simultaneously), limiting the scope of its operation; the system is best suited for controlled two-way communications such as by telephone, radio, or computer.

Nuclear Fusion is created

by...*↺ _____

SORRY, HUMANITY MIGHT NOT BE READY FOR THIS YET.

TROUBLESOME QUOTES

"Further global progress is now possible only through a quest for universal consensus in the movement towards a new world order."
Mikhail Gorbachev, before the UN, December 7, 1988

"We shall have World Government, whether or not we like it. The only question is whether World Government will be achieved by conquest or consent."
James Paul Warburg, while speaking before the United States Senate, February 17, 1950

"There will be, in the next generation or so, a pharmacological method of making people love their servitude, and producing dictatorship without tears, so to speak, producing a kind of painless concentration camp for entire societies, so that people will in fact have their liberties taken away from them, but will rather enjoy it, because they will be distracted from any desire to rebel by propaganda

or brainwashing, or brainwashing enhanced by pharmacological methods. And this seems to be the final revolution."
Aldous Huxley's lecture to The California Medical School in San Francisco in 1961

"History records that the money changers have used every form of abuse, intrigue, deceit, and violent means possible to maintain their control over governments by controlling the money and its issuance."
James Madison (1751–1836), Father of the Constitution for the USA, 4th US President

"Complete and accurate surveillance as a means of control is probably a practical impossibility. What is much more likely is a loss of privacy and constant inconvenience as the wrong people gain access to information, as one wastes time convincing the inquisitors that one is in fact innocent, or as one struggles to untangle the errors of the errant machine."
Victor Ferkiss, Technological Man: The Myth and the Reality, 1969

"There will be, in the next generation or so, a pharmacological method of making people love their servitude, and producing dictatorship without tears, so to speak, producing a kind of painless concentration camp for entire societies, so that people will in fact have their liberties taken away from them, but will rather enjoy it, because they will be distracted from any desire to rebel by propaganda or brainwashing, or brainwashing is enhanced by pharmacological methods. And this seems to be the final revolution."
Aldous Huxley's lecture to The California Medical School in San Francisco in 1961

"One-fourth of humanity must be eliminated from the social body. We are in charge of God's selection process for planet earth. He selects, we destroy. We are the riders of the pale horse, Death."
Psychologist Barbara Marx Hubbard—member and futurist/strategist of Task Force Delta; a United States Army think tank

"…In short, the 'house of world order' will have to be built from the bottom up rather than from the top down. It will look like a great 'booming, buzzing confusion,' to use William James' famous description of reality, but an end run around national sovereignty, eroding it piece by piece, will accomplish much more than the old-fashioned frontal assault."
Richard N. Gardner, in "Foreign Affairs," April 1974

"There ought to be limits to freedom."
Governor George W Bush, May 21, 1999

"When we got organized as a country and we wrote a fairly radical Constitution with a radical Bill of Rights, giving a radical amount of individual freedom to Americans...And so a lot of people say there's too much personal freedom. When personal freedom's being abused, you have to move to limit it. That's what we did in the announcement I made last weekend on the public housing projects, about how we're going to have weapon sweeps and more things like that to try to make people safer in their communities."
President Bill Clinton, 3-22-94, MTV's "Enough is Enough"

"The Trilateral Commission doesn't run the world, the Council on Foreign Relations does that!"
Winston Lord, Assistant Secretary of State, the U. S. State Department

SECRET WEAPONS

(Public Information)

In 1958, the chief White House advisor on weather modification, Captain Howard T. Orville, said the U.S. Department of Defense was studying "ways to manipulate the Ionic's of the Earths atmosphere so as to affect the weather" by using an electric beam to ionize or de-ionize the atmosphere over a given area. Just like science fiction stories like Star Trek, they have invented the hand-held plasma gun. Weapons like those tend to get some attention, but the following is much more dangerous. In 1966, Professor Gordon J.F. MacDonald was an Associate Director of the U.S. Institute of Geophysics and Planetary Physics at the University of California, Los Angeles, a President's Science Advisory Committee, and later a member of the President's Council on Environmental Quality.

He published papers on the use of environmental-control technologies for military purposes. MacDonald said: "The key to geophysical warfare is the identification of environmental instabilities to which the addition of a small amount of energy would release vastly greater amounts of energy." A scientist named MacDonald had a number of ideas for using the environment as a weapon system.

He wrote a chapter called "How to Wreck the Environment" for the book "Unless Peace Comes." The description of the use of weather manipulation, climate modification, polar ice cap melting, destabilization, ozone-depletion techniques, earthquake engineering, ocean-wave control and brainwave manipulation using the planet's energy fields. He also said that these types of weapons would be developed and, when used, would be virtually undetectable by their victims. A weapon called HAARP is such a project. The U.S. military's intention to do environmental engineering is well documented.

For public record, the U.S. Congress subcommittee hearing on Oceans and International Environment looked into military weather and climate modification research conducted between 1972–1974. "What emerged was an awesome picture of research and experimentation by the Department of Defense into ways environmental tampering could be used as a weapon." HAARP zaps unstable areas of the active electrical shield protecting the planet from the constant bombardment of high-energy particles from space, called the ionosphere. "If the ionosphere is disturbed, the atmosphere below is traumatized." Energy blasted upward from an ionosphere heater is not much compared to the total in the ionosphere, but HAARP documents admit that thousand fold greater amounts of energy can be released in the ionosphere than injected.

The Department of Defense (HAARP-program):

1.) Give the military a tool to replace the electromagnetic pulse effect of atmospheric thermonuclear devices;

2.) Replace the huge Extremely Low Frequency (ELF) submarine communication system operating in Michigan and Wisconsin with a new and more compact technology;

3.) Be used to replace the over-the-horizon radar system that was once planned for the current location of HAARP with a more flexible and accurate system;

4.) Provide a way to wipe out communications over an extremely large area, while keeping the military's own communications systems working;

5.) Provide a wide-area Earth-penetrating tomography which, if combined with the computing abilities of EMASS and Cray computers, would make it possible to verify many parts of nuclear nonproliferation and peace agreements;

6.) Be a tool for geophysical probing to find oil, gas and mineral deposits over a large area; and

7.) Be used to detect incoming low-level planes and cruise missiles, making other technologies obsolete.

As another form of disrespect for nature, the results of this would be cataclysmic disorder and natural retaliation. Life is a circle, what goes around, comes around. Independent scientists told Begich and Manning that a HAARP-type "sky buster" with its unforeseen effects could be an act of global vandalism.

HAARP HISTORY

The patents illustrated below were the package of ideas, which were originally controlled by ARCO Power Technologies Incorporated (APTI), a subsidiary of Atlantic Richfield Company, one of the prime oil companies in the world. APTI was the contractor that fabricated the HAARP facility. ARCO sold this subsidiary, the patents and the second-phase construction contract to E-Systems in June 1994. E-Systems have been one of the major intelligence contractors in the world, doing labor for the CIA, defense intelligence organizations and others. Eighteen billion dollars of their annual vending are to these organizations, with $800 million for black projects—projects so secret that even the United States Congress isn't told how the money is being spent. The Reagan, and Bush presidencies placed in-ordinate funds into projects like this.

U.S. Air Force documents reveal that a system has been developed for manipulating and disrupting human mental processes through pulsed radio-frequency radiation (the stuff of HAARP) over large geographical areas. The most telling material about this technology came from writings of Zbigniew Brzezinski (former National Security Advisor to President Carter) and J.F. MacDonald (Science Advisor to President Johnson and a Professor of Geophysics at UCLA), as they wrote about use of power-beaming transmitters for geophysical and environmental warfare. The documents showed how these effects might be caused, and the negative effects on human health and thinking. Animal brains; like humans, are effected by electromagnetic fields over time.

The mental-disruption possibilities for HAARP are the most disturbing. More than 40 pages of the book, with dozens of footnotes, chronicle the work of Harvard professors, military planners and scientists as they plan and test this use of the electromagnetic technology. For example, one of the papers describing this came from the International Red Cross in Geneva. It even gave the frequency ranges where these effects could occur the same ranges, which HAARP is capable of broadcasting. The following statement was made more than 25 years ago in a book that Brzezinski wrote while a professor at Columbia University:

"Since 1966, several U.N. political strategists were tempted to exploit research on the brain and human behavior. Geophysicist Gordon J. F. MacDonald, specialist in problems of warfare, said artificially excited electrical strokes in the ionosphere could develop oscillations that produce relatively high power levels over certain regions of the Earth. In this way, one could develop a system that would seriously impair the neural performance of very large populations in selected regions over an extended period…' No matter how deeply disturbing the thought of using the environment to manipulate behavior for national advantages, to some the technology permitting such use will very probably develop within the next few decades."

In 1966, MacDonald was a member of the President's Science Advisory Committee and later a member of the President's Council on Environmental Quality. He published papers on the use of environmental-control technologies for military purposes. The most profound comment he made as a geophysicist was: "The key to geophysical warfare is the identification of environmental instabilities to which the addition of a small amount of energy would release vastly greater amounts of energy." This is another Pandora's box.

An educated man named "Zbigniew Brzezinski" predicted a "more controlled and directed society" that would gradually appear, linked to technology. An elite group that impresses voters by allegedly superior scientific know-how would dominate this society. Angels Don't Play This HAARP further quotes Brzezinski: "Unhindered by the restraints of traditional liberal values, this elite would not hesitate to achieve its political ends by using the latest modern techniques for influencing public behavior and keeping society under close surveillance and control. Technical and scientific momentum would then feed on the situation it exploits."

His forecasts are accurate! Today, a number of new tools for the "elite" are emerging, and the temptation to use them increases steadily. The policies to permit the tools to be used are already in place. How could the United States be changed, bit-by-bit, into the predicted, highly controlled technocracy? Among the "stepping stones" Brzezinski expected were persisting social crises and use of the mass media to gain the public's confidence. Encouragement of terrorist activities, planned accidents, planned environmental problems, etc., are among the activities setting an obvious pattern.

In another document prepared by the government, the U.S. Air Force claims: "The potential applications of artificial electromagnetic fields are wide-ranging and can be used in many military or quasi military situations. Some of these potential uses include dealing with terrorist groups, crowd control, controlling breaches of security at military installations, and antipersonnel techniques in tactical warfare. In all of these cases the EM (electromagnetic) systems would be used to produce mild to severe physiological disruption or perceptual distortion or disorientation. In addition, the ability of individuals to function could be degraded to such a point that they would be combat-ineffective. Another advantage of electromagnetic systems is that they can provide coverage over large areas with a single system. They are silent, and countermeasures to them may be difficult to develop. One last area where electromagnetic radiation may prove of some value is in enhancing abilities of individuals for anomalous phenomena."

The U.S. Department of Defense sampled lightning and hurricane manipulation studies in Project Sky fire and Project Storm fury. And they looked at some complicated technologies that would give big effects. Angels Don't Play This HAARP cites an expert who says the military studied both lasers and chemicals, which they figured, could damage the ozone layer over an enemy. In 1994 the U.S. Air Force revealed its Spacecast 2020 master plan, which included the arrogant stupidity of <u>weather control</u>. Scientists have experimented with weather control since the 1940's, but Spacecast 2020 noted, "Using environmental modification techniques to destroy, damage or injure another state [is] prohibited." {This government's history does not state any positive encouragement to state prohibition would be followed, neither does the intent of its development.}

The book Angels Don't Play This HAARP: Advances in Tesla Technology is available from Earth pulse Press for $14.95 plus postage and handling ($1.50 U.S.; $4 international). Dr. Nick Begich is an Anchorage, Alaska-based independent researcher and activist and former president of the Alaska Federation of Teachers and the Anchorage Council of Education. Jeane Manning is a reporter and editor residing in Vancouver, Canada.

A decade of researching no conventional energy technologies has culminated in her forthcoming book The Coming Energy Revolution (Avery Publishing Group, New York, 1996). She contributed to the book: "Suppressed Inventions and Other Discoveries" (Auckland Institute of Technology Press, New Zealand). The intention of test detonating weapons in the Antarctic is unconfirmed, but likely. Some of the worlds governments already test explode weapons, and discard materials in the open ocean. Ever wonder where? (Info, courtesy of the freedom of info act.)

MICROCHIP IMPLANTS

Since the 1970's, Silicon, and later made of gallium arsenide implants were made small enough to be inserted just under the skin of a persons wrist, scalp, etc., with or without the consent of the subject. They can conceivabley be inserted into organs that are set for transplant, in stitsches, or other forms of surgery; even by doctors performing the operations. It is now almost impossible to detect or remove them. It is technically possible for every newborn to be injected with a microchip, which could then function to identify the person for the rest of his or her life. Such plans were secretly being discussed in the U.S. at high government levels, without any real consideration of the privacy issues involved.

In Sweden, Prime Minister Olof Palme gave permission in 1973 to implant prisoners, and Data Inspection's ex-Director General Jan Freese revealed that nursing-home patients were implanted in the mid-1980s. The technology is revealed in the 1972:47 Swedish state report, *Statens Officiella Utradninger* (SOU). Implanted human beings can be followed almost anywhere. Brain functions can be remotely monitored by supercomputers and even altered through the changing of frequencies emitted. Secret experiments have included prisoners, soldiers, poor minorities, mental patients, handicapped children, deaf, and blind people, homosexuals, single women, the elderly, school children, and any group of people considered "marginal" by the elite experimenters. A high percentage of the persons in these groups are African American, Native American, or from Arabic countries. Asian persons have been targeted more in the 90's. MRI's, CAT scans, and X-Rays, may detect the chips, but most examiners are trained to not recognize them as an anomoly.

Today's microchips operate by means of low-frequency radio waves that target them. With the help of the military and spy satellites, the implanted person can be tracked anywhere on the globe. Such a technique was among a number tested in the Iraq war, according to Dr. Carl Sanders, who invented the intelligence-manned interface (IMI) biotic, which is injected into people. (Earlier during the Vietnam War, some soldiers were injected with the Rambo chip, designed to increase adrenaline flow into the bloodstream, many others were provided with drugs.) The 20-billion-bit/second supercomputers at the U.S. National Security Agency (NSA) can now "see and hear" what soldiers experience in the battlefield with a remote monitoring system (RMS).

When a 5-micromillimeter microchip (the diameter of a strand of hair is 50 micromillimeters) is placed into optical nerve of the eye, it draws neuroimpulses from the brain that embody the experiences, smells, sights, and voice of the implanted person. Once transferred and stored in a computer, these neuroimpulses can be projected back to the person's brain via the microchip to be reexperienced. Using a RMS, a land-based computer operator can send electromagnetic messages (encoded as signals) to the nervous system, affecting the target's performance. With RMS, healthy persons can be induced to see hallucinations and to hear voices in their heads.

Every thought, reaction, hearing, and visual observation causes a certain neurological potential, spikes, and patterns in the brain and its electromagnetic fields, which can now be decoded into thoughts, pictures, and voices. Electromagnetic stimulation can therefore change a person's brainwaves and affect muscular activity, causing painful muscular cramps experienced as torture. The NSA's electronic surveillance system can simultaneously follow and handle millions of people. Each of us has a unique bioelectrical resonance frequency in the brain, just as we have unique fingerprints. With electromagnetic frequency (EMF) brain stimulation fully coded, pulsating electromagnetic signals can be sent to the brain, causing the desired voice and visual effects to be experienced by the target. This is a form of electronic warfare that can also manipulate voting.

The Washington Post reported in May 1995 that Prince William of Great Britain was implanted at the age of 12. Thus, if he were ever kidnapped, a radio wave with a specific frequency could be targeted to his microchip. The chip's signal would be routed through a satellite to the computer screen of police headquarters, where the Prince's movements could be followed. He could actually be located anywhere on the globe.

The mass media has not reported that an implanted person's privacy vanishes for the rest of his or her life. S/he can be manipulated in many ways. Theoretically using different frequencies, the secret controller of this equipment could change a person's emotional life. S/he can be made aggressive or lethargic. Sexuality can be artificially influenced. Thought signals and subconscious thinking can be read, dreams affected and even induced, all without the knowledge or consent of the implanted person.

A perfect cyber-soldier can thus be created. This secret technology has been used by military forces in certain NATO countries since the 1980s without civilian and academic populations having heard anything about it. Thus, little information about such invasive mind-control systems is available in professional and academic journals. The NSA's Signals Intelligence group can remotely monitor information from human brains by decoding the evoked potentials (3.50 HZ, 5 milliwatt) emitted by the brain. Prisoner experimentees in both Gothenburg, Sweden and Vienna, Austria have been found to have evident brain lesions.

All international human rights agreements forbid non consensual manipulation of human beings—even in prisons, not to speak of civilian populations. Under an initiative of U.S. Senator John Glenn, discussions commenced in January 1997 about the dangers of radiating civilian populations. The U.S., E.U., and Israel, pose the gravest threats to humanity, as they are the greatest supporters. The latest supercomputers are powerful enough to monitor the whole world's population. What will happen when people are tempted by false premises to allow microchips into their bodies; such as cecretly curable health problems, kidnapping, etc.? One lure is a microchip identity card. Compulsory legislation has even been secretly proposed in the U.S. to criminalize removal of an ID implant, by elitist intentions. All there waiting for is a natural, or planned disaster, that will motivate mass acceptance in a few years, or is it months?

When your brain functions are connected to supercomputers by means of EM radio implants and microchips, it will be too late for protest. This threat can be defeated partially by the education of the public, using available literature on biotelemetry, and information exchanged at international congresses. One reason this technology has remained a state secret is the widespread prestige of the psychiatric *Diagnostic Statistical Manual IV* produced by the U.S. American Psychiatric Association (APA) and printed in 18 languages.

Bad psychiatrists working for U.S. intelligence agencies participated in writing and revising this manual. This psychiatric "bible" covers up the secret development of MC technologies by labeling some of their effects as symptoms of paranoid schizophrenia.
http://www.worldnetdaily.com/news/article.asp?ARTICLE_ID=15185 (Sept-3. 2004)

A Corresponding Prophesy being followed:

"…and cause that as many as would not worship the image of the beast should be killed. And he causeth all, both small and great, rich and poor, free and bond, to receive a mark in their right hand, or in their foreheads: and that no man might buy or sell, save he that had the mark, or the name of the beast, or the number of his name."

Revelation 13:15-17

The cost of ammunition, if raised considerably, could result in reasonable reductions of unnecessary deaths and injuries. Along with information sharing and historical accuracy, the costs of war must become more expensive, than the costs of peace. Those that profit from deaths willingly against the innocent must be waived from significance of existence. Those that serve the path to justice of the people should receive benefits on their path.

POSITIVE QUOTES

"…Amen-Ra, who was the first king, the god of the earliest time, and he who remains the prime minister of the poor. Amen-Ra accepts no bribes from the guilty; he takes no testimony from the witness, and pays no attention to one who promises. He speaks to the heart and judges the guilty. He assigns the guilty to the fire of the east, and the righteous to the peace of the west.

…The Husia

"…. Be skilled in speech so that you will succeed. The tongue of one is as a sword, and effective speech is stronger than all fighting. None can overcome the skillful. A wise person is a school for the nobles, and those who are aware of the knowledge do not attack them. No evil takes place when the teacher is near. Truth comes to him in its essential form, shaped in the sayings of the ancestors.

…(Kemet) Book of Kheti.

"..Sincerity is the way of heaven, and to think the way of the sincere is the way of humanity. Never was there one possessed of complete sincerity who did not move others. Never was there one without sincerity who was able to move others.

…Modern translation of Confucianism

-Whenever there is tension or fighting between groups, individuals, or peoples, it means that a time of mutual understanding has been lost, and channels of communication have not been used.

-Inner life is the basis for outer activity. A person's actions are a mirror of the inner self.

-Our activities and successes are based on our inner strength and wholeness of self. To grow, it is necessary for us to recognize and correct our own faults. When we gain the ability to understand and correct our negative habits, and our intent is to be greater, we make strides to become happier in life.

"…If you love others, and the affection is not returned, look into your love. If you rule others and they are unruly, look into your wisdom. If you treat others politely and they do not return your politeness, look into your respect. If your desires are not fulfilled, turn inward and examine yourself.

…Modern translation of Confucianism

"…Riches are not from an abundance of worldly goods, but from a contented mind.

…Islam

The fullest expressions of the divine are found in loving relationships, acts of kindness, and caring of the nature around you. Individual religions and cultures have unique characteristics. The fundamental principles for wisdom, happiness, and health, are universal. For this reason, in part, no people should seek to emulate another. Uniqueness is a vehicle to enhance understanding of all.

".....with the ancient is wisdom; and in length of days understanding.

…Judaism

-Education is our passport to the future, for tomorrow belongs to those that prepare for it today.…

Malcolm X

-It is not only important to ask what do you know, it is important to ask…. "How do you know?"

…Prof. Manu Ampim

-Each of us possesses the potential for a winning life. Within each of us is the ability to have fulfilling relationships, to enjoy good health and prosperity, to feel and show true compassion for others, and the power to face and surmount our deepest problems.

…Dr. Daisaku Ikeda

U.S. MARSHAL LAW QUALIFICATIONS

Executive Orders associated with **FEMA** that would suspend the **U.S. Constitution** and the **Bill of Rights**. These and new Executive Orders have been on record for over 30 years and could be enacted by the stroke of a Presidential Pen:

EXECUTIVE ORDER 10990 Allows the government to take over all modes of transportation and control of highways and seaports.

EXECUTIVE ORDER 10995 Allows the government to seize and control the communication media.

EXECUTIVE ORDER 10997 Allows the government to take over all electrical power, gas, petroleum, fuels and minerals.

EXECUTIVE ORDER 10998 Allows the government to seize all means of transportation, including personal cars, trucks or vehicles of any kind and total control over all highways, seaports, and waterways.

EXECUTIVE ORDER 10999 Allows the government to take over all food resources and farms.

EXECUTIVE ORDER 11000 Allows the government to mobilize civilians into work brigades under government supervision.

EXECUTIVE ORDER 11001 Allows the government to take over all health, education and welfare functions.

EXECUTIVE ORDER 11002 Designates the Postmaster General to operate a national registration of all persons.

EXECUTIVE ORDER 11003 Allows the government to take over all airports and aircraft, including commercial aircraft.

EXECUTIVE ORDER 11004 Allows the Housing and Finance Authority to relocate communities, build new housing with public Funds, designate areas to be abandoned, and establish new locations for populations.

EXECUTIVE ORDER 11005 Allows the government to take over railroads, inland waterways and public storage facilities.

EXECUTIVE ORDER 11051 Specifies the responsibility of the Office of Emergency Planning and gives authorization to put all Executive Orders into effect in times of increased international tensions and economic or financial crisis.

EXECUTIVE ORDER 11310 Grants authority to the Department of Justice to enforce the plans set out in Executive Orders, to institute industrial support, to establish judicial and legislative liaison, to control all aliens, to operate penal and correctional institutions, and to advise and assist the President.

EXECUTIVE ORDER 11049 Assigns emergency preparedness function to federal departments and agencies, consolidating 21 operative Executive Orders issued over a fifteen-year period.

EXECUTIVE ORDER 11921 Allows the Federal Emergency Preparedness Agency to develop plans to establish control over the mechanisms of production and distribution, of energy sources, wages, salaries, credit and the flow of money in U.S. financial institution in any undefined national emergency. It also provides that when the President declares a state of emergency, Congress cannot review the action for six months. The Federal Emergency Management Agency has broad powers in every aspect of the nation.

National Security Act of 1947 Allows for the strategic relocation of industries, services, government and other essential economic activities, and to rationalize the requirements for manpower, resources and production facilities.

International Emergency Economic Powers Act Enables the President to seize the property of a foreign country or national. These powers were transferred to FEMA in a sweeping consolidation in 1979.

THE DRAFT: A PLAN FOR FORCED MILITARY LABOR

About $28 million has been added to the 2004 Selective Service System (SSS) budget, to prepare for a military draft that could start as early as June 15, 2005. SSS must report to Bush on March 31, 2005 that the system, which has lain dormant for decades, is ready for activation. Or is it for implant technology? Please see website: www.sss.gov/perfplan fy2004.html to view the SSS Annual Performance Plan—fiscal year 2004. The Pentagon has quietly begun a public campaign to fill all 10,350 draft board positions and 11,070 appeals board slots nationwide. Though an unpopular election year topic, military experts and influential members of Congress are suggesting that if Rumsfeld's prediction of a "long, hard slog" in Iraq and Afghanistan [and a permanent state of war on "terrorism"] proves accurate, the U.S. may have no choice but to draft. www.informationclearinghouse.info/article5146.htm.

On the horizon are a multitude of military operations and social reconstruction projects on the minds of these officials.

The chief of the Selective Service System has proposed registering women for the military draft. The age requirements for draft registration to 34 years old, up from 25 are also under serious consideration. The Selective Service System plan, obtained under the Freedom of Information Act, highlights the extent to which agency officials have planned for an expanded military draft in case the administration and Congress would authorize one in the future.

Congress brought twin bills, S. 89 and H.R. 163 forward this year, entitled the Universal National Service Act of 2003, "To provide for the common defense by requiring that all young persons [age 18–26] in the United States, including women, perform a period of military service or a period of civilian service in furtherance of the national defense and homeland security, and for other purposes." These active bills currently sit in the Committee on Armed Services.

Dodging the draft will be more difficult than those from the Vietnam era remember next time. College and Canada will not be options. In December 2001, Canada and the US signed a "Smart Border Declaration," which could be used to keep would-be draft dodgers in. Signed by Canada's Minister of Foreign Affairs, John Manley, and US Homeland Security Director—Tom Ridge, the declaration involves a 30-point plan which implements, among other things, a "pre-clearance agreement" of people entering and departing each country. Reforms aimed at making the draft equitable along gender, and class lines, also eliminates higher education as a shelter. Undergraduates would only be able to postpone service until the end of their current semester. Seniors in High School would have until the end of the academic year. Some of the few prospective safe areas from unwanted military forced labor are the Peace Corps, service in certain federal jobs, dual-citizenship, or certain restricting medical conditions, if you are on the list.

THE OLYMPICS

The Greeks did not invent Olympic Athletic Contests. Like most of the aspects of Greek society, the Kemetic (Egyptians) had large public games, which is also is an imitation of earlier African games from the south. Several other cultures like those in what is called "Mesoamerica," also had large game events in similar fashion earlier in time than the Greeks. The Mayan city of Copan (now located in Honduras), Timbuktu (now in the location called Mali), Beijing (in ancient Chinese dynasties), are among the many other places multi-societal/national-type peoples gathered for large spectacle games and competitions. Carved and script writings depicting sports events, have been found in virtually all advanced civilizations, as part of the norm of societal entertainment, or ritual. In Ancient (Kemet) Egypt, acrobats, who displayed high physical agility and strength, were seen as performers.

Most Nubian/Kemetic acrobats were women that performed alone or in groups. The Martial Arts were preserved only for military. Young Nubian boys also participated in acrobatics, and played games with hoops. Wrestling, and an original Kung Fu type of martial arts were part of Egyptian Military Training. Ancient Nubians also participated in various running activities. One of the kingdom's most important festivals was the "jubilee celebration," a festival first celebrated on the 30th anniversary of the reign of Amenophis III, and celebrated continuously in three-year intervals. In the "ritual run", an integral part of the celebration, the current king would run between two sets of three semicircles, the semicircles being cosmic references to the order of the universe.

Physical evidence of the "ritual run" exists at the pyramid complex of King Djoser, where you can find traces of the world's first sports facilities, complete with the running track for the "ritual run." The Egyptians participated in running, jumping (seldom as a discipline, rather in the context of children's games), wrestling (in pairs of competitors), stick fighting, boxing, swimming, and rowing as general social games.

The word "Olympic" was taken from a Greek god. The first Greek Olympic Games at Olympia were held in the year 776 BC. Leaders Hippias of Elis compiled a list of Olympic victors in 400 BC, of the stadium running race. They were organized into festivals held every four years as a result of a peace agreement between the city-states of Elis and Pisa.

SOME COOKING INFO

<u>SPINACH STEW:</u> A dinner from Ghana (This is a very quick and economical dish)

- 3/4 cup of vegetable oil—(Heat oil over medium heat for 1-minute on stove)
- 1-small peeled & cubed onion—(Add onions and sauté' until transparent)
- 1-small tomato, cubed.—
- 3-ounces of tomato paste—add both tomato ingredients and cook for 5-minutes.

After 5-minutes, add all of the following ingredients:

- 1-pound of fresh spinach (chopped to small bits)
- Ground Fish (any), or one 12-ounce can of corned beef
- 1-teaspoon of ground red pepper
- 1-teaspoon of salt

Cook for 30–35 minutes over medium-low heat in a large pan....Serves-5 with rice.

STEAMED OKRA: (All of Africa)

- 1-pound of Okra
- 1-cup of water
- 1-teaspoon of lemon (mixed, covered, and cooked at medium heat for 5-minutes) Serves-4

MAFE'—"Peanut Butter Stew": (Senegal)

- This is considered one of the favorite stews on the continent. This is in almost every African cookbook. An international gourmet delicacy.

Spices, Herbs, Vegetables, Fruits, & Grains of Africa used <u>in the U.S.A.</u>, etc...

Anise, Peanuts, Caraway, Cardamom, Coffee, Ginger, Black-Eye Peas, Tamarind, Couscous, Cumin, Garlic, Fenugreek, Collard Greens, Licorice, Millet, Okra, Onions, Plantains, Spinach, Sorghum, Watermelon, Cantaloupe, Yam, Sesame, Kale, Rice, Pumpkin, Cotton, Ambary Hemp, etc.

Use of tomato, corn, refined sugar, sweet potatoes, and oranges came from ancient trade & commerce with the Indigenous People of the America's & Polynesians.

==

GINGER BEER: (An extremely powerful non-alcoholic soda from Nubia)

½ pound or more of ginger root (Wash & Grate into a large bowl)
2-Limes (Juice the limes over the grated ginger)
1–½ cups of brown sugar/or ½ cup of honey (pour over ginger)
½ teaspoon "cream of tarter" (pour over the sugar)
8-cups of boiling water (All the above contents are to be mixed while boiling for 1-minute)
Let mixture cool for 2 ½ hours
½ teaspoon of yeast (Sprinkle over drink while cooling)

Add ½ teaspoon of baking yeast when soda is at room temperature, no warmer. Cover and leave at room temperature for 24-hours. Strain particles, chill, and serve. This drink is guaranteed to drop your blood pressure, for a short time.

===

Jamaican Jerk Chicken Makes 6 servings
Cook Time: 1 Hour
Ready in: 3 Hours 20 Minutes
4-limes, juiced + 1-cup of water
6-chicken breast halves—(cut into chunks, pour juice & water over chicken)
2 teaspoons ground allspice
1/2 teaspoon ground nutmeg
1-teaspoon salt
1-teaspoon brown sugar
2 teaspoons dried thyme
1-teaspoon ground ginger
1 1/2 teaspoons ground black pepper
2 tablespoons vegetable oil
2 onions, chopped
1 1/2 cups chopped green onions
6 cloves garlic, chopped
2-5 Habanero peppers, chopped.

In a blender or food processor, place allspice, nutmeg, salt, brown sugar, thyme, ginger, black pepper and vegetable oil. Blend it with the white onions, green onions, garlic & Habanero peppers until pasty. Pour the blended marinade mixture into bowl with chicken. Cover and marinate in the refrigerator at least 2 hours. Preheat an outdoor grill for medium heat and lightly oil grate. Cook chicken slowly on the preheated grill. Turn frequently, basting often with remaining marinade mixture. Cook to desired tenderness.

The Africa Cookbook: The taste of a continent. By. Dorinda Hafner
The Griots Cookbook. By—Alice McGill
Cooking the West African Way. By. Bertha V. Montgomery
South of the Sahara. By. Elizabeth A. Jackson

THE FUTURE

All futures are made by you and I…. "Eternity is not the future, eternity is not a period of time, eternity is here, now, and forever in this dimension of existence." Virtually all-spiritual leaders and the people within their religions must learn the rights and wrongs expressed towards humanity by all players in world history. This must include recognition of every negative action of there own philosophies. Only then can each group talk about repairing the wounds they and/or others have created to our civilizations. Even with the likely hit of an asteroid in 2029, other astronomical events, meteorological actions, and geological activities, changes applied naturally should not be worsened by unnaturally produced ones. Nature's plans do not include things like biological genocide, nuclear weapons, biological weapons, current ecological destruction, or chemical weapons.

> *The best way to deal with force is to avoid it! Perceive the way of nature, and no force of man can harm you! You do not have to stop force. It is easier to redirect it.—Learn more ways to preserve or change, rather than destroy; check, rather than hurt; hurt, rather than mame; mame, rather than kill.*
>
> *(Kung Fu)*

What religions aspire for unfounded war, genocide, destruction of nature, denial of open dialogue, or suppression of women? We determine how we live according to our individual and collective nature. Transformation of a society may only take 1/8 of a generation, and 1–2 generations to form a new civilization. Even in a college environment, sometimes it only takes the actions a one, or a few students to change the social picture. We are in a society of the earth, not a nation, or state!

SLEEP DEPRIVATION

For virtually all life forms; including humans, sleep is one of the essential functions of living. Worldwide, sleep deprivation is becoming an epidemic way of life. Many people are living off balance and not paying attention to the needs their own bodies are calling forth to be satisfied. Melanin is an essential for the health of all people, but many chemicals of today are designed to attack those cells, also effecting sleep. General human behavior and physical degradations are altered as sleep deprivation is extended. In tasks requiring judgment, poor behaviors transpire as sleep duration is limited more than an hour per night, over time.

The act of sleeping only one-hour a night over many nights generates subtle cognitive impairments. Greater reductions of sleep lead to extreme cognitive deficits. It is obvious that you may be lacking sleep if you feel drowsy during the day, dose off during normal awakened time, you of course know you are sleep-deprived and the body is trying to do its job. Bad social behavior in particular societies tend to also reflect the sleep hour adequateness of the people. Children are the most effected of the population. Besides adults not being able to function correctly in their daily tasks, school children are endangered by the confusion of determined needs for night hourly sleep, and nap time.

The amount of sleep a child from toddler to teen may need seems to be a general minimum of 10–11 hours for every 24 hours. The average teenager's body tends to need a minimum of 8–9 hours, and remains the same until the age of about 45. From this age on, the human body, according to historical trends, has a need for sleep similar to that of a toddler. A return to the use of nap-time throughout pre-school to high school years may benefit the average student, along with appropriate eating schedules and diet. Academic performance would likely increase 10x, above the average scores of today, if these simple measures were taken.

There are studies that show younger children who don't get enough sleep are at a higher risk for accidents, learning difficulties, as well as greater behavior problems. Sleep-deprived kids have been considered to have the false disease called attention-deficit hyperactivity disorder (ADHD), because the symptoms of sleep deprivation, low serotonin, and other deficiencies closely mirror the pharmaceutically manufactured profit gaining so-called chemically curable problem.

A related issue to this has been high blood pressure. The manufactured ban on the sale of "tryptophan," seemed to be done when it was found to have better & longer-term B.P. lowering effects than the drugs from the USFDA/FTC/Cartel, partially due to findings about serotonin and melanin on a variety of ailments.

THE BIG FIX

Each of the known world religions, contain faults and strengths, which can be altered to form a great religion all can share. It is possible to create other religions that can embody the full existence of each group of people on earth; indeed, many of the current religions claim that they are the answer to all problems. The power of faith is a common factor of Faith in each religion, but differs according to development of the historical context it comes from. Billions of people, impending natural disasters, and diversity of perceptions are factors for today's changes. Again, I must mention that transformation of a society only takes as much as one to two generations, as history has explained countless times. Billions of women are living in non-supporting societies in terms of child support.

This is mostly true in paternal capitalist cultures, but exists elsewhere too. A society that is collective-communal would have as a basic tenet, the support of the raising of each child through engagement of the entire community. The ways and means for the support of the children in a society have historically been formed with the support of many family members and friends, throughout human history. Discipline, diet, education, and security are the means of care that until recently, have been the responsibility of more than the family model of mom and/or dad only.

The violence & discrimination promoting game, **Grand Theft Auto: Vice City**, instructs players to "kill the Haitians," hurt or kill innocent people to take their property, kill public officers of local law & safety, endanger children, and awards points for each kill of the innocent. These types of games are actually purchased by so-called parents, guardians, and group homes. These types of media also provide an avenue to discuss ways people try to find happiness in life.

Movies and other media shown as popular from the USA and other places, with culturally degrading images, promote cultural degradation efforts of foreign intentions, especially among the youth of various places like Eastern Europe, among indigenous Africans, south-east Asia, Japan, etc., looking for role models. Intended images from the actors to spread a message to reach for positive growth are shown out of context to promote acceptance of casual violence, rape, and gain dependence on co-opted information, against actual scholarly and spiritual information from their own people. The recent moves to show 70's black exploitation films throughout Africa as an image of how to be a wealthy black person in white controlled cities in Africa are firm examples. Movies like Sankofa, Hotel Rwanda, Malcolm X, Panther, and Posse are among those that are resisted frequently from public view in the U.S., South America, and especially throughout Africa. In addition, media role models from many movies and music are the main icons of today, and probably tomorrow. Understanding of self in the realm of the classical of the individual's heritage is essential.

THE U.S. CONSTITUTION IS "NOT FULLY AMERICAN"

The U.S. Constitution is not a purely "American," it is constructed from elements of the wisdom of many cultures; including those of Ancient Egypt, Native Americans, Greece, Rome, Renaissance Europe, and Persia. Within most governments, there are repressive and/or hateful governing bodies that do not provide capable means to greater qualities of life. The promise of "liberty and justice for all," is inaccurate towards the realities of its creation and daily Faith. Keep in mind that several ancient civilizations existed for eons with very advanced principles and laws. Most have declined due to issues from outside, not within. By far, the majority of its foundation was from the indigenous peoples.

The African Constitution went this way, in part:

- The land belongs to no one, but each family has the right to land use sufficient for Self-Sustenance.

- The people are the first and final source of power.

- The Government and the people are one and the same.
  (Check "The Destruction of Black Civilization"
  By: Dr. Chancellor Williams)

When you speak, you are a voice of the earth. When you listen, you are the ears of the earth. When you touch, you are the skin of the earth. When you think in this manner, you begin to become aware of your place in existence. Movements towards a common world are being made many peoples, in many ways. Several examples of the process in progress are the revolutionary reconstruction of the indigenous peoples of Africa, and the America's, over the last few years. For example; the correlation of the popular rebellious music of the 50's, influenced the social change attitudes of the 60's, the liberation songs during slavery, and currently those from conscious hip-hop are influencing transformations of the youth worldwide.

The current 4th—12th graders in many public schools are getting a much better social studies education than most of the rest of the people in the U.S. have had. It is easy for an adult to feel envy for this, but everyone should feel proud of this recent advancement, as it is a product of the multiculturalism revolution of the 80's–90. Some major people to thank for the current status of progressed education are Prof. Leonard Jeffries—from Cuny University of New York, activist people, Dr. Molefi Asante of Temple University, Ishakamusa Barashango of

Baltimore-Maryland, Prof. Manu Ampim of Advancing the Research: Oakland, CA., Dr. Maulana Karenga of Los Angeles, CA, Dr. Ivan Van Sertima or New Jersey, Dr. Boyd Graves, Dr. Frances Cress Welsing. These are some of the most important people of the late 20th and early 21st centuries.

The African Union in 2004, as a whole has agreed, and is actively participating in forming a United Federation of African States, leading to a much more powerful stateless African Union. This is in accordance with the will and gradual re-education of the people on the true history of division, degradation, and civilization structure before Islamic and European damage to their civilizations. The same is true among the growing reunion of the native peoples of the America's. (International Indian Treaty Council, Anahuac Nation, etc.)

Civilizations have existed in several different ways for many centuries. The people of today should learn the spiritual and economic support systems of past civilizations, and compare them with the imperialist founded system of economics that they now follow. For a clear majority, most still live in the same spiritual body that supported the social character that made yesterday evil, and occurs today. Application of a new world order, or just beginning your own, will begin to take form when the youth of the society are aware, and ready to take over, not by crisis, or coerced force by any government leader or system. Resistance to truth is only a trial and test of directed resolve for change. Truth requires acceptance of duty to correct wrongs set on life indigenous to the place and time considered for the past, present, and future.

> "History is a clock that people use to tell their political and cultural time of day. It is also a compass that people use to find themselves on the map of human geography. The role of history is to tell a people what they have been, and where they have been, what they are and where they are. The most important role that history plays is that it has the function of telling a people where they still must go and what they still must be."
>
> **(The Late Honorable) Professor. John Henrik Clarke,**
> **African Historian**

Flag of the International Indian Treaty Council & the African Union

RESEARCH SUGGESTIONS

1. The Destruction of Black Civilization: Great Issues of a Race 4500b.c.-2000a.d.
   By. Dr. Chancellor Williams

2. Race Matters—By: Cornel West

3. Black Indians.—By: Lorenz Waltz

4. In the Black: A History of African Americans on Wall Street—By: Gregory S. Bell

5. Middle Egyptian: An Introduction to the Language and Culture of Hieroglyphs
   By: James P. Allen (Author)

6. Eyes on the Prize: America's Civil Rights Years, 1954–1965—By: Juan Williams.

7. Dirty Little Secrets About Black History: Its Heroes & Other Troublemakers
   By: Claud Anderson.

8. Songs of West Africa: A Collection of over 80 Traditional West African Folk Songs and Chants in 6 Languages With Translations, Annotations
   By: Dan Gorlin

9. Erasing Racism: The Survival of the American Nation—By: Molefi Kete Asante

10. African Dance—By: Kariamu Weish Asante

11. Cycles: A View of Planet Earth

12. Towards Black Community Development—By: Prof. Manu Ampim

13. <u>The Rhythms of Black Folk: Race, Religion, and Pan-Africanism</u>—By: Jon Michael Spencer

14. <u>Africanisms in Afro-American Language Varieties</u>—By: Salikoko S. Mufwene (Editor)

15. <u>500 Nations: An Illustrated History of North American Indians</u>—By: Alvin M., Jr. Josephy

16. <u>Cherokee Connections</u>—By: Myra Vanderpool Gormley

17. <u>Dark Alliance: The CIA, the Contras, and the Crack Cocaine Explosion</u>— By: Gary Webb

18. <u>Killing Hope: US Military and CIA Interventions Since World War II</u> By: William Blum. Portions available at: http://members.aol. com/bblum6/American holocaust.html.

19. <u>The Immaculate Deception: The Bush Crime Family Exposed</u>—By: Russell S. Bowen

20. <u>Symbolism Revisited</u>—By: Edgar J. Riley

21. <u>Oneness: Great Principles Shared By: all Religions</u>—By: Jeffrey Moses

22. <u>Selections from the Husia: Sacred Wisdom from Ancient Egypt</u>—By: Maulana Karenga

23. <u>Hero with a Thousand Faces</u>—By: Joseph Cambell

24. <u>The Final Battle</u>—By: Hal Lindsey

25. <u>Is Religion Killing Us?</u>—By: Jack Nelson-Pallmeyer

26. <u>The complete idiots guide to: Women's Spirituality</u>—By: Mary Faulkner

27. <u>In All Her Names: Explorations of the Feminine Divinity</u>—By: Joseph Cambell

28. <u>Material World: A Global Family Portrait</u>—By: Peter Menzel

29. <u>The Hip Hop Generation</u>—By: Bakari Kitwana

30. <u>Black Excellence: African-Americans on Striving and Excellence</u>—By: Sonya Tinsley

31. <u>Majority-Minority Relations: 4th edition</u>—By: John E. Farley

32. <u>Metu Neter: vol. 1 & 2</u>—By: Ra Un Nefer Amen

33. <u>Introduction to Social Problems: 7th edition</u>—By: Thomas J. Sullivan

34. <u>Boys and Girls Learn Differently</u>—By: Michael Gurian

35. <u>African Presence in Early Europe</u>—By: Ivan Van Sertima

36. <u>The Iceman Inheritance: Prehistoric Sources of Western Man's Racism, Sexism, and Aggression</u>—By: Michael Bradley

37. <u>Black Historical facts of the life of Jesus</u>—By: Rev Dr. Ishakamusa Barashango

38. <u>The Passover Plot</u>—By: Hugh J.Shonefield

39. <u>Jesus and the Zealots</u>—By: S.G.F. Brandon

40. <u>History of the African-Olmecs: Black civilizations of America from Pre-Historic Times to the Present</u>
By: Paul Alfred Barton

41. <u>Introduction to African Civilizations</u>—By: John G. Jackson.

42. <u>Stolen Legacy.</u>—By: George G. M. James

43. <u>World's Great Men of Color, Volumes I & II.</u>—By: Rogers, J. A.

44. <u>They Came Before Columbus.</u>—By: Dr. Ivan Van Sertima

45. <u>The Teachings of Ptahhotep The oldest Book in the world.</u>
By: Hilliard, A. L. Williams and N. Damali. Eds. Atlanta: Blackwood Press, 1987.

46. <u>Kemet and the African World View.</u>
By: Dr. Maulana Karenga. Los Angeles: University of Sankore Press, 1986.

47. <u>Africa: Mother of Western Civilization.</u>—By: Yosef Ben-Jochannan.

48. <u>Black Women in Antiquity.</u>—By: *Dr. Ivan* Van Sertima.

49. <u>New Dimensions in African History</u>—By: Dr. John Henrik Clarke and Yosef Ben-Jochannan.

50. <u>Rachel's Tears: The Spiritual Journey of Columbine Martyr.</u>—By: Beth and Darryl Scott

51. <u>http://www.matrixinstitute.com/futuremap.html</u>

Rosedale KS 66103
1-800-879-0543
http://www.cartserver.com/sc/cart.cgi

SOME AFRICAN FRUITS, VEGGIES, SPICES, AND HERBS USED WORLDWIDE

Ginger, Coffee, Peanuts, Lime, Fig, Olives, Watermelon, Kola Nut, Dates, Pumpkins, Cantaloupes, Cucumbers, Rice, Cayenne Peppers, Cassava (Tapioca), Sesame Seeds, Kale, Greens, Spinach, Yams, Pinto, Anise, Plantains, Caraway, Cardamom, Ginger, Black-Eye Peas, Tamarind, Okra, Couscous, Cumin, Garlic, Fenugreek, Collard Greens, Licorice, Millet, Okra, Onions, Palm Oil, Pumpkin, Amaranth, etc...<u>Export and use adapted into other cultures over several centuries, prior to European and Islamic expansionism.</u>
Use of tomato, corn, Papaya's, and oranges came from ancient trade & commerce with the Indigenous People of the America's & Polynesians.

One of many common African Hairstyles   Pharaoh Aménophis III

UNIVERSAL DECLARATION OF HUMAN RIGHTS & RESPONSIBILITIES

All life is to be treated with dignity, equality, and rights equal to all members of the human family. Only life designated By: individual cultures as food sources, shall be allowed to be quartered, and of these maximum life supporting percentages for the wild must remain in the environment it is indigenous from. All nations must absolve territorial political perceptions for Earth Unification. Governance of humanity shall consist of multi-culture elected representatives from the peoples, which will elect continental councils. Each continental council shall be governed By: the people elected judicial council that will be the highest level of governance, below the power of the people. Free higher education, freedom of choice, freedom of expression, free healthcare, and the ability to vote are the rights of all persons upon the age of 20. All persons from birth to age 20 have shall have free healthcare, right to highest quality education, right to safety & protection for full development, right to participate in governance from age 12–20, right to full knowledge of all issues that may effect the future upon the time of their age of voting.

All human beings shall enjoy these rights as designated and proclaimed as the highest aspartameiration of the common people. The people have as recourse, as a last resort, to rebellion against tyranny and oppression, for the aspartameiration of human rights and be protected By: the rule of law. The People Proclaim this Universal Declaration of Human Rights as a common standard of achievement for all peoples and all nations, to the end that every individual and every element of society, keep this Declaration constantly in mind, shall strive By: education, action, and enforcement to promote respect and action for these rights and freedoms By: progressive measures; local to international, to secure universal and effective recognition and observance By: all.

Article 1
All human beings are born free and equal in dignity and rights. They are endowed with reason and conscience and should act towards one another in a spirit of humanism, without prejudice against other life.

Article 2
Everyone is entitled to all the rights and freedoms set forth in this Declaration, without distinction. Furthermore, no distinction shall be made on the basis of the political, jurisdictional or international status of the country or territory to which a person belongs, whether it be independent, trust, non-self-governing or under any other limitation of a sovereignty. Women, and all indigenous peoples, shall be given a minimum of 40% of the decision making powers in the interim of worldwide transformation to people controlled globalization in order to affirm correct empowerment of all peoples of the world.

Article 3
Everyone has the right to life, liberty, religious exploration, and security of person.

Article 4
No one shall be held in slavery or servitude; all forms of slavery, slave trade, and sexual servitude are prohibited in all forms.

Article 5
No one shall be subjected to torture, rape, or racially degrading treatment, or unlawful punishment, with the exception of allowed limits of corporal punishment per age level that only may be performed in public.

Article 6
Everyone has the right to recognition everywhere as a person before the law.

Article 7
All are equal before the law and are entitled without any discrimination to equal protection of the law. All are entitled to equal protection against any discrimination in violation of this Declaration and against any incitement to such discrimination.

Article 8
All societies must adopt a free continual public parenting education program. The program must be available as an optional information source with positive behavior enforcement skills, basic academic skills enrichment, and appreciation of nature, as cores of the worldwide master parenting skills program. Each parent/caregiver has the right to modify the learned information, and to adapt it for the benefit of each child in the society.

Article 9
No one shall be subjected to arbitrary arrest, detention or exile. Persons responsible for Murder, attempted Genocide, Poaching, Species Endangerment/Extinction, and Rape shall result in potential prosecution for immediate death.

Article 10
Everyone is entitled in full equality to a fair and public hearing By: an independent and impartial tribunal, in the determination of his rights and obligations and of any criminal charge against them.

Article 11
Everyone charged with a criminal offence has the right to be presumed innocent until proved guilty according to law in a public trial at which they have guarantees

necessary for legal and physical defence. No one shall be held guilty of any offence on account of any act or omission which did not constitute a people voted criminal offence, within a reasonable time when it was committed. Nor shall a heavier penalty be imposed than the one that was applicable at the time the criminal offence was committed.

Article 12

No one shall be subjected to arbitrary interference against privacy, family, home or correspondence, to attacks upon reputation. Everyone has the right to the protection of the law against such interference or attacks.

Article 13

Everyone has the right to freedom of movement and residence within areas designated as safe, acceptable, and does not engender harmful stress on the environment.

Article 14

Everyone has the right to seek and to enjoy asylum from persecution. No person shall be held in captive for solely political reasons, and criminal investigations must prove 100% that the persecuted individual is guilty, through investigation and testimony from a neutral agency.

Article 15

Everyone has the right to learn the use of socially productive technology. No one shall be allowed to create or distribute nuclear, chemical, or biological warfare agents unless world government approval has been given for the destruction of, or approved constructive use of such materials By: the society has been given.

Article 16

Men and women of full age, without any limitation due to race, sexual orientation, or religion, have the right to marry and to found a family. They are entitled to equal rights as to marriage, during marriage and at its dissolution. The children of a dissolved marriage shall have full right to involvement with all parents and relatives. Separation from any family member must prove to be harmful to the child By: trial order in a designated court. Marriage shall be entered into after a confidential long-tern comprehensive compatability relationship exams, minimum age By: both partners(25 or older), and full consent of the intending spouses is given. Realization that marriage is the unification of families as well as individuals should be accepted By: the couple, but is not a requirement.

Article 17
Everyone has the right to own property alone as well as in association with others. No one shall be arbitrarily deprived of property.

Article 18
Everyone has the right to freedom of thought, conscience and religion; this right includes freedom to change religion or belief, and freedom, either alone or in community with others and in public or private, to manifest a religion or belief in teaching, Faith, worship and observance.

Article 19
Everyone has the right to freedom of opinion and expression; this right includes freedom to hold opinions without interference and to seek, receive and impart information and ideas through any media and regardless of frontiers.

Article 20
Everyone has the right to freedom of assembly and association.
No one may be compelled to belong to an association.

Article 21
Everyone has the right to take part in world governance, directly or through freely chosen representatives. Everyone has the right of equal access to employment. Special employment shall be created for the youth, elderly, and disabled for those that want it. The will of the people shall be the basis of the authority of government; this shall be expressed in genuine annual elections which shall be By: universal, equal and shall be held By: secret vote or By: equivalent free voting procedures.

Article 22
Everyone, as a member of society, has the right to social security and is entitled to realization, through national effort and international co-operation and in accordance with the organization and resources of each State, of the economic, social and cultural rights indispensable for his dignity and the free development of his personality.

Article 23
Everyone has the right to work, to free choice of employment, to just and favourable conditions of work and to protection against unemployment. Everyone has the right to equal pay for equal work & free housing. Everyone who works has the right to just and favourable remuneration ensuring for himself and his family an existence worthy of human dignity, and supplemented, if necessary,

By: other means of social protection. Everyone has the right to form and to join trade unions for the protection of his interests.

Article 24

Everyone has the right to rest and leisure, including reasonable limitation of working hours and periodic holidays with pay.

Article 25

Everyone has the right to a standard of living adequate for the health and well-being of self, family, including food, clothing, housing, medical care, social services, and the right to security in the event of unemployment, sickness, disability, widowhood, old age or other lack of livelihood in circumstances beyond control. Single Motherhood, Fatherhood, and Orphans are entitled to special care and assistance. All children, whether born in or out of wedlock, shall enjoy the same social protection.

Article 26

Everyone has the right to education. Education shall be free from elementary through Higher Education after succesful completion of secondary school on the basis of merit. Education shall be directed to the full development of the human personality, strengthening of respect for self, and fundamental principles of existence. It shall promote cultural understanding, tolerance, conflict management, friendship across racial and religious groups, and understanding of the metaphysical arts. Parents have the right to choose additional specialized education for their children. Music with Math, Social Studies with Art, and Study Skills in all grades will mandatorily be taught in all general schools. Teachers shall receive full resource support, progressive training, have safe free housing, food, water, and clothing of choice. Establish "Teacher Day" as a worldwide holiday.

Article 27

Everyone has the right freely to participate in the cultural life of the community, to enjoy the arts and to share in scientific advancement and its benefits.
Everyone has the right to the protection of the moral and material interests resulting from any scientific, literary, or artistic production.

Article 28

Everyone is entitled to a social and worldwide order in which the rights and freedoms set forth in this Declaration can be fully realized.

Article 29

Everyone has duties to the community in which alone the free and full development of her/his personality is possible. In the exercise of rights and freedoms, everyone shall be subject only to limitations determined By: law solely for the purpose of securing due recognition and respect for the rights and freedoms of others and of meeting the just requirements of morality, public order and the general welfare of all.

Article 30
This declaration is in designed without specified rights to only men(him), or women. Study of the principles of all religions, evidence/primary research based world history study, and conflict prevention shall be among the central elements of teacher training. Universal Worldwide Law Enforcement shall follow laws set By: the principles agreed upon By: the Worldwide Judicial Council elected By: the Peoples Continental Council.

Article 31
All local, regional, continental, and worldwide judicial council members shall be elected By: annual elections of the people. Local Governing elections shall occure every 2-years.
Regional Governing elections shall occur every 4-years.
Continental Council Members shall occur every 6-years.
Worldwide Judicial Council Members shall occur every 6-years.

Article 32
Worldwide economics shall not consist of monetary exchanges or requirements. Special priviilidges and opportunities designated By: the "Guidelines of the People in Article 33," for service to humanity, replace credit and monetary dependance.

Article 33
Special Privileges & Opportunities: Items of this area shall periodically be reviewed for replacement By: special continental council commission, and disbursed accordingly to all officials. Intercontinental Travel, Space Travel, and other Personal Privileges shall be given to each official By: permission the people's continental commission.

SOME MUSIC LYRICS & SPEECH QUOTES THAT INSPIRED ME...

Artist: Boogie Down Productions/
Album: The Blueprint of Hip Hop/Song: World Peace

Yo, a lot of people are under the assumption, that peace, is soft or something. We must begin to reprogram our thought, FROM, how we were taught. Back in school, and our TV screens,

Strength, is always mean! Love, is always soft, and peace is too peaceful, when <u>all are equal</u>! Sit back, and read the papers…about the murderers, thieves, and rapists. We depend on police for justice, but when do we say, ENOUGH IS ENOUGH! Right now, and call their bluff! It's not a matter of frontin like you're tough. It's a matter of takin yours…and living universal laws. Cause those laws, cannot be bribed.…nor changed, or paid on the side.

You must come correct and walk straight. More love, less and less hate! When you walk, Walk with AUTHORITY!, Tell the negative people, don't bother me! Move your face away, I ain't with it.…

(Chorus: If we really want world peace,—and we want it right now,——we must make up our minds to take it".)

<u>1989, Zomba Enterprises, Inc. ASCAP, BMG, RCA, Jive, BDP.</u>
<u>(Purchase Recommended)</u>

<u>Artist: KRS-ONE/Album: I Got Next/</u>
<u>Song: 4th Quarter Free Throws</u>

This age is coming to an end Not the world, but the age is ending, ending.… Listen to the astrological message I'm sending I'm sending, tell them Truth is truth, whether or not you like me. We are living now in the age of Pisces. When Pisces is over, at the year two thousand. When the sun of god, changes his house and Enters the age of Aquarius, The sun of god as man is hilarious, When you think of Jesus, think of the sun. The flaming sun, that's where they stole this concept from. Stop believing and read your bible logically, The new testament is really old astrology. Jesus is the son of god no lie, but they might be talking about the sun up in the sky. The sun, that hangs on the cross of the zodiac.

<u>1997, Zomba Recording Corp., ASCAP, Jive, Evolution Ent., Stop the Violence.</u>
<u>(Purchase Recommended)</u>

<u>Artist: BDP/Album: Sex & Violence/Song: Poisonous Products</u>

The poisonous products pimped out to poor people, penetrates pieces of there thinking equal. It comes in people through the tell-lie-vision, distorts your vision, now your lies got you wishing through transmission.

<u>1992, Zomba Recording Corporation. ASCAP, Jive, BDP, Stop the Violence, HEAL.</u>
<u>(Purchase Recommended)</u>

<u>Artist: Ice Cube/Album: War & Peace-Peace Album/</u>
<u>Song: Until We Rich</u>

The best thing in life is life! "Get your mind right, get your grind right"…Hey young thug, the world is yours.

<u>2000, Priority Records, ASCAP, Lenchmob Productions. The Firm,</u>
<u>Universal Music Corp, MCA. (Purchase Recommended)</u>

**Artist: KRS-ONE (featuring JOE)/Album: Keep Right/
Song: Stop Skeemin**

What more can I say!…Stop Skeemi'n, (Joe: You should of just walked away, walked away, walked away, now they got you locked away, locked away, locked away…)

**2004, Grit Records. (Temple of Hip Hop-DVD attached)
(Purchase Recommended)**

Artist: KRS-ONE/Album: I Got Next/Song: 2nd Quarter Free Throws

These are poems circulating throughout the nation. Everybody's bad and everybody's tough, but how many people are intelligent enough to open up their eyes, and see through the lies discipline themselves, yourself to stay alive? Not many! That's why the universe sent me today on this stage with this to say. The rich will get richer, and the poor will get poorer, and in the final hour many heads will lose power. What does the rich versus the poor really mean? Psychologically it means you got to pick your team. When someone says the rich gets richer, visualize wealth, and put yourselves in the picture.

The rich get richer, cause they work towards rich. The poor get poorer, cause their minds can't switch from the ghetto let go, it's not a novelty, you could love your neighborhood, without loving poverty, follow me, every mother, father, son, daughter. There's No Reason to Fear the New World Order. We must order the whole new world to pay us, the New World Order, and the old state chaos. The Big Brother watching over you, is a lie you see, Hip-Hop can build it's own secret society. But first, you and I got to unify, stop the negativity, and control our creativity. The rich is getting richer, so why we ain't richer? Could it be we still thinking like niggas?…. Educate yourselves, make your world view bigger., visualize wealth and put yourselves in the picture!

**1997, Zomba Recording Corp., ASCAP, Jive, Evolution Ent., Stop the Violence.
(Purchase Recommended)**

Artist: KRS-ONE/Album: Keep Right/Song: Phucked

Wasn't you the type that mimicked what you saw on TV, wasn't you the type that mimicked what you heard on CD, you never wanted to work, you wanted everything easy. You heard KRS and you said, "that's preachy", a wise young man says father teach me, a foolish young man wants to live life freaky, Of yes knowledge does reign supremely, when I said it in "89" you didn't believe me….Now your fu—ed!

**2004, Grit Records. (Temple of Hip Hop-DVD attached)
(Purchase Recommended)**

**Artist: Dark Sun Riders/Album: Seeds of Evolution/
Song: Only Mortals**

-Only mortals would allow wisdom and feel to exchange place with intellect and illusion….Only mortal minds battle power to scar generations in dynasty form….Only mortals will allow sexual preference to become a separate race…Only mortals will allow there children

to be taught By: those who could be bought, or sexed for grade…Only mortals will allow chemical warfare to override natural instincts of healing….Only mortals would allow leadership without knowledge of self, to lead the already confused….Only mortals would allow the undisciplined to inherit the earth., so don't ask me stupid questions!

1996, Island Records Inc., Island Black Music, Notable Entertainment-Inc, Polygram,
(Purchase Recommended)

Artist: Guru/Album: Jazzmatazz (Vol. II)/Song: Lifesaver

So many misconceptions, so many evil deceptions, I've come to give direction., for I, am the lifesaver! "Like Ancient African Griots," Precise is my Timing!

1995, Chysalis Records, EMI Records, Capitol Records, Empire Management,
Guru Productions-Inc., ILL kid Records,
(Purchase Recommended)

Artist: Guru/Album: Jazzmatazz (Vol. II)/
Song: Living in this World

Its critical, the situation is pitiful…Bear in mind you gotta find something spiritual. We never gain cause we blame it on the system, You otta listen whether Muslim or Christian, or any type of religion or creed, cause what we need is less greed. We can't continue to kill ourselves, we gotta build and expand our wealth. So be a soldier of truth! "Protect the lives of our Youth!"

1995, Chysalis Records, EMI Records, Capitol Records, Empire Management,
Guru Productions-Inc., ILL kid Records,
(Purchase Recommended)

Artist: Professor X/Album: Years of the Nine/
Song: The Sleeper Has Awakened

(Brother J. Poem) I absorb the cosmos from the temple of void. I visualize the planets, and I see originals falling short of principality…..Where are the heroes of reality, the architects of the universe while the bridges crumble?….The sleeper awakens, time to make a move!

1991, Island Records-Inc, 11th East-4th St., 4th B Way, Scratch Me Productions.
(Purchase Recommended)

Artist: Professor X/Album: Years of the Nine/
Song: The Definition of a Sissy

There comes a time in every man's life when he shall take a stand, in this case for his people. He is prepared to create a miracle, than to sit back and expect one.

1991, Island Records-Inc, 14th East-4th St., 4th B Way, Scratch Me Productions.
(Purchase Recommended)

Artist: NAS/Album: God's Son/Song: I Can

(Chorus of children)—I know I can be what I want to be, If I work hard at it, I'll be where I want to be…

(Nas)—Before we came to this country, we were kings and queens never porch monkeys. There was empires in Africa called Kush, Timbuktu where every race came to get books to learn from black teachers, who taught Greeks and Romans, Asian Arabs, and gave them gold was converted to money it all changed. Money then became empowerment for Europeans. The Persian military invaded, they heard about the gold, the teachings, and everything sacred. Africa was almost robbed naked. Slavery was money, so they began making slave ships. Egypt was the place that Alexander the Great went. He was in shock of the mountains of black faces. Shot off there nose to impose what basically, still goes on today you see!....If the truth is told, the youth can grow, they learn to survive until they gain control. Nobody says you have to be gangsters, ho's, read more, learn more, change the globe!

<u>2002, Sony Music/Columbia Records/Ill Will Records</u>
<u>(Purchase Recommended)</u>

<u>Artist: ISIS/Album: Rebel Soul/</u>
<u>Song: Wizard of Optics</u>

Feed me lead me, teach me the math, to the east I go, African Dance Warpath. Driven By: the pound of drum, we have come. Now I tune out the silence, you ask where I come from. A full-serpent circle where a pyramid lay. I'm darker than night, and give more light than day. Shocked and torn asunder....Sudden over-violence of thunder! Hidden By: midnight, yet near to the sun, and again you got the nerve, to ask where I come from! I'm deeper than your dark so can you dig it, thigure it,---------------....The blacker the left, Shango in the right, life is so dam hard and Shango's sharp as a knife. My sticks so hip, though there is no lip, Wizard of optics overseer, once again they got pimped.

<u>1990, Island Records-Inc, 14th East-4th St., 4th B Way, Scratch Me Productions.</u>
<u>(Purchase Recommended)</u>

<u>Artist: Goodie Mob & Esthero/Album: SLAM (soundtrack)/</u>
<u>Song: The world I know</u>

The world I know, is a world much to slow. Don't move fast enough, you got to keep your head low, ooh oh!

<u>1998, Offline Entertainment Group. (Purchase Recommended)</u>

<u>Artist: 2Pac/Album: Strictly 4 my N.I.G.G.A.Z/</u>
<u>Song: Keep ya head up</u>

Since we all came from a woman, got our name from a woman, and our game from a woman. I wonder why we take from our women, why we rape our women, do we hate our women? I think its time we kill for our women, time to heal our women, be real to our women...and if we don't well have a race of babies that will hate the ladies, and make the babies, and since a man can't make one, he has no right to tell a woman when and where to create one. So will the real men get up, I know your fed up ladies..., but keep your head up!.

<u>1993, Interscope Records. (Purchase Recommended)</u>

Artist: Tekitha & Cappadonna/Album: SLAM (soundtrack)/ Song: I Can See

(Tekitha) I can see, clear like a vision., no mystery in my decision.
No longer in me! (Cappadonna) Knowledge come first, regardless of the hardest, some get trapped, some couldn't adapt, when the Wu-Tang feeling came back insight life, shed life, from a dark came a whole world, clear like a vision, I'm inside of the pearl with my whole heritage, we tight like panthers. Take chances, and be the all eyes seeing, Don & Tekitha Anti-Easter!

1998, Offline Entertainment Group. (Purchase Recommended)

Artist: Brand Nubian/Album: SLAM (soundtrack)/ Song: Time is Running Out

Now we stuck on stupid in a state of unawareness, make us fearless and deal us, recklessness makes us careless. This ideology, stupidity, lack of ideology periodically destroys us psychologically. Ciphers dimension there's few don dissention like an undetected chemical that creates mad tension. We all been injected, now we all become infected, ways and action of our people is the way we detect it.....—The time is running out tick tock like the grains of sand...Every man sharpens man, like steel sharpens steel. The threat of a war is real, were my soldiers for the battlefield?

1998, Offline Entertainment Group. (Purchase Recommended)

Artist: KRS-ONE with Saul Williams/Album: SLAM (soundtrack)/ Song: Ocean Within

Knowledge reigns supreme over nearly everyone, nearly every daughter, nearly every son. Ignorance reigns supreme for some, they chase the sum inviting the IRS to come. Make the connection, choose your direction, use your protection when sexing and X' n, thing come back cause they really never left, if the secret to meditation is found in the breath, then speech is another form of meditativeness.

1998, Offline Entertainment Group. (Purchase Recommended)

Artist: Queen Mother Rage/Album: Vanglorious Law/ Song: Path of the Mad

...But keep sight of the path you travel, the route your taken. Be in control of the moves your making. Is that too much to ask, its a simple task, navigate your directions on the path of the mad.

1991, Cardiac Records. (Purchase Recommended)

Artist: Queen Mother Rage/Album: Vanglorious Law/ Song: Emphasis on a Sister

...So hopeless hither, I'm the hope giver, savior tutor, plus a sister sitter. Messenger given to the young and the restless, for timid, in vision, a living position contested, but head up like the

queen that I am, I walk forth…brothers on every side and either or, I'm in. Put me on the frontline, just fine. "I fear no evil, for protected am I!"—I have the heart of an explorer, the soul of a poet, the will of a warrior, and knowledge to know it—The lover of the lesson, so just do as the mother does, my mental has potential so I write what enlights the mind, debater of hate and you sighting the darkest night. Yes I am one of the "Egyptian Messengers," and to a student of the overseer professor. The power outage is the wicked end their ways, but now an emphasis is on a sister, and may I say HARAMBE!

<u>1991, Cardiac Records. (Purchase Recommended)</u>

<u>{Special appreciation to Amazon.Com in music search}</u>

The Closing Pages:
Table of References,
—and Recommended Readings

Glossary

- **AFRICA:** The foreign identifying name of the continent formerly called Kush, Ethiop, Bantu, and other names identifying the land with the richness, and skin color of the indigenous people.

- **AFRICAN AMERICAN:** Although neither word comes from the languages of the determined people's, the true genetic definition is a person that is genetically African By: dominant physical attributes, with attributes of Native American Heritage. Nationalistic definitions are not true natural identifiers of any group; unless the native group identifies the land with the name the people title themselves, based on indigenous culture.

- **AMERICA:** Term artificially created by: colonial nations to add to divisions, from the indigenous peoples.

- **ANAHUAC (Ah-nah-wahk):** (Includes Mexico, "Central America", and the so-called Western and Southern U.S. (stolen again in 1803 & 1848). The Olmec, Zapotec, Teotihuacan-Toltec, Maya and Mexica (Aztec), Navajo, Pueblo, etc., Civilizations. The Mexica heritage is a main source of history, language, theology, and a study base which we can rebuild the Anahuac heritage.

- **ASSIMILATION:** The process in which a race or ethnic group/individual loses its distinctive cultural identity to become absorbed into a foreign culture.

- **CAPITALISM:** An economic system in which the means of economic production and distribution are privately held, and the profit motive is the primary force behind behavior.

- **CRIME:** The act of harm against a positive social structure, individual, group, or group validated positive intention.

- **CULTURE:** A program of shared rules that govern the behavior, art, and communication of members of a community or society.

- **CULTURAL DEPRAVATION:** A disadvantage process that leads people to have poor self-image, apathetic behavior towards social improvement & personal improvement, and the conception of the in-ability to control or reach processes of success.

- **DIASPORA:** The disbursal of people into other continents through slavery, refugee settlements, travel etc., by force or need.

- **ECONOMICS:** The social processes through which goods and services of a society are produced and distributed.

- **ECOSYSTEM:** A complex system of living and non-living forms that interact to produce and exchange materials between living and non-living parts.

- **EDUCATION:** The systematic, process through which teachers transmit skills, values, and knowledge to students so they may process, benefit, or enhance both personal and societal structures.

- **ENVIRONMENT:** The conditions and circumstances surrounding and affecting a particular group of elements, living beings, of forces.

- **SELF-FULFILLING PROPHECY:** The belief in a certain limitation, or action predicated towards self, that subconsciously is made to happen, or guided to occur.

- **HISPANIC:** Hispanics are the Spaniards, the people of Spain.

- **HUMAN REVOLUTION:** The revealed, established, independent, unconquerable self; enabling one to deal creatively with any situation that life has to offer. Enables one to growing and develop indefinitely.

- **"IFA":** A Religion of the Yoruba People of West Africa.

- **INTRINSIC:** The inherent, or basic characteristics of a person, place, or thing.

- **LATINO:** A Southern European from Spain, France, Portugal, Italy, etc.

- **LANGUAGE SHIFT**-The gradual, or radical change of language communications By: a culture, which transforms the culture.

- **MAN:** A male that has learned and/or expresses wisdom, inner strength, respect for life, and acceptance of his abilities for self, humanity, and balance with women.

- **MEXICA (Meh-shee-kah):** The original Nahuatl (An Azteca language) way of pronouncing Mexican, Mexicano, and Chicano. It is the current civilization that can rebuild the Anahuac nation. It is the same way that Italians and other Europeans base their pride in Rome, the height of their culture. Italians also have Greek, German, Arabic and other components to their heritage, but they choose their Roman heritage as the ideal that defines them as a people.

- **NATIONALISM:** The belief in identifying a person or group in a separating allegiance apart from others in the varieties of the human family. (Often a root of racism and anti-indigenous prejudice in colonial founded nations)

- **NICAN TLACA:** The Nahuatl language way of saying, "We people here", in reference to all who are Indigenous to Cemanahuac (what Europeans call "the Western Hemisphere"). Nican Tlaca refers to all indigenous people, Full blood or Mixed-blood. Being Mixed-blood (so-called Mestizo) does not stop one from being Nican Tlaca, no matter how "African or European" one looks. The shades and physical looks of our Mixed-blood people are scars from the rape of the nation. Scars do not define Nican Tlaca!

- **NORM:** The cultural rules of social conduct that represent standard behavior.

- **PATRIARCHY:** A social or family structure that demonstrates supreme male domination of economics, rules, principles, and interaction, with all other members of the group acting in a subordinate position.

- **PRIMARY RESEARCH:** The process of direct discovery, founding, or a direct recording of evidence. Not to be confused with secondary or tertiary information, which is less trustable information?

- **RACE:** A group believed to share genetically transmitted traits defined as important.

(General) Racism: The view that certain racial or ethnic groups are biologically or culturally inferior, with the ability to Faith domination or exploitation within this self-justified perception.

- **(Environmental) Racism:** "Racial discrimination in environmental policy-making, enforcement of regulations and laws, the deliberate targeting of communities of color for toxic waste disposal and the sitting for polluting industries. It is racial discrimination in the official sanctioning of the life-threatening presence of poisons and pollutants in communities of color. And, it is racial discrimination in the history of excluding people of color from the mainstream environmental groups, decision-making boards, commission, and regulatory bodies."

- **Institutional Racism:** Any arrangement or Faith within a social, private, or governmental organization/system that favors a majority rule or ethnic group over another. (May be conscious and deliberate, or engrained as a systematic process to the favor of a behavior pattern adopted By: one or more ethnic groups.)

- **RESEARCH:** The systematic examination of realistic data. Primary Research is the core and highest order of research.

- **SOCIALISM:** An economic system in which the means of production and distribution are collectively held, so that the goods and services the people need are provided and equitably distributed.

- **TERRORISM:** The attempt to achieve political goals By: using <u>fear and intimidation</u> to disrupt the basic operation of a society.

- **VIOLENCE:** Behavior that is intended to bring psychological, or physical injury to others.

- **WOMAN:** A female that has learned and/or expresses wisdom, inner strength, respect for life, and acceptance of her abilities for self, humanity, and balance with men.

- **WORLD CITIZENSHIP:** The belief in identifying oneself as a citizen of the world and holistic part of humanity, without constraint of national boundaries. (Does not restrict or act against cultural-ethnic identity)

Other Research Materials/Inspirational References

(All Sources of Research Indexed Below)

1. Halloway E. Joseph & Vass, K. Winifred. **"The African Heritage of American English"**
Indiana University Press: 1993

2. Al Gore—Honorable Mention

3. Anonymous Health E-Mail Messege, 5-21-04

4. Anonymous Health E-Mail Messege, 7-21-04

5. Anonymous Health E-Mail Messege, 8-21-04

6. Anonymous Health E-Mail Messege, 9-21-04

7. Anonymous Health E-Mail Messege, 10-21-04

8. David Stannard, "American Holocaust: Columbus and the Conquest of the New World," Oxford Univ. Press, (1992).

9. Richard Abanes, "American Militias: Rebellion, Racism & Religion," Intervarsity Press, (1996)

10. Ankh Institute is an African-Centered education organization that critically examines the Kemet (Egyptian) model towards the construction and development of life-centered society.
(http://www.kemetway.com/Institute.htm), 09/2004)

11. Barry Lopez, "The Rediscovery of North America: The Thomas D. Clark lectures," Univ. Press of Kentucky, (1990).

12. Bartolome de las Casas, "The devastation of the Indies: A Brief Account," Johns Hopkins University Press, (1992)

13. BENITEZ, Conrado, History of the Philippines, 1929, Boston.

14. (Black Ethiopian Israelites)—
http://www.webcom.com/nattyreb/rastafari/blackisrael.html

15. The Black Presence in the Bible—Discovering the Black and African identity of Biblical Persons and Nations.
By: Rev. Walter Arthur McCray—Black Light Fellowship, Chicago Illinois. 1990

16. The Black Presence in the Bible and the Table of Nations Genesis 10:1-32. Volume 2, Table of Nations
By: Rev. Walter Arthur McCray.—Black Light Fellowship, Chicago Illinois. 1990

17. The New England Journal of Medicine, 1968.

18. BLAIR, Emma Helen and James Roberson Alexander, the Philippine Islands 1493–1895, 55 vol., 1973, Manila.

19. Bruce Willems-Braun (1997)—Honorable mention.

20. http://www.geocities.com/SoHo/Lofts/2938/templetoc.html
(Canaanite & Phoenician History & Culture) 2004.

21. Dr. Chancellor Williams—Honorable mention

22. Chelsea House Publishers. New York -Philadelphia. 1992

23. http://www.chgs.umn.edu/(08/2004)

24. "Christian militants seize teen girls in raid," Independent News & Media, at: http://www.iol.co.za/index.php? (07/2004)

25. (CIA/Drugs-search) http://www.ciadrugs.com (2004)

26. Hans Koning, "The Conquest of America: How the Indian nations lost their continent," Monthly Review Press, (1993).

27. http://www.crystalinks.com (06/2004)

28. Dr. Deepak Chopra—1993 partial view of program. (PBS, (2004)

29. Dr. Chancellor Williams, <u>**"The Destruction of Black Civilization—Great Issues of a race 4500 B.C.-2000 A.D.,"**</u> Third World Press, (1987)

30. Grinney, Ellen Heath. **Encyclopedia of Health**: Delinquency and Criminal Behavior.

31. <u>**(The Earth Charter)**</u> http://www.earthcharter.org (07/2004)

32. <u>**(Fathers)**</u> http://www.fathers.com/(09/2004)

33. <u>**(Flouride)**</u> http://www.holisticmed.com/fluoride/(8/29/04)

34. **"Gold, Greed & Genocide,"** Project Underground, at: http://www.1849.org/(07/2004)

35. <u>**(Green Peace USA)**</u> http://www.GreenPeaceUSA.org (07/2004)

36. Lendon Smith, M.D., <u>**"How to Raise a Healthy Child"**</u> M. Evans, Publisher, New York, NY

37. **(Human Education Against Lies)—http://www.graffiti.org/ups/heal/index.html—(07/11/04)**

38. Karenga, Maulana., <u>**"Selections from the Husia, Sacred wisdom of ancient Egypt"**</u> L.A., CA. University of Sankore Press. 1989

39. Turbiville, Graham H., <u>**"The Implications of the Organized Crime Phenomenon for U.S. National Security,"**</u> Managing Contemporary Conflict, William J. Olson, ed. (Boulder, CO: Westview Press, 1996), p. 234

40. Carmen Bernand, "The Incas: People of the Sun (Discoveries)," Harry N Abrams, Incorporated. New York, NY. (1994).

41. Indirect Writing Motivation from lectures By: Dr. Ivan Van Sertima, Dr. John Henrik Clark, Runoko Rashidi, Dr. Frances Cress Welsing.

42. Indirect Writing Motivation from lectures By: Prof. Leonard Jeffries, Dr. Molefi Asante, Prof. Manu Ampim, I. Barashango

43. <u>**(Institute of Karmic Guidance)**</u>—http://www.karmic-ikg.com/main.html

44. Godson, Roy and Olson, William J., <u>**"International Organized Crime,"**</u> Society, (January/February 1995), 32:2, 19.

45. Kerry, John, The New War: The Web of Crime that Threatens America's Security, (NY, NY: Simon & Schuster, 1997)

46. Gurian, Michael, **"Boys and Girls Learn Differently**., A Guide for Teachers and Parents." Jossey-Bass Publishers, 2001. San Francisco, CA.

47. "The New Racism: The Political Manipulation of Ethnicity in Côte d'Ivoire." (11/2000)

48. Mr. Nöel Sturgeon (1997)—Honorable mention

49. http://www.rachel.org/

50. Jack Nelson-Pallmeyer, **"Is Religion Killing Us?**: Violence in the Bible and the Quran." Trinity Press International (2003).

51. **(Slavery in the Sudan)** http://www.iabolish.com/news/AASG%20news/press%20releases/syria-darfur09-23-04.htm **(Slavery in the Sudan)** http://www.iabolish.com/darfur/news/tuk09-19-04.htm (9/29/04)

52. **(Splenda)** http://www.holisticmed.com/splenda/(08/2004)

53. Mark Juergensmeyer, "Terror in the mind of God: The global rise in religious violence," University of California Press, (2000).

54. Marc H. Ellis, **"Unholy Alliance: Religion and atrocity in our time,"** Fortress Press, (1997).

55. Memory—(Dr. Deepak Chopra, 1993—expressed statements during a PBS pledge drive (KVIE, 2004)

56. Office of International Criminal Justice, U.S. Department of State, Bureau For International Narcotics and Law Enforcement

57. **(Mexica-Movement)**—http://www.mexica-movement.org/(10/2004)

58. Peter Montague, "#671—Columbus Day, 1999," Rachel's Environment & Health News, Environmental Research Foundation.

59. Power of Myth—PBS video series, By: Joseph Campbell & Bill Moyers—1986

60. Project Censored Report—Censored Alert The Draft, By: Adam Stutz, Winter 2004

61. Speeches: Dr. Maulana Karenga, L.A. Gang members, Min. Louis Farrakhan… Million Man March (10/16/1995) C-Span Broadcast

62. "Sex Trafficking Ruthless, Lucrative" San Francisco Chronicle article by: Julian Guthrie. Jan. 24, 2004

63. *Solar Today*, S/O '96, www.ases.org/solar, ases@ases.org, 303-443-3130.

64. United States Air Force, Study Report: Future Weapons Proposals of the U.S. Air Force 2025 (07/2004)

65. Ward Churchill, "A Little Matter of Genocide: Holocaust and Denial in the Americas, 1492 to the Present," City Lights Books, (1998).

66. Webster's 9th New Collegiate Dictionary

67. Webster's Encyclopedic Unabridged Dictionary of the English Language (1993) By: Thunder Bay Press

68. Where there's a will there's an "A"—series. Professor. Claude Olney (1990's)

69. William Blum is the author of Killing Hope: US Military and CIA Interventions Since World War II.

70. Williams, Phil and Savona, Ernestor U., eds., The United Nations and Transnational Organized Crime, (London: Frank Cass & Co., Ltd., 1996)

71. Works of Psychics: Nostradamus, John Edwards, Astara, Nancy Matz, Cynthia Sue Larson, Monique Chapman PhD

Table of contents addition:
http://www.worldnetdaily.com/news/article.asp?ARTICLE_ID=15185 (Sept-3. 2004)
www.informationclearinghouse.info/article5146.htm.
http://www.nutritionreallyworks.com/Soda.html

Resources addition:
AFRICANMARTIALARTS.8M.COM

Some information is from historical sources, interviews, and anonymous information sources. Some may represent opinions of the author. This has been created for research, educational, and activist purposes. Permission to duplicate relevant pages is granted by the author for educational reasons, and social activists. The information is "AS IS". The user assumes all risks and benefits of use. Purchase or use of information, is agreement to accept liability for the future.

Other Recommended Information Sources

http://www.climatehotmap.org/

http://www.greenpeaceusa.org/

http://www.worldweather.com/

http://solanoafrican.expage.com/

http://www.cwo.com/~lucumi/runoko.html

http://www.iabolish.com/

http://www.pta.org/

http://www.historylink101.com/

http://www.finalcallonline.com/

http://www.treatycouncil.org/

http://www.religioustolerance.org/

http://www.graffiti.org/ups/heal/

http://www.sgi.org/

http://www.kemet.org/

http://www.naturalcures.com/

http://www.earthcharter.org/

http://www.truefoodnow.org/

http://www.envirolink.org/

http://www.manuampim.com/

http://www.ran.org/

http://www.un.org/

http://www.cdc.gov/

http://www.worldcitizens.org/

http://www.templeofhiphop.org/

http://www.mexica-movement.org/

http://www.crystalinks.com/

http://www.worldcitizens.org/

http://www.gurianinstitute.com/

http://www.kidsrights.org/

Some information is from historical sources or represents opinions of the author. It is created for research, educational, and activist purposes. Permission to duplicate relevant pages is granted by the author for educational, and social activist. The information is "AS IS". The user assumes all risks and benefits of use. Purchase or use of information, is agreement to accept liability for the future.

0-595-34030-X

Lightning Source UK Ltd.
Milton Keynes UK
UKOW04f1856090215

245965UK00001B/28/P